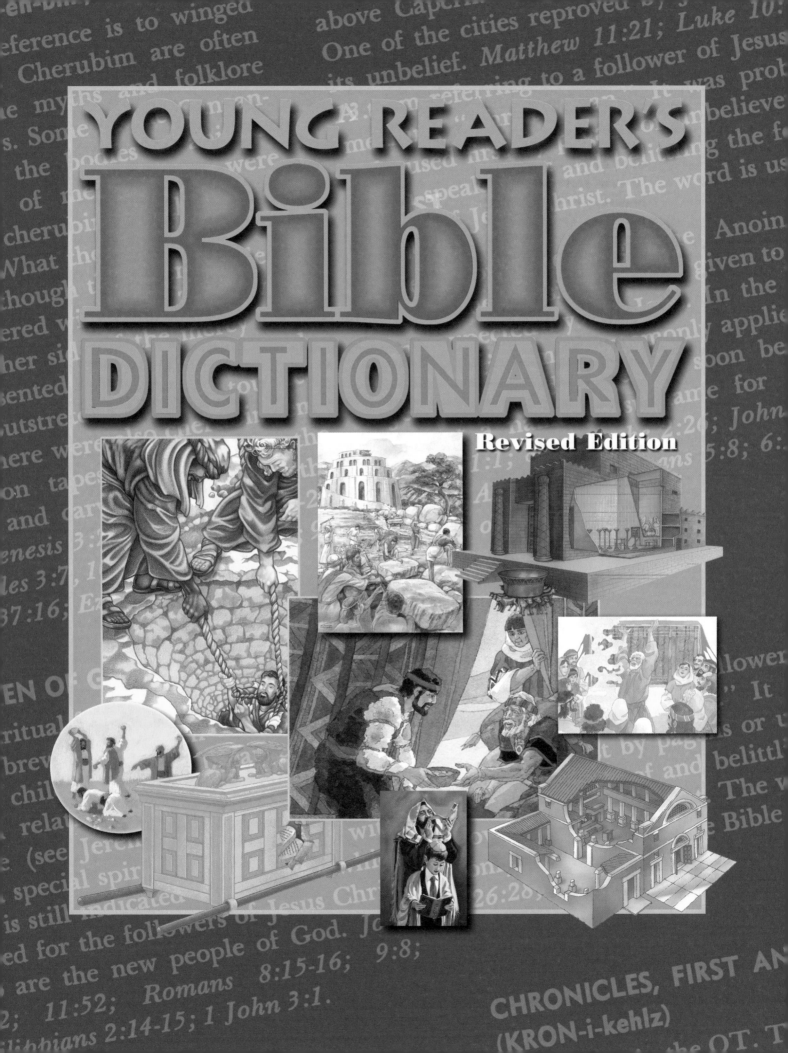

YOUNG READER'S Bible DICTIONARY

Revised Edition

YOUNG READER'S Bible DICTIONARY

Revised Edition

Abingdon Press
Nashville

00 01 02 03 04 05 06 07 08 09 — 10 9 8 7 6 5 4 3 2 1

MANUFACTURED IN SPAIN

Table of Illustrations

Abingdon Press wishes to acknowledge our indebtedness
to the following:

The original editorial committee consisting of Carolyn M.
Wolcott, Margie McCarty, Loma Mae Jones, and Paul W. Koper,
and those persons who provided invaluable assistance in the
preparation of the original manuscript; Harriett Roorbach,
Rosemary Roorbach, Marion Armstrong, and Mary Alice Jones.

This revised edition was edited by Peg Augustine and Gary
Flegal. Peg Augustine is a writer and editor specializing in
Christian education materials for children. Dr. Gary Flegal,
Ph.D., is a Certified Lay Speaker in The United Methodist
Church. He is a regular contributor to several publications,
including Church Musician Today and Senior Musician. He has
served as a consultant on a number of curriculum projects for
Abingdon Press.

Introduction

This dictionary has been prepared to help you learn about the persons, places, events, ideas, and unfamiliar terms in the Bible. Most of these words can be found either in the New Revised Standard Version of the Bible or the New International Version of the Bible; occasionally however, entry words from the King James Version and other popular versions are included because of their rich historical significance. Each definition includes references to passages in the Bible where the word appears. The entries also include a guide for pronouncing each proper name and for other difficult words.

Alphabetical sections are color-coded for ease of use. Entries appear in the same color as the section in which they fall. The phonetic pronunciation of the entry word appears in boldtype just under the entry word. Scripture passages where the entry word will be found appear in italic type at the end of the entry.

Colorful artwork throughout will help you see what life was like during Bible times. When you read the text and look at the illustrations, you will experience day-to-day activities, occupations, and living conditions of people who lived in Bible lands.

AARON
(AIR-uhn)

The elder brother of Moses. Aaron served as spokesman for his brother when Moses asked the Pharaoh to let the Israelites leave Egypt, and he assisted Moses in helping the Israelites escape from Egyptian slavery. During the Israelites' long stay in the wilderness Moses anointed Aaron priest of the tabernacle, the tent of meeting in which the ark with the Ten Commandments was kept. Descendants of Aaron also became priests. In the OT they are sometimes referred to as Levites—from Levi, the family or tribal name. (See *Ark of the Covenant, Levi, Priests and Levites, Tabernacle.*) *Exodus 6:20-29; 28:1-4; 29:4-7; 32:1-5; and other references.*

ABADDON
(uh-BAD-uhn)

A poetic name used in the OT to indicate a place under the earth where the dead were supposed to dwell. It was also called Sheol. Other early peoples had similar ideas about the dwelling places of the dead. *Job 26:6; 28:22; 31:12; Psalm 88:11; Proverbs 15:11; 27:20.*

ABBA
(AH-buh)

An Aramaic word meaning "the father," "my father," or "our father." In the NT Jesus used this word as a familiar name for God, the Father. *Mark 14:36; Romans 8:15; Galatians 4:6.*

ABEDNEGO

See *Shadrach, Meshach, Abednego.*

ABEL
(AY-bul)

The second son of Adam and Eve. In the OT story Abel, said to have been a shepherd, was murdered by his brother Cain. The NT mentions Abel as the first person to die for his faith. *Genesis 4:1-9; Hebrews 11:4.*

ABIATHAR
(uh-BYE-uh-thar)

A priest of David's time. After David's death Abiathar and the priest Zadok disagreed over which of David's sons should be made king. Zadok anointed Solomon king, and Abiathar was sent into exile in the city of Anathoth. It is possible that Abiathar, his son, and Zadok's son were responsible for some of the records preserved in the Books of Samuel. *1 Samuel 22:20-23; 23:6-14; 2 Samuel 15:24-29; 1 Kings 2:26-27; Mark 2:23-28. (Here Abiathar is mentioned as high priest when David ate the bread of the Presence in the house of God. In 1 Samuel 21:5-6 Ahimelech is named as the one who gave David the bread. See Ahimelech.)*

ABIGAIL
(AB-i-gale)

Wife of Nabal the owner of large flocks of sheep and goats. When Nabal refused to invite David to his sheepshearing feast or to give him and his men any food, Abigail rode to meet David and apologize, asking him not to harm her husband. David respected her wishes. After Nabal's

death David married Abigail. Also the name of one of David's sisters. *1 Samuel 25:1-42; 1 Chronicles 2:16-17.*

ABIJAM
(uh-BYE-juhm)

King of Judah from about 913 to 911 B.C. He was the son and successor of Rehoboam. His name also appears as Abijah. *1 Kings 14:31-15:8; 2 Chronicles 13:1-22.*

ABIMELECH
(uh-BIM-uh-lek)

One of the seventy sons of Gideon (or Jerubbaal). He persuaded the men of Shechem to help him become king after his father's death. He murdered all of his brothers except the youngest, Jotham, who told a fable warning the people that Abimelech would be a cruel king. The bramble in Jotham's fable represents Abimelech. *Judges 9:1-57.*

ABIGAIL HONORS DAVID

12

ABISHAI
(AB-i-shye)

A nephew of David. He is remembered as one of David's brave and loyal men who volunteered to go with David on a dangerous and daring venture. *1 Samuel 26:6-9; 2 Samuel 23:18-19.*

ABLUTION
(ab-LOO-shuhn)

Ceremonial or symbolic washing of hands, cups, pots, or other utensils to make these objects fit for use in worship, or fit for a place in the religious life of the community. *Matthew 15:1-20; 23:25-26; Mark 7:1-23; Hebrews 6:2, 9:10.*

ABNER
(AB-nur)

Commander of the Israelite army under Saul, he fought in the battles against the Philistines. At the festival of the new moon he was seated in the place of honor beside King Saul. Abner introduced David to Saul. *1 Samuel 14:50; 17:55-58; 20:25; 26:5, 2 Samuel 2:8-10; 3:17-39; and other references.*

ABRAHAM OR ABRAM
(AY-bruh-ham, AY-bruhm)

OT patriarch known as the father, or ancestor, of the Hebrew people. He was noted for his obedience to God. Born near Ur in Mesopotamia, Abraham wandered with his family close to Haran. Abraham, in obedience to God, left Haran and led his family to Canaan, the Land of Promise. God made a covenant, or agreement, with Abraham promising that he would be the father of a great nation, and that through him God would bless all the families of the earth. A son, Isaac, was born to Abraham's wife, Sarah. The faith of Abraham was tested when God asked

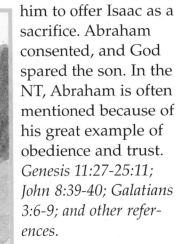

ABRAHAM AND ISAAC

him to offer Isaac as a sacrifice. Abraham consented, and God spared the son. In the NT, Abraham is often mentioned because of his great example of obedience and trust. *Genesis 11:27-25:11; John 8:39-40; Galatians 3:6-9; and other references.*

ABSALOM
(AB-suh-luhm)

The third son of King David. Absalom was handsome and ambitious. He led a revolt against his father and tried to take the throne. *2 Samuel 13:1-19:8.*

ABYSS
(uh-BISS)

An unmeasured, deep, bottomless pit. This word is used in the NT to refer to the place of the dead. (See *Sheol, Abaddon.*) *Luke 8:31; Romans 10:7.*

ACACIA
(uh-KAY-sh)
A hard, close-grained, orange-brown wood sometimes called shittim wood. It was used in building the ark of the covenant and is still common in the desert regions of Negeb and Sinai. The tree has sweet-smelling yellow blossoms and soft green leaves. Acacia trees also grow in the United States. *Exodus 25:3-5, 10, 13, 23; Deuteronomy 10:3; Isaiah 41:19.*

ACHAIA
(uh-KAY-uh)
The Roman province that made up most of ancient Greece. Achaia is mentioned frequently in the NT in connection with Paul and the early Christian churches. *Acts 18:12, 27; 19:21; Romans 15:26; 1 Corinthians 16:15; 2 Corinthians 1:1; 9:2; 11:10; 1 Thessalonians 1:7-8.*

ACTS OF THE APOSTLES
(uh-Pah-suhl)
The fifth book in the NT. It was written as a sequel to the Gospel of Luke. Acts records many of the experiences of Jesus' followers after the Resurrection and describes how the Christian church began and spread. *See the book itself.*

ADAM
(AD-uhm)
A Hebrew word meaning "man." This is the name given the first man in the stories of creation. In the NT Adam is spoken of as representing all humankind. *Genesis 2:7-5:5; Romans 5:14; 1 Corinthians 15:22, 45.*

ADONIJAH
(ad-uh-Nye-juh)
The fourth son of David whose plot to take over the throne, as the old king lay dying, failed and led finally to his own destruction. Since his older brothers were dead, Adonijah claimed the right to reign after David. Solomon, aided by his mother, by Zadok the priest, and by the prophet Nathan, took the reign away from Adonijah. *2 Samuel 3:4; 1 Kings 1:5-2:25.*

ADULLAM
(uh-DUL-uhm)
An OT town which was in the territory of the tribe of Judah. Joshua defeated the king of Adullam during the Hebrew conquest of Canaan. In a cave near Adullam David took refuge when Saul was trying to kill him. *Joshua 12:15; 1 Samuel 22:1-2.*

ADULTERY
(uh-DUHL-tur-ee)
Intimate and sinful physical relations between a married man and a woman who is not his wife, or between a married woman and a man who is not her husband. In both the OT and NT adultery is a most serious offense against God, and because it damaged the life of families, it was seen as an offense against the whole community. *Exodus 20:14; Leviticus 20:10; Matthew 5:27-28; Mark 10:2-12.*

AGAPE

(uh-GAh-pay)

This Greek word does not appear in the Bible, but it was used by Christians to mean the love of God. When early Christians broke bread and ate together, the meal was sometimes called "the Agape." (See *Love*.)

AGRIPPA

(uh-GRIP-uh)

Agrippa II was the king of Judea before whom Paul made his defense after the Jewish authorities accused him of crimes against the laws of the Jews and of Caesar. *Acts 25:13-26:32.*

AHAB

(AY-hab)

Seventh king of the northern kingdom of Israel. He reigned for twenty years from about 874 to 853 B.C. During most of his reign he was at war with the Assyrians. Probably influenced by his Baal-worshiping wife, Jezebel, Ahab built a temple to Baal, erected an altar, and worshiped this god. Ahab was condemned by the prophet Elijah. One of the stories about Ahab's reign tells of Elijah's triumph over the prophets of Baal in a contest to prove to the people that the Lord was God. Ahab was fatally wounded in a battle with the King of Syria (not the same as Assyria) even though he had disguised himself so no one would recognize him. He died in his capital city, Samaria. (See *Elijah, Jezebel*.) *1 Kings 16:29-22:40.*

AHASUERUS

(ah-hah-zhoo-AIR-uhss)

A king of the Persian Empire, who made Esther, a Jewess, his wife. (See *Esther*.) *Ezra 4:6; Esther 1:1-10:3.*

AHAZ

(AY-haz)

King of the southern kingdom of Judah from about 732 to 716 B.C. His reign had important and long-lasting results for the religious and political life of Judah, and also for Israel. The kings of Israel and Syria joined forces and invaded Judah, besieging Jerusalem. It is reported that Ahaz burned his son as an offering, which was probably a desperate attempt to avoid defeat. When this failed, Ahaz appealed to Tiglath-pileser, king of Assyria, for help. The Assyrian king responded quickly and began the campaigns which finally ended in the destruction of the northern kingdom of Israel. Judah, however, was forced to pay heavy tribute to the Assyrians. Ahaz also introduced Assyrian worship into the temple. *2 Kings 16:1-20; 2 Chronicles 28:1-6, 16-27; Isaiah 1:1; 7:1-17.*

AHAZIAH

(ay-huh-Zye-uh)

1. King of Israel from about 853 to 852 B.C. He was the son and successor of Ahab. *1 Kings 22:49-53; 2 Kings 1:2-17.*
2. See *Jehozhaz* (1).

AHIJAH
(uh-Hye-juh)

A priest and prophet from the town of Shiloh. Meeting Jeroboam on the road outside Jerusalem, Ahijah foretold one of the most important events in the history of Israel, the division of Solomon's kingdom into two separate kingdoms. *1 Kings 11:29-40; 12:12-15; 2 Chronicles 9:29.*

AHIMELECH
(uh-HIM-uh-lek)

A priest of the sanctuary at Nob who helped David when he was fleeing from Saul by giving him the holy bread of the sanctuary and the sword of Goliath. When Saul heard of this, he was very angry and had Ahimelech and all the other priests put to death. (See *Abiathar.*) *1 Samuel 2:1–22:23; and other references.*

ALABASTER
(AL-uh-bas-ter)

A soft calcite stone, light and creamy in color and often having a banded or striped appearance that adds to its beauty. In Bible times it was most frequently used for vases and for flasks or boxes to hold perfume and precious ointments. *Song of Solomon 5:15; Matthew 26:7; Mark 14:3; Luke 7:37.*

ALEXANDRIA
(al-ig-ZAN-dri-uh)

The capital city and great seaport of Egypt. This city was built by Alexander the Great in 331 B.C. Many Jews settled there at that time, and the OT was translated into Greek there. It had a great library and became a center of learning. Next to Rome it was the most important city in NT times. *Acts 18:24; 27:6; 28:11.*

ALLEGORY
(AL-uh-goh-ri)

A story with a double meaning. In the Bible there are some stories in which the characters and events tell one obvious story, but because these characters and events also have a hidden meaning, there is another story below the surface. (See *Fable, Myth, Parable.*) *Judges 9:7-15; 2 Samuel 12:1-4 are examples of allegory.*

ALLOTMENT

In early OT times the portion of land distributed or assigned by lot to each of the tribes occupying Canaan. The Hebrews had a very special attitude toward their land. They lived in Canaan, the Promised Land, promised by God to Abraham and his descendants. For this reason they thought of God as their landlord, that is, God was the owner of the land. As the years went by, the people lost sight of this idea. *Joshua 11:23; 16:1-3; Ezekiel 48:10-13.*

ALMIGHTY

Having absolute power. The word is often used as an adjective with "God" to show his greatness, power, and might. As a noun it is a synonym for God, and "the Almighty" is often used in hymns and psalms in place of the word "God." *Genesis 17:1; Psalm 91:1; Revelation 4:8; and other references.*

ALMS
(ahlmz)
Gifts given to the poor. OT laws directed the Hebrews to be generous to the poor (see Deuteronomy 15:7-11). The NT records the directions of Jesus and the apostles for remembering the needy. *Matthew 6:2-4; Luke 12:33; Acts 3:2-3.*

ALMUG
(AL-muhg)
A special kind of sweet-scented wood used in musical instruments such as lyres and harps. It was also used in the construction of Solomon's temple. Almug may have been sandalwood, but this is uncertain. *1 Kings 10:11-12.*

ALTAR

ALOES
(AL-ohz)
A spicy substance from the resin of a tree. This type of aloes was used for perfume and incense. Another type of aloes, which came from a plant rather than a tree, was the source of a bitter medicine. When mixed with myrrh it was used for the preparation of a body for burial. *Numbers 24:6; Psalm 45:8; Proverbs 7:17; John 19:39.*

ALPHA AND OMEGA
(AL-fuh, oh-MAY-guh)
The first and last letters of the Greek alphabet. In the NT the two letters are always used together as symbols for God and for Jesus Christ. They indicate that in God all things begin and end, but God himself is without beginning or end. *Revelation 1:8; 21:6; 22:13.*

ALTAR
(AHL-tur)
In early OT times this was usually a mound of earth or a block of stone supported by a pile of smaller stones. Often these were built in a place where God had made himself known. Sacrificial offerings of animals were made to God on the altar, and often incense was burned. In later OT times altars were more elaborate and were often of great size. Other people than the Hebrews also built altars for their gods. *Genesis 8:20; 12:7; 26:23-25; 35:1; Exodus 17:15; Matthew 5:23-24; Acts 17:22-23.*

AMALEKITES
(uh-MAL-uh-kites)
A nomadic desert tribe in the OT, descendants of Esau. The Amalekites continually raided and threatened the Israelites in the time of Moses. Later they were badly defeated by King Saul and were completely wiped out in Hezekiah's reign. *Numbers 13:29; 14:42-45; 1 Samuel 15:4-8; 1 Chronicles 4:43.*

AMAZIAH

(am-uh-ZYE-uh)

1. King of the southern kingdom of Judah from about 797 to 792 B.C., son of King Joash. *2 Chronicles 25:1-28.*
2. Priest of the shrine at Bethel. It was this Amaziah who tried to keep the prophet Amos from coming to Bethel and denouncing the sins of the people. *Amos 7:10-15.*

AMBUSH

Lying in wait in a hiding place in order to attack an enemy by surprise. Also, the place where one lies in wait. *Judges 9:25, 34-35; Acts 25:2-3.*

AMEN

(ah-MEN or ay-MEN)

A Hebrew word meaning "truly" or "surely." In the Bible its use signified the listener's willingness to acknowledge and agree with the statement or the prayer of a previous speaker. Often it was used as a blessing at the end of a letter. "Amen" is usually used today at the end of a prayer or a hymn. It signifies that the one who uses the word sincerely means what he has said or sung. *Deuteronomy 27:15-26; 1 Kings 1:36; 1 Chronicles 16:36; Nehemiah 8:6; 1 Corinthians 14:16; 2 Corinthians 1:20; Ephesians 3:20-21.*

AMON

(AY-muhn)

1. Governor of the city of Samaria during the reign of Ahab. He was in charge of the prophet Micaiah who had been imprisoned after predicting the failure of Ahab's expedition against Ramoth-gilead. *2 Chronicles 18:25-27.*

2. King of Judah from about 643 to 641 B.C. He was the son of Manasseh and apparently continued in the ways of his father worshiping the Assyrian gods. He was murdered by his servants. *2 Kings 21:19-26; 2 Chronicles 33:21-25.*

AMOS

(AY-muhss)

A prophet who lived in Tekoa, a town in Judah. He made his prophecies sometime between 760 and 745 B.C. Amos was a shepherd and also "a dresser of sycamore trees." The sycamores mentioned in the Bible are a type of fig-mulberry tree common in Palestine. Just before the fruit ripens it is necessary for the dresser to pinch or pierce the fruit to allow insects to escape. Otherwise the fruit will not be edible. When Amos took his produce to the marketplaces of the cities, he saw the dishonesty of the people and the way the rich mistreated the poor. In the marketplace at Bethel in the northern kingdom of Israel he warned the people that they could not please God by worship if they continued to be dishonest and unjust to the poor, for God was a holy and just God. "Hate the evil and love the good and establish justice and God will be with you," Amos declared. (See *Amos, Book of.*)

AMOS, BOOK OF

A prophetic book in the OT. The messages of Amos were the first prophetic messages to be gathered into a book. His brief book is included among the last twelve books in the OT, known as the Minor Prophets. *See the book itself.*

ANATHOTH
(AN-uh-thoth)
In the OT a priestly city near Jerusalem. Jeremiah the prophet was born there and in this city made his first prophecies. The citizens were so angry with the prophet that they threatened his life (see *Jeremiah*). *1 Kings 2:26; Isaiah 10:30; Jeremiah 1:1; 11:21-23.*

ANDREW
(AN-droo)
A fisherman from Capernaum and a brother of Simon Peter. Andrew was one of Jesus' first disciples and was one of the twelve apostles. *Matthew 4:18-20; 10:2; Mark 1:16.*

ANGEL
In Bible usage a spiritual being or messenger from God sometimes said to appear in human form. Angels are reported as announcing special events and giving help in time of crisis. In the OT angels are mentioned in the stories of Abraham. In the NT angels appear in the accounts of Jesus' birth and his temptation. *Genesis 22:11; 31:11; Exodus 3:2; 23:20-24; 1 Kings 19:5; Psalm 91:11; Matthew 4:6, 11; Luke 1:26-38; 2:9-15.*

ANNUNCIATION
(a-nuhn-si-AY-shuhn)
In the NT the angel Gabriel's

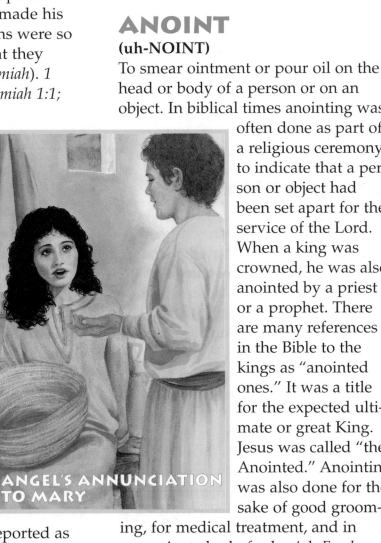

ANGEL'S ANNUNCIATION TO MARY

announcement to Mary that she would give birth to a son whose name was to be Jesus. *Luke 1:26-38.*

ANOINT
(uh-NOINT)
To smear ointment or pour oil on the head or body of a person or on an object. In biblical times anointing was often done as part of a religious ceremony to indicate that a person or object had been set apart for the service of the Lord. When a king was crowned, he was also anointed by a priest or a prophet. There are many references in the Bible to the kings as "anointed ones." It was a title for the expected ultimate or great King. Jesus was called "the Anointed." Anointing was also done for the sake of good grooming, for medical treatment, and in preparing a body for burial. *Exodus 29:36; 30:30; Ruth 3:3; 1 Samuel 9:15-16; 2 Kings 9:1-3; Matthew 6:17; Mark 16:1; Luke 7:44-46.*

ANTICHRIST
(AN-tye-kriste)
As used in the NT a demonic being in opposition to the Christ. The word is also used to refer to actual historical rulers who fight against the faithful. *1 John 2:18, 22; 4:3; 2 John 1:7.*

ANTIOCH
(AN-tee-ok)

1. A city near the seacoast north of Israel. It was the third largest city in the Roman Empire. It was in Antioch that the followers of Christ first came to be called Christians and from Antioch that Paul set out on his missionary journeys. *Acts 11:19-30.*
2. A Greek city in Pisidia also visited by Paul. *Acts 13:14.*

APOCRYPHA
(uh-POK-reh-feh)

The title given to fourteen or fifteen books written during the last two centuries B.C. and the first century A.D. but not included in the Hebrew scriptures when these scriptures were made official by the Council of Jamnia about A.D. 90. These books were, however, included in the Septuagint, or Greek translation of the OT. The word originally meant "hidden books." "Hidden" referred to the secret wisdom they contained. Gradually the word came to refer to books not in the canon, that is, not officially recognized as sacred scripture. When any apocryphal books appear in Protestant Bibles, they are usually placed between the OT and NT.

APOLLOS
(uh-Pahl-uhss)

An important member and worker in the early Christian church. He was an evangelist and a scholarly and fluent preacher. *Acts 18:24–19:1; 1 Corinthians 1:12; 3:4-9; 4:6; 16:12.*

APOSTLE
(eh-POS-ehl)

A title meaning "messenger" or "someone who is sent." It was the title applied to the twelve disciples sent out by Jesus. It was also used to refer to Paul, and to certain other first-generation leaders in the early church. *Matthew 10:1-5; Mark 6:30; Luke 6:13-16; 9:10; Acts 14:4, 14; Romans 16:7; 1 Corinthians 15:9; Ephesians 4:11.*

AQUILA AND PRISCILLA
(AK-weh-leh, pri-SIL-eh)

A husband and wife who were companions of Paul in Corinth and Ephesus and like Paul were tentmakers. They became partners with Paul in his missionary work, possibly as teachers. *Acts 18:2-3, 16, 26; Romans 16:3-4; 1 Corinthians 16:19.*

ARABAH
(AR-uh-buh)

One of the main regions of Israel lying below sea level. It contains the Jordan Valley, Sea of Galilee, the Dead Sea, and the land south to the Gulf of Aqabah. In the Bible "the Arabah" meant any part of this long valley. The southern Arabah was one of the areas through which the Israelites traveled on their journey from Egypt to Canaan. *Deuteronomy 1:1; 2:8; 4:9; Joshua 8:14; Ezekiel 47:8.*

ARABIA
(uh-RAY-bee-uh)

A large peninsula in southwest Asia. Its present-day boundaries are: the

Red Sea on the west, the Gulf of Adan and the Indian Ocean on the south, the Gulf of Uman and the Persian Gulf on the east, and by Jordan, Syria, and Iraq on the north. The name probably means "desert." Arabia is often mentioned in the Bible as the source of gold, silver, precious stones, perfumes, and spices. The northwest portion of Arabia was the scene of some important biblical events. *1 Kings 10:14-15; 2 Chronicles 9:13-14; Isaiah 21:13; Jeremiah 25:24; Ezekiel 27:21; Galatians 1:17; 4:25.*

ARAM, ARAMEANS
(AIR-uhm, ar-uh-MEE-uhnz)
See *Syria, Syrians.*

ARAMAIC
(ar-uh-MAY-ik)
The name of a group of dialects closely related to the Hebrew language. In the time of Jesus it was the everyday language of the Jews and was spoken by Jesus and the disciples. It still survives in a few villages in the eastern mountain range running parallel to Lebanon and called the Anti-Lebanon. Some parts of the OT were originally written in Aramaic. *2 Kings 18:26; Ezra 4:7; Isaiah 36:11.*

ARARAT
(AIR-uh-rat)
A country in the region of Armenia. It refers to the mountains located in this region that emerged first from the waters in the OT account of the Flood. The Assyrian name was Urartu. *Genesis 8:4; Jeremiah 51:27.*

ARCHANGEL
(ARK-ayn-juhl)
As used in the Bible a chief angel. *1 Thessalonians 4:16; Jude 1:9.*

ARCHAEOLOGY
(ahr-ki-OL-eh-ji)
Study of humanity's past made through the examination of artifacts that have been left behind. These remains are found by digging in the places where ancient towns or burial grounds once were located. Bowls, baskets, tools, tablets of writing, jewelry, and many things of this kind give valuable clues to the history of the people. Archaeologists have made important discoveries that have helped in an understanding of biblical history.

ARCHIVES, HOUSE OF THE
(AHR-kighvz)
Meaning "house of books." In the OT, the house of the archives was the place where historical documents, public records, and probably worn out scrolls were stored. *Ezra 5:17–6:1.*

AREOPAGUS
(AIR-ee-AP-puh-guhss)
A rocky hill in Athens, Greece. It is also the name for a council or court that met there in NT times. Paul was taken to the Areopagus for questioning about his teaching. *Acts 17:19.*

ARIMATHEA
(air-i-muh-THEE-uh)

A town where the Jewish official Joseph lived. After the crucifixion of Jesus, Joseph asked for the body, and he took it and buried it in his own tomb. The location of the town is uncertain. *Matthew 27:57-60; Mark 15:43-46; Luke 23:50-53; John 19:38.*

ARISTARCHUS
(air-i-STAR-kuhss)

A Gentile Christian from Thessalonica who was closely associated with Paul from the time of Paul's missionary journey in Macedonia until Paul's death. Tradition says Aristarchus was martyred in Rome under the emperor Nero. *Acts 19:29; 20:4; Colossians 4:10; Philemon 1:24.*

ARK OF NOAH
(NOH-uh)

In the OT account a floating vessel like a houseboat in which Noah, his family, and at least one pair each of all living creatures took refuge during the Great Flood. *Genesis 6:14–8:19.*

ARK OF THE COVENANT
(KUH-vuh-nuhnt)

A box or chest of acacia wood overlaid with gold. It was too holy to be touched and so was carried by priests and Levites on poles. Inside the ark the stone tablet containing the Ten Commandments were kept. On the ark was the mercy seat, which represented the throne of God and signified God's presence and guidance. For this

ARK OF NOAH

reason the Israelites carried it with them during their wanderings in the wilderness and when they went into battle. Later when Solomon built the temple in Jerusalem, the ark was placed in it. *Exodus 25:10-22; Numbers 10:35-36; Deuteronomy 10:1-5; 1 Samuel 4:4–7:2; 1 Kings 8:6-21; 2 Chronicles 5:2-10.*

Later Artaxerxes stopped the reconstruction of Jerusalem for a while. But he later permitted Nehemiah, his cupbearer, to go to Jerusalem to direct the rebuilding. Artaxerxes decreed that exiles in Babylonia could freely return to Jerusalem. *Ezra 4:11-13, 23-24; 7:1, 7-8, 11-26; Nehemiah 2:1.*

ARMLET

In the OT a metal ring or band worn on the upper arm as jewelry. Armlets were worn by kings and other persons in authority. *Exodus 35:22; Numbers 31:50; 2 Samuel 1:10; Isaiah 3:20.*

ARK OF THE COVENANT

ARMOR OF GOD

A figurative, or pictorial, way of speaking of the protection God gives the faithful to stand against evil. Armor was actually part of the protective equipment of a soldier. It consisted of helmet, girdle, shield, breastplate, mail, and leg guards. These protected the soldier from the blows of his enemies. The armor of God refers to truth, righteousness, peace, faith, and prayer, which strengthen a person to stand against evil. *Ephesians 6:11, 13.*

ARTAXERXES

(ahr-tuh-ZURK-seez)
King of Persia who reigned in the fifth century B.C. It was this king who gave Ezra permission to go to Jerusalem.

ARTEMIS

(AR-tuh-mis)
A goddess worshiped more widely than any other goddess in the Greek world. She was called Diana by the Romans. The NT mentions "silver shrines of Artemis" made in the city of Ephesus by Demetrius, a worker in silver. These were probably small silver pieces made to resemble the shrine of the goddess. The temple to Artemis of the Ephesians was an elaborate building, one of the wonders of the ancient world. It contained a "sacred stone that fell from the sky," which was probably a meteorite. *Acts 19:23-40.*

ASA
(AY-suh)

King of Judah from about 911 to 870 B.C. He undertook to rid the land of idols and incense altars to foreign gods, and to restore the worship of the Lord to its rightful place among the Hebrews. *1 Kings 15:9-24; 2 Chronicles 14:1–16:14.*

ASCENTS, SONG OF
(uh-SENTZ)

Title of Psalms 120–34. Probably the songs the people chanted when going up to Jerusalem at festival times or in procession going up to the temple. The word "ascent" means "a going up."

ASHDOD
(ASH-dod)

One of the five principal cities of the Philistines in OT times. At one time the ark of the covenant was captured by the Philistines and brought to Ashdod and placed beside the pagan god Dagon. *Joshua 13:3; 1 Samuel 5:1-8; 2 Chronicles 26:6.*

ASHERAH
(ash-UR-uh)

Hebrew name for an Amorite or Canaanite goddess associated with the worship of Baal. The word also means an image of Asherah. *Judges 6:25-30; 2 Kings 23:4; 2 Chronicles 33:3.*

ASHKELON
(ASH-kuh-lon)

One of the five principal cities of the Philistines in OT times. It was the only one located on the shores of the Mediterranean Sea. The Israelites captured and held Ashkelon for a brief time. *Joshua 13:3; Judges 1:18; 1 Samuel 6:17; 2 Samuel 1:20.*

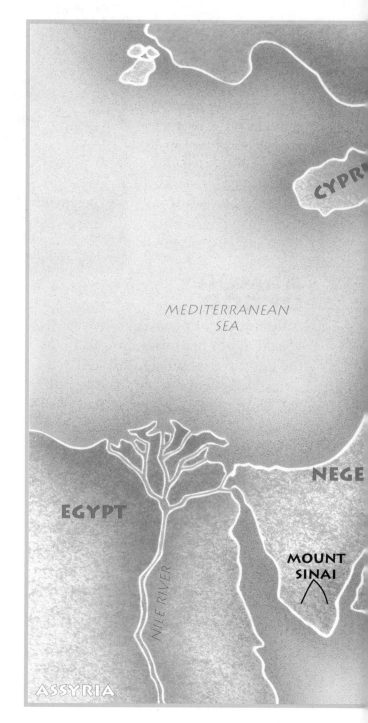

ASSYRIA
(uh-SIHR-ee-uh)

An ancient civilization in Mesopotamia east of the Tigris River. The territory now lies within the borders of Iraq. The Assyrians had many kings who were able military leaders. These people were noted for their cruelty to their captives, often skinning them alive. The Assyrian armies with their horses and chariots often invaded the lands of the Israelites. The Assyrians achieved a strong empire which dominated the world in the eighth century B.C. At this time they destroyed the northern kingdom of Israel and deported the people into other countries. *2 Kings 17:1-6; 18:13–19:36; Psalm 83:8.*

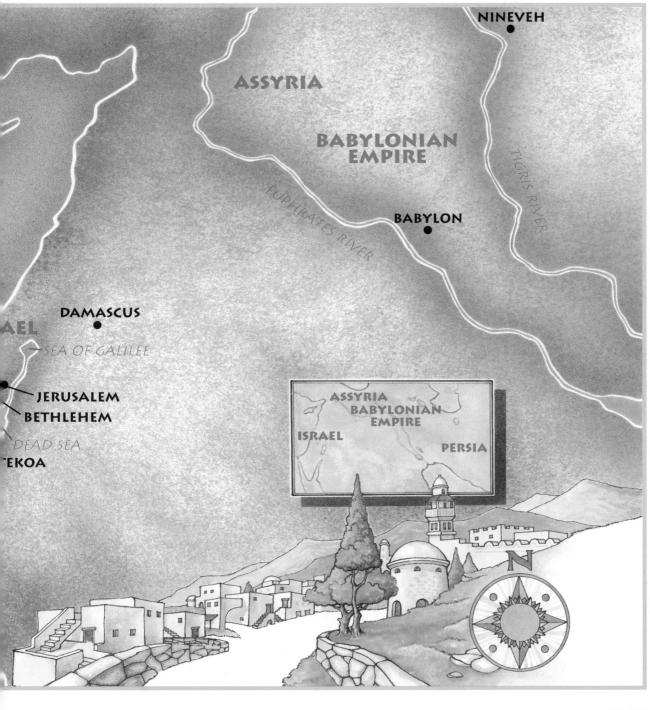

ATHALIAH

(ATH-uh-lye-uh)

Wife of Jehoram (Joram) and daughter of Ahab and Jezebel. She reigned as queen over the northern kingdom of Israel from about 797 to 792 B.C. She was a worshiper of Baal and seems to have had much influence over the life of Israel as the power behind the throne of her son Ahaziah. She seized the throne when he died. The OT account gives the picture of a cold-blooded and ruthless woman. There was a revolt against her led by the priest Jehoida. He and his wife had taken the infant son of Ahaziah and hidden him away. They raised him in secret and had him anointed king when he was seven years old. *2 Kings 11:1-21; 2 Chronicles 22:10-15.*

ATHENS

(ATH-enz)

Chief city of the ancient district of Atica, now the capital of modern Greece. In NT times Paul visited this old city and spoke in the marketplace and in the Aeropagus (see *Aeropagus*). *Acts 17:15-22; 18:1; 1 Thessalonians 3:1.*

ATONEMENT

(uh-TOHN-ment)

The achievement of a state of harmony, or the overcoming of conflict or separation. In the biblical accounts, the Hebrews were deeply conscious of humanity's separation from God due to humanity's sin. The Hebrews made sacrifices and offerings to the Lord to achieve reconciliation. These sacrifices, usually animals, symbolized the unworthiness of the person who made the offering and also that person's desire to be united with God (see *Reconciliation*.) *Exodus 29:33; Leviticus 4:20; 16:1-22; 23:27-28; Numbers 29:11; Nehemiah 10:32-33.*

ATONEMENT, DAY OF

For the Hebrews a day of fasting and repentance. In OT times this was the one day of the year when the most holy place of the temple was entered, and then only by the high priest. Here he sprinkled the blood of a sacrifice to atone for the sins of all the people. As a symbol that the people were cleansed of their sins, a goat, called the scapegoat, was led through the wilderness and pushed over a precipice. Still a most solemn holy day for Jews everywhere, the Day of Atonement (Yom Kippur) comes in the autumn. *Leviticus 16:1-34; 25:9.*

AUGUSTUS, CAESAR

(uh-GUHS-tuhss, SEE-zur)

Founder of the Roman Empire and ruler over it when Jesus Christ was born. *Luke 2:1.*

AZARIAH

(az-uh-RYE-uh)

See *Uzziah.*

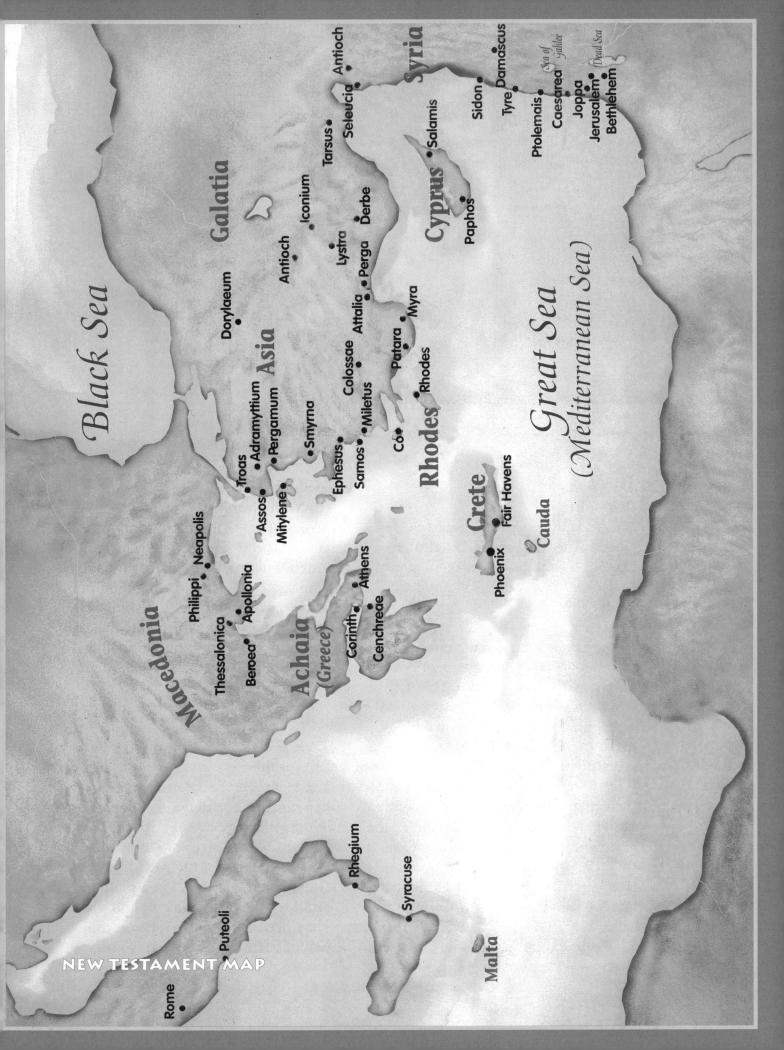

NEW TESTAMENT MAP

Bb

BAAL
(BAY-uhl)

A Canaanite word which means "lord." The Canaanites called their chief god Baal, but there were many less important gods also known as Baals. These were connected with a particular place. The high places and the pagan ceremonies which the OT prophets cried out against were connected with Baal worship. The Israelites were often tempted by Baal worship. Jezebel, King Ahab's wife, tried to persuade Ahab to make the worship of Baal the official religion of Israel. The names of many places in Palestine were combined with Baal to indicate that the place belonged to the god. Some of the Hebrews even called their children by names ending in Baal, such as Eshbaal and Meribbaal (see 1 Chronicles 8:33-34). *Deuteronomy 4:1-3; Judges 2:11-13; 8:33; 1 Kings 16:31-32; Psalm 106:28; Hosea 2:17.*

BAASHA
(BAY-uh-shuh)

King of the northern kingdom of Israel about 909 to 886 B.C. He became king following the reign of Nadab, whom he murdered during a military campaign against the Philistines. He reigned at Tirzah, which was the capital of the northern kingdom before Omri built up Samaria. *1 Kings 15:27-30, 33; 16:1-7.*

BABEL
(BAY-bhul)

The Hebrew form of the name Babylon. Also, a play on a Hebrew word meaning "to mix." The OT account of the tower of Babel tells how the people of the world, after the Great Flood, gathered on a plain to build for themselves a city and unite. They decided to make a tower that would reach to heaven. This was the

28

occasion for the mixing of their languages so that they no longer understood one another. It is interesting to note that the Babylonians worshiped their god Marduk in a tower-like structure. *Genesis 11:1-9.*

BABYLON

(BAB-uh-lawn)

An ancient city of Mesopotamia whose ruins are situated on the lower Euphrates River. It lies southwest of Baghdad in modern Iraq. Babylon was the capital city of the great Babylonian Empire under King Nebuchadnezzar. When Nebuchadnezzar captured Judah, the Hebrew people were taken as captives to Babylonia. *2 Kings 24:1–25:30.*

BACKSLIDING

A term used by the prophets to describe the Hebrew people's rejection of and disobedience to God. The word means "sliding back from" or "turning away from" what the people knew to be right. *Isaiah 57:17; Jeremiah 8:5.*

BALAAM

(BAY-luhm)

A prophet in early OT times. When Balak, king of Moab, feared an invasion of the Israelites, he summoned Balaam to pronounce a curse on them. Instead Balaam, even though he was not an Israelite, uttered a blessing as God commanded him. There is also a story about Balaam's talking donkey. NT references to Balaam are unfavorable. *Numbers 22:5–24:25;*

31:8, 16; Deuteronomy 23:4-5; Joshua 13:22; 24:9-10; Nehemiah 13:2; Micah 6:5; 2 Peter 2:15; Jude 1:11; Revelation 2:14.

BALANCES

A type of scale made by hanging two pans from each end of a beam which is balanced by being suspended on a cord or from a shaft. To weigh metal or grain, blocks or stones of a given size were put in one pan and the material to be weighed in the other. Material or weights were added until the pans hung evenly. Hebrew law required honest balances. The term is used as a figure of speech in Hebrew poetry to express the idea that people must be "weighed," or measured, against the standards of goodness. *Leviticus 19:35-36; Isaiah 40:12; Amos 8:5; Daniel 5:27.*

TOWER OF BABEL

BANKING

The business of making loans, receiving deposits of money, and changing the money of one nation to the money of another. In NT times bankers carried on their business at tables in the market-place. *Matthew 25:27; Luke 19:23.*

BANNER

A sign, symbol, or standard held high on a pole as the emblem of a tribe (see Numbers 2:10). Troops of soldiers used banners rather like flags to rally the men, and trumpets were sounded when the banners were raised or paraded (see Isaiah 18:3). The Egyptians, Assyrians, Babylonians, Persians, and Romans all had banners which they carried. The eagle was used on the banners of imperial Rome; the god Asher drawing a bow was used on the banners of Assyria. *Exodus 17:15-16; Song of Solomon 6:4, 10; Jeremiah 50:2.*

BANQUET
(BANG-kwit)

A meal consisting of large quantities of rich foods. The prophet Amos described banquet customs in OT times when guests would eat lying on beds, or couches, of ivory (see Amos 6:4-6). Banquets were held on many occasions such as harvests, birthdays, weddings, and important national occasions like the crowning of a king or the signing of a treaty. *Esther 1:1-9; 2:18; Mark 6:21; Luke 14:12-24.*

BAPTISM
(BAP-tiz-uhm)

A ceremonial act using water to sym-bolize washing or making pure in the sight of God. In the NT John the Baptist used baptism as a sign of repentance. Later Jesus' disciples used baptism as an outward sign of belief in Jesus Christ and the new, clean life of faith. This ceremony marks a per-son's acceptance into the fellowship of the Christian community. Most Christian churches baptize either by sprinkling water on the head, by immersion where the whole body is lowered under the water, or by pouring water over the head or body. *Matthew 28:18-20; Mark 1:4-5, 9-11; Luke 3:3; Acts 2:37-38, 41; 8:12; 16:14-15.*

BARABBAS
(buh-RAB-uhss)

A prisoner of the Roman authorities at the time of Jesus' trial. The Roman rulers made it a practice at times, espe-cially on holidays, to please the people by freeing a prisoner. During the feast of the Passover, Jesus and Barabbas were among those from whom one was to be chosen. The people, urged on by the chief priests and other leaders, chose Barabbas to be set free. Jesus was crucified. *Matthew 27:15-21; Mark 15:6-15; Luke 23:18-19; John 18:39-40.*

BARAK
(BAIR-uhk)

A Hebrew leader during the time of the judges who with the prophetess Deborah, led an Israelite army in a vic-torious campaign against the Canaanites. Barak is also mentioned in a NT list of ancient people whose faithfulness was commendable. *Judges 4:6–5:15; Hebrews 11:32.*

BARBARIAN
(bar-BUHR-i-an)
Originally someone who spoke a different language; in the NT the word means "foreigner"—someone neither Greek nor Jew. Paul used the term "barbarian" when he said that he was under obligation to preach the gospel to all. *Romans 1:14; Colossians 3:11.*

BARLEY
An important grain or cereal in Bible times that was cheaper than wheat and ripened earlier. It was used as food for animals and humans and was especially important to the poor. At the beginning of the barley harvest, the people brought a sheaf of the first fruits to the priest (see Leviticus 23:10-14) as a dedication of the entire harvest. *Exodus 9:31; Deuteronomy 8:7-10; Judges 7:13; Ruth 1:22; 2:17; 2 Samuel 17:27-29; 1 Kings 4:28; 2 Kings 7:1, 16, 18; 2 Chronicles 2:10, 15.*

BARNABAS
(BAR-nuh-buhss)
One of the first men in Jerusalem to accept Christianity. His first home was on the island of Cyprus. After the crucifixion of Jesus, Barnabas worked with the apostles and later became a leader of the Antioch church. He introduced Paul to the disciples in Jerusalem and was Paul's companion on several missionary journeys. His name meant "son of encouragement," and his work was important in his homeland of Cyprus. *Acts 4:36-37; 9:26-30; 11:22-30; 13:1-4; and other places in Acts; 1 Corinthians 9:6; Galatians 2:1, 9, 13.*

BARNABAS PREACHING

BARRACKS

Buildings for lodging soldiers. In the NT these were headquarters of Roman officers stationed in Jerusalem. Paul was taken to the barracks for protection when he was seized in Jerusalem. *Acts 21:30-37; 22:24; 23:10, 16, 21.*

BARTHOLOMEW

(bar-THOL-uh-myoo)
One of the twelve apostles. His name meant "son of Talmai." He may also have been known as Nathanael (see John 1:45-51). In the Armenian church there is a tradition that the gospel was brought to Armenia by Thaddeus and Bartholomew. *Matthew 10:3; Mark 3:18; Luke 6:14; Acts 1:13.*

BARTIMAEUS

(bar-ti-MAY-uhss)
A blind beggar of Jericho. He was healed by Jesus. *Mark 10:46-52.*

BARUCH

(bah-ROOK)
Scribe of secretary to the prophet Jeremiah. It is likely that some of the scrolls which Jeremiah dictated to Baruch are part of the book of Jeremiah. Baruch may also have written some of the material himself. *Jeremiah 32:12-16; 36:4-32.*

BASHAN

(BAY-shuhn)
A wide, fertile plain in the northern part of the land east of the Jordan River. A seminomadic people called Amorites or Westerners settled here in 2000 B.C. The area was well suited for growing wheat and raising cattle, and reference to this often appears in the poetry of the Bible. Bashan was taken by the Israelites and divided among the tribes of Israel. *Deuteronomy 3:1-14; Joshua 9:9-10; 1 Kings 4:13, 19; 2 Kings 10:32-33; 1 Chronicles 5:11; Psalms 22:12; 68:15, 22; Isaiah 2:13; Amos 4:1.*

BASIN

A bowl-like vessel of any size. The words "basin" and "bowl" are often used to indicate the same thing in the Bible. Basins of many sizes and types were used in making sacrifices. These vessels were also used for table service and for cleaning, much as they are used today. Small bowls were placed on tables for washing before meals. Water was poured from a pitcher over the hands and caught in the bowls. Basins were placed at the doors of houses for washing dusty feet before entering. *Exodus 12:22; 24:6; Numbers 4:14; 7:83; John 13:5.*

BATHSHEBA

(bath-SHEE-buh)
The beautiful wife of Uriah, a soldier in the army of King David. The king desired to make Bathsheba his wife, and so he ordered that Uriah be put in a dangerous spot in battle so that he would be killed. When this happened, David took the woman as his own wife. The prophet Nathan condemned this sinful affair. Solomon, who later became king, was the son of Bathsheba and David. (See *Solomon, Uriah*). *2 Samuel 11:1-17, 26-27; 1 Kings 1:11-40; 2:13-25.*

BATTERING RAM

An antique engine of warfare. It was used by the Assyrians. The battering ram was a large pole with a heavy head supported in a framework set on wheels so that it could be rammed against the gates and walls of a city to break them down (see 2 Samuel 20:15). *Ezekiel 4:2; 21:22; 26:9.*

BEARD

The hair growing on a man's face. Hebrew men wore full beards and cut them only in times of mourning. The Egyptians and Romans shaved their faces, and the pharaohs sometimes wore artificial beards. *Leviticus 14:9; 19:27; 2 Samuel 19:24; Isaiah 7:20; 15:2.*

BEATEN OIL

The high quality olive oil made by crushing ripe olives in a mortar. This oil was used in the lamp in the sanctuary and with the daily sacrifices. *Exodus 27:20; 29:40; 1 Kings 5:11.*

BEATITUDE
(bee-AT-i-tud)

A form of writing which begins with the word "blessed." There are beatitudes in the OT and NT, but the most familiar are those in the Sermon on the Mount. (See Psalms 1:1; 119:1-2; Isaiah 56:2; Matthew 5:3-12.)

BEELZEBUL
(bee-EL-zuh-buhl)

A name for Satan, also spelled Beelzebub. *Matthew 10:25; 12:24, 27; Mark 3:22; Luke 11:15, 18-19.*

BEER
(BEE-uhr)

A word meaning "well" that is often used in combination with place names as in the name Beer-sheba. Also the place where the Israelites dug a well which offered such an adequate water supply that the people sang praises to it. *Numbers 21:16-18; Judges 9:21.*

BASIN

BEERSHEBA
(bihr-SHEE-buh)

The principal city of the Negeb in the southern part of Palestine. In the time of Abraham a religious sanctuary was located there. Beersheba was at the southern tip of the Israelite country while Dan was at the northern tip, so the expression "from Dan to Beersheba" meant the entire nation. There is an important modern city just west of the old site. (See *Beer.*) *Genesis 21:25-33; 26:32-33; 46:1, 5; Judges 20:1; 1 Samuel 3:20; 8:2; 1 Kings 4:25; 19:3; 2 Kings 12:1; Nehemiah 11:27, 30.*

BELIAL
(BEE-lee-uhl)

Meaning worthless or ungodly. In the OT it is used in such Hebrew expressions as son, daughter, or man of Belial and is translated as "worthless one," or something similar. (See 1 Samuel 2:12; Job 34:18.) In the NT it refers to Satan or an enemy of Christ. *2 Corinthians 6:15.*

BENEDICTION
(ben-uh-DIK-shuhn)

A prayer for God's blessing. Several NT letters close with benedictions. *Numbers 6:24-26; Romans 15:13; 2 Corinthians 13:14; Hebrews 13:20-21.*

BENJAMIN
(BEN-juh-min)

A son of Jacob for whom one of the twelve tribes of Israel was named. As a son of Rachel, the favored wife, he was especially loved by his father. The name also refers to the territory occupied by the Benjamites. *Genesis 35:16-18, 24; 42:4, 36; 43:14-16, 34; 44:12; 45:12, 14, 22; Joshua 18:11-20.*

BETHANY
(BETH-uh-nee)

A small village just under two miles from Jerusalem, near the Mount of Olives. It was the home of Mary, Martha, and Lazarus, close friends of Jesus with whom he sometimes stayed. *Matthew 21:17; 26:6; Mark 11:1, 11-12; 14:3; Luke 24:50; John 11:1, 18.*

BETHEL
(BETH-uhl)

Meaning "house of God." A city of major importance mentioned in the OT. It was located on a major road running along the ridge where the territories of Ephraim and Benjamin met. When Abraham stopped near Bethel, he built an altar to God. Three years later, Jacob's name was changed to Israel. *Genesis 12:8; 13:3; 28:10-22; 31:13; 35:1-15; Judges 1:22-26; 20:18-28; 1 Kings 12:28-33; 2 Kings 2:2-3; 1 Chronicles 7:28; 2 Chronicles 13:19; Amos 7:12-13.*

BETHLEHEM
(BETH-luh-hem)

A town in Judah about six miles south of Jerusalem. Most of the story in the book of Ruth took place in and near Bethlehem. It was also the home of David. It is best known as the birthplace of Jesus. *Genesis 35:19; Judges 17:7-9; Ruth 1:1-2, 19, 22; 2:4; 4:11; 1 Samuel 16:1-4, 18; 17:12, 15; 20:6, 28; 2 Samuel 16:1-4, 18; 17:12, 15; 20:6, 28; 2 Samuel 23:14-16; 1 Chronicles 11:16-18;*

2 Chronicles 11:6; Micah 5:2; Matthew 2:1-16; John 7:42.

BETHPAGE
(BETH-fayj)

A village near Jerusalem, probably east of Bethany. The name means "house of unripe figs," referring to a kind of fig which never looks ripe, even when ready to eat. Bethphage is mentioned in the report of Palm Sunday, that is, Jesus' entry into Jerusalem the week before he was crucified. Bethpage was probably the village where the disciples found the colt on which Jesus rode into the city. *Matthew 21:1; Mark 11:1; Luke 19:29.*

BETHSAIDA
(beth-SAY-duh)

Meaning "house of the fisher," it was a town in NT times, located on the shore of the Sea of Galilee. Bethsaida is mentioned several times in connec-tion with the ministry of Jesus, and it was probably close to this town that the feeding of five thousand people with the loaves and fishes took place. *Matthew 11:21; Mark 6:45; 8:22; Luke 9:10-17; John 1:44.*

BEZALEL
(BEZ-uh-lel)

A skilled and inspired craftsman from the tribe of Judah who was put in charge of making the tabernacle in the wilderness and the ark, altars, tables, and other equipment. He created artistic designs in metal, stone, and wood for decorating the ancient sanctuary. His name means "in the shadow or protection of God." (See *Tabernacle, Ark of the Covenant.*) *Exodus 31:1-5; 35:30–36:2; 37:1; 38:22; 1 Chronicles 2:20; 2 Chronicles 1:5.*

BETHLEHEM

BIRTHRIGHT

The special rights and privileges of the firstborn or eldest son. In OT times the eldest son inherited more of his father's wealth than did his younger brothers and became head of the family after his father's death (see *Firstborn*). The OT reports that Jacob deceived his father to obtain the birthright that was rightly his brother's. In the NT Paul's Roman citizenship is mentioned as his birthright. (See Acts 22:28). *Genesis 25:29-34; 43:33; Hebrews 12:16.*

BITTER HERBS

Herbs eaten with lamb during the Passover as a reminder of the bitter experience of the Israelites during the Exodus. Horseradish is the herb commonly used with lamb when Jews eat the Passover meal today. *Exodus 12:8.*

BITUMEN

(bi-TOO-muhn)
Mineral tar asphalt found in wells. Bitumen was mentioned in the OT story of the Tower of Babel as being used for mortar in the building of a city on the Plain of Shinar. It was also used to seal and waterproof the basket of bulrushes in which the infant Moses was placed. *Genesis 11:3; 14:10; Exodus 2:3.*

BLASPHEMY

(BLAS-fuh-mee)
Any dishonoring of the name of God by slandering, cursing, or an act of irreverence. For the Hebrews the name of God was so sacred that it could be spoken only with great reverence, and to use the name of God for a wrong or foolish purpose was a serious sin. In the NT some of the religious leaders of the Jews accused Jesus of blasphemy because he spoke of a familiar relationship with God. In the early church blasphemy included active interference with the preaching of the gospel of Jesus Christ. *Leviticus 24:11; 1 Samuel 3:13; Nehemiah 9:18-19; Matthew 12:31; 26:63-65; Mark 14:61-64; John 10:33-36; Romans 2:24; 1 Timothy 1:12-13; James 2:7.*

BLESSED

To be favored with spiritual happiness. In the OT the term usually included in its meaning long life and prosperity in harmony with God and God's law. When "blessed" is applied to God, it is an exclamation of worship. In the NT "blessed" is used for faithful Christians, especially those who suffer for their faithfulness. (See *Beatitude*.) *Genesis 48:14-15; 2 Samuel 6:11; Psalms 1:1-2; 28:6; Matthew 13:16; 16:17; Luke 6:20-23; 1 Timothy 1:11; 6:15; James 1:12.*

BLIND

Without sight. The blind had a difficult life in Bible times. They could only beg for a living. Many times people considered that such afflictions were caused by sin, so the blind were often outcasts. *Leviticus 19:14; Deuteronomy 27:18; Luke 4:18-19; John 9:1-41.*

BLOODGUILT

The guilt of one who shed the blood of an innocent person, even if the killing was accidental. This guilt could not be atoned for or taken away by offering a sacrifice. By OT law the entire community shared in the bloodguilt, and for this reason everyone helped find the killer and saw that the punishment required by law was carried out.

If the killing was intentional, the murderer must die. If accidental, the killer could serve a period of time in a city of refuge. (See *Cities of Refuge*.) *Exodus 22:2-3; Deuteronomy 19:8-10; 1 Samuel 25:26, 33; Psalm 51:14.*

JACOB STEALS ESAU'S BIRTHRIGHT

BOAT

A small open vessel, usually a sailboat and sometimes having oars, used for fishing on the Sea of Galilee. Also a smaller craft used for ferrying across the Jordan River. *Matthew 4:21-22; Mark 3:9; Luke 5:1-3; John 6:22-24.*

BOAZ

(BOH-az)
A wealthy landowner of Bethlehem. He married Ruth, the Moabitess, and became the great grandfather of David. *Ruth 2:1–4:22; Matthew 1:5.*

BODY

In the OT "body" refers to the whole physical makeup of a person. In the NT the word has added spiritual meanings. Jesus used bread as a symbol of his body. Paul talked about disciplining the body because physical desires often interfere with a person's good intentions. The church is called the body of Christ. *Job 14:22; Psalm 109:24; Matthew 6:22; 26:26; Luke 12:22-23; 1 Corinthians 6:19; 10:16-17; 12:12-27; Ephesians 2:3; James 3:2-3.*

BOOK

In Bible times a strip of leather or papyrus upon which were written laws, history, stories, prophecies, and other literary compositions. These were rolled up and often sealed. Several books which are not part of the Bible are mentioned by name in the OT, for example the "Book of Jashar." *Exodus 24:7; Joshua 10:13; 2 Kings 22:8; 2 Chronicles 27:7.*

BOOTHS, FEAST OF

One of Israel's three great festivals. It was celebrated with joy and thanksgiving at the end of the harvest season. Each family built a booth of branches and vines as the harvest time approached. The father and older son slept in it to guard the ripening grain. At the time of the feast the family ate meals in the booth for seven days. The celebration also recalled the wilderness life of the Israelites during their long journey from Egypt to Canaan. The festival is also known as the Feast of Tabernacles, the Feast of Ingathering, and the Feast of the Lord. *Leviticus 23:34, 39-43; Deuteronomy 16:13-17; Ezra 3:4; Nehemiah 8:13-18; Zechariah 14:16-19.*

BOW AND ARROW

A weapon used by hunters and warriors. In Bible times the bow was made of wood or bone with a gut or hide string. The arrows were made of a shaft of reed or light wood to which a pointed head of flint, bone, or metal was fastened. Sometimes the arrows were given barbs or dipped in poison to make them more painful or deadly. *Genesis 21:20; Isaiah 7:24; Hosea 1:7.*

BREAD

An important item of food made from wheat or barley flour, mixed with water, kneaded, and baked. People who were wandering nomads did not have much bread since they did not raise the grain needed to make flour or meal. However, for settled people of all periods in history bread has been a basic food. This was true in OT and NT times. Bread also had a religious use. In OT times the Hebrews made offerings of flour alone or of loaves. In NT times it was unleavened bread that Jesus used as a symbol of his body. *Genesis 14:18; 18:5-6; 41:54; Leviticus 23:17; Psalm 104:15; Mark 14:22; Luke 22:19.*

BREAD OF THE PRESENCE

Also called showbread. Twelve loaves of bread made of fine flour, arranged in two rows on a table in the temple or sanctuary as an offering to God. The number twelve suggested the twelve tribes of Israel. Fresh loaves were brought each sabbath, and the old loaves were eaten by the priests (see Leviticus 24:5-9). This offering of holy bread was required to be in the sanctuary continually. *Exodus 25:30; 1 Samuel 21:6; 1 Kings 7:48; 1 Chronicles 9:32; 2 Chronicles 4:19; 13:11; Matthew 12:1-4.*

BREASTPIECE

An ornamental piece of folded material attached by golden rings to the ephod, a garment worn by the high priest in the sanctuary. It had four rows of three jewels each, set in gold. Each jewel represented one of the tribes of Israel. This pouchlike piece carried the Urim and Thummim (probably stones and sticks of uneven lengths) with which the priest, in the early days, determined by lot God's judgments on the people. (See *Ephod, Urim and Thummim.*) *Exodus 28:4, 15-30.*

BREASTPLATE

A piece of armor made of solid metal, attached to or worn over a tunic to protect the chest, shoulders, and back of a soldier. Before the use of metal, leather or padded cloth was used. *1 Kings 22:34; 2 Chronicles 18:33; Isaiah 59:17; Ephesians 6:14; 1 Thessalonians 5:8.*

FEAST OF BOOTHS

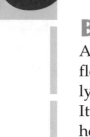

BRICK

The most common building material of the Bible lands. Clay was shaped into blocks and dried in the sun or in an oven called a kiln. During their stay in Egypt the Hebrews were forced to make bricks of clay, bound with straw, for the pharaoh. *Exodus 1:14, 5:7-19.*

BROOM TREE

A desert shrub or bush with pale pink flowers like pea blossoms. It frequently grows large enough to offer shade. Its roots and foilage burn with intense heat and make a fine charcoal. *1 Kings 19:5; Job 30:4; Psalm 120:4.*

BROTHERS AND SISTERS

In the NT Jesus looked upon all believers who wanted to do God's will as his brothers and sisters. Paul addressed the people in the Christian churches as brothers and sisters. *1 Corinthians 1:10-13*

BUCKLER

(BUHK-ler)
A shield. The words "shield" and "buckler" were used to refer to the same thing. In OT times it was a small, movable guard made of leather or metal and carried in the hand or worn on one arm of a soldier while he carried his weapon in the other. With this movable shield the soldier protected parts of his body not covered with armor and warded off the blows and weapons of his enemies. The terms "shield" and "buckler" were some-times used as figures of speech for God's protection and God's truth. (See *Armor of God.*) *1 Kings 10:16-17; 2 Chronicles 14:8; Psalms 35:2; 91:4.*

BULL

Male bovine animal, such as an ox or bull, used for sacrifice in the temple. *Exodus 29:1, and other verses; Leviticus 1:5; and other places in Leviticus; Numbers 7:15; and other references.*

BULRUSH

A kind of reed that grows in swampy places and beside streams. Baskets were woven from bulrushes. It was also called papyrus plant (see Isaiah 18:2), and from it came the earliest known material for the making of paper. *Exodus 2:3.*

BULWARK

(BUHL-werk)
A wall or barrier built for defense purposes, sometimes called a rampant. In the OT "bulwark" is used in figures of speech to describe God's protection. The church is sometimes called a bulwark of truth. *Psalm 8:2; Jeremiah 50:15; 1 Timothy 3:15.*

BUSH, THE BURNING

The flaming bush through which Moses became aware of God's presence and God's plans for Israel. *Exodus 3:2–4:17.*

CAESAR

(SEE-zur)

The family name of Julius Caesar. The name was taken by his adopted son, Octavius or Octavian, who was also Julius Caesar's grandnephew. Octavian became the first emperor of the Roman Empire, and the title Caesar Augustus was conferred on him by the Roman Senate. The term became the title of all succeeding Roman emperors. Caesar Augustus ruled from 27 B.C. to A.D. 14 and was the emperor when Jesus was born. Several other Caesars are mentioned in the NT. Caesar Augustus—*Luke 2:1-7*; Tiberius Caesar—*Mark 12:14-17; Luke 3:1; 23:2; John 19:12-15*; Claudius Caesar—*Acts 18:2*; Nero (probably)—*Acts 25:8-12; 28:17-19*.

CAESAREA

(sess-uh-REE-uh)

A city of NT times on the coast of Judea, twenty-three miles south of Mt. Carmel. The city was rebuilt in Greek style by Herod the Great and named in honor of Caesar Augustus. Caesarea was the headquarters of the Roman government in Judea. The city is mentioned in the stories of Paul. *Acts 8:40; 9:30; 1:1, 24; 11:11; 18:22; 21:8; 23:23; 25:13.*

CAESAREA PHILIPPI

(sess-uh-REE-uh, FIL-i-pye)

A city located in NT times on the southwestern slope of Mt. Hermon in Judea. The city probably controlled a large area around it, for there are references in the NT to districts and villages of Caesarea Philippi. It was here that Jesus asked Peter and the other disciples the question, "But who do you say that I am?" *Matthew 16:13-20; Mark 8:27-30.*

CAIAPHAS
(KYE-uh-fuhss)

The high priest before whom Jesus was brought to trial (see mark 14:53; Luke 22:54). He is also named among those who plotted the arrest and crucifixion of Jesus. *Matthew 26:3-4, 57; John 11:47-50; 18:13-14.*

CAIN
(kane)

Eldest son of Adam and Eve. Cain became jealous of his brother Abel and murdered him. He was punished by being exiled from his land. *Genesis 4:1-16.*

CALEB
(KAY-leb)

One of the spies sent into Canaan by Moses to find out more about the land before the people of Israel tried to enter it. *Numbers 13:1-30.*

CALF, GOLDEN

In the OT an image of a bull made of wood and overlaid with gold before which the people made sacrifices and offerings and indulged in heathen celebrations—especially the calf image made by Aaron while the people of Israel camped near Mt. Sinai. It was also called "molten calf." *Exodus 32:3-6; Deuteronomy 9:16, 21; 2 Kings 10:29; 17:16; 2 Chronicles 11:15; 13:8; Nehemiah 9:18; Psalm 106:19.*

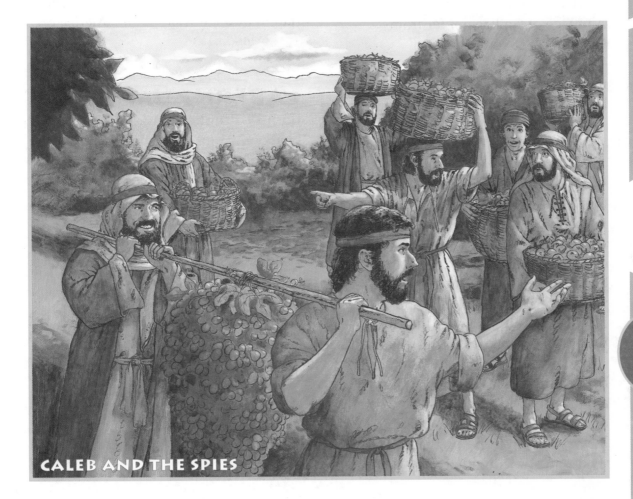

CALEB AND THE SPIES

CAMEL

A large animal used as a beast of burden and for travel in the desert. The camel is a cud-chewing mammal that is well suited to desert life. It thrives on desert plants and goes several days without water. Its flat feet keep it from sinking as it walks in sand. The Hebrews did not eat camel meat though other people of the Middle East did. Camel milk was used, however, and camel hair was woven into wool for tents and clothing. Most of the biblical references are to the one-humped Arabian camel. *Genesis 24:10-11; 32:15; Leviticus 11:4; Deuteronomy 14:7; 2 Kings 8:9; Matthew 19:24.*

CANA
(KAY-nuh)

A village of Galilee not far from Nazareth. It was the home of Nathanael, one of the disciples. It was the scene of Jesus' first miracle, when he turned water into wine. *John 2:1-11; 4:46; 21:2.*

CANAAN
(KAY-nuhn)

In the OT the territory bounded on the west by the Mediterranean Sea, on the east by the Jordan River, on the south by Sinai, and on the north by Syria. It was sometimes called the Land of Promise because this was the land promised to Abraham. This was the territory invaded and finally conquered by the Israelites after they left Egypt and crossed the wilderness. The people of the land were called Canaanites, and they spoke a Semitic language. The whole area was divided into several local kingdoms which had strongly fortified cities. When conquered, some Canaanites remained in the land and others migrated to Phoenicia. Canaan came to be called Palestine. The area today includes the countries of Israel, Lebanon, and part of Jordan (see *Palestine*). *Genesis 12:5-7; Deuteronomy 32:48-49; Joshua 14:1; Psalm 105:8-11.*

CANANAEAN
(kay-nuhn-NEE-uhn)

A name given to a certain Simon, a disciple of Jesus, to distinguish him from Simon Peter. In Luke 6:15 and Acts 1:13 Simon is referred to as the Zealot. Cananaean means "zealot." This may indicate that he was a member of one of the Jewish political parties that grew up in protest against the Roman domination of the Jewish nation. *Matthew 10:4; Mark 3:18.*

CAPERNAUM
(kuh-PUR-nuhm)

One of the most important cities on the shore of the Sea of Galilee. Capernaum was the scene for much of Jesus' teaching and healing and is the only place where Jesus is said to be "at home." It was the home of Peter, Andrew, James, and John and probably the home of Matthew (Levi). *Matthew 4:13; 8:5-6; 11:23; 17:24; Mark 1:21; 2:1; 9:33; Luke 4:23, 31; 10:15; John 2:12; 4:46; 6:16, 24, 59.*

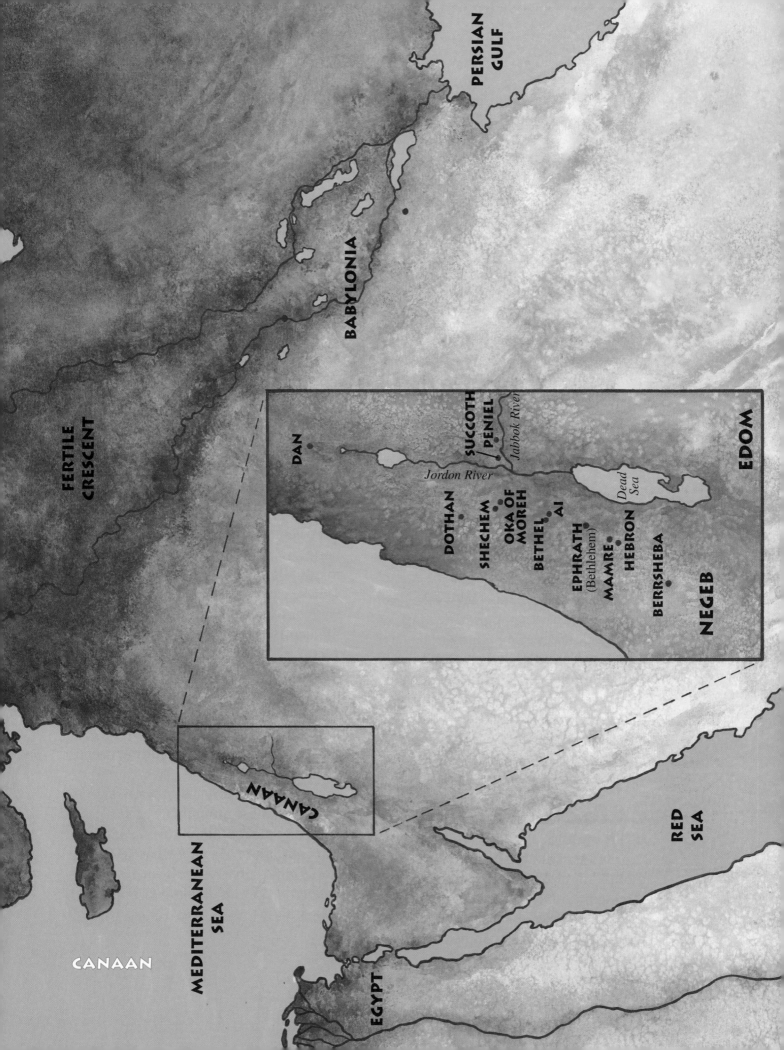

PERSIAN GULF

BABYLONIA

FERTILE CRESCENT

DAN

SUCCOTH
PENIEL

Jabbok River

Jordon River

Dead Sea

EDOM

DOTHAN

SHECHEM

OKA OF
MOREH

BETHEL

AI

EPHRATH
(Bethlehem)

MAMRE

HEBRON

BERRSHEBA

NEGEB

CANAAN

MEDITERRANEAN
SEA

CANAAN

EGYPT

RED
SEA

CAPTAIN

A person having authority over others. This word is applied in the Bible to many different kinds of people: heads of the camps in the wilderness, men in charge of armies, and priests in charge of the temple guards were all called captains. *1 Samuel 22:2; 2 Kings 1:9-14; Acts 4:1, 5:24.*

CAPTIVITY

Being taken and kept imprisoned or enslaved by force, especially being taken from one's own country and made to live in another land. In the OT it usually refers to the Babylonian captivity when the people of Judah were conquered by Nebuchadnezzar and carried off to Babylon in the sixth century B.C. (See *Exile.*) *2 Kings 24:15; Ezra 3:8; Nehemiah 8:17.*

CARAVAN
(KAR-uh-van)

A group of people, especially merchants with pack animals, traveling together, often through dangerous territory. Caravan routes crisscrossed the ancient world. Asses and camels were used to transport goods, and it may be that there were escorts or guards mounted on horses. *Genesis 37:25; Judges 5:6; 8:11; Job 6:18-19.*

CARMEL, MOUNT
(KAR-muhl)

A prominent mountain at the head of a mountain range on the eastern coast of the Mediterranean Sea which divides the coastal plain of Palestine into two parts. It was the scene of the contest between the prophets of Baal and the prophet Elijah. *Joshua 19:26; 1 Kings 18:19-20; Jeremiah 46:18.*

CARPENTER

In Bible times a craftsman who worked with wood, making yokes, plows, threshing boards, benches, beds, chests, boats. The workshop was usually in the home. Carpenters also worked on the upper stories of stone houses and sometimes repaired gates. Jesus was closely connected with the trade and was probably trained in it since Joseph was a carpenter. *2 Samuel 5:11; 2 Kings 12:11; 1 Chronicles 14:1; 22:15; 2 Chronicles 34:11; Isaiah 44:13; Matthew 13:55; Mark 6:3.*

CASSIA
(kash-UH)

An oriental tree with sweet-smelling bark, probably used in making anointing oil. Buds of the tree were used as we use cloves to season food, and the smaller leaves and pods were used in medicines. *Exodus 30:24; Psalm 45:8; Ezekiel 27:19.*

CATTLE

In biblical usage a general term for domesticated animals including sheep, goats, cows, oxen, asses, and camels. Possession of many cattle was a sign of wealth as these animals were the source of meat, milk, hides, wool, and transportation. They also had an important place in sacrificial worship. *Numbers 31:9, 33; Psalms 50:10; 144:14; John 4:12.*

CEDAR

An evergreen tree with fragrant and beautiful wood which is long lasting. The trees usually grow to a height of twenty feet, but the cedars of Lebanon grew to as much as 120 to 140 feet. Cedar wood was used in burning sacrifices in the temple. A great deal of cedar was used in the building of the temple. The large logs needed for this were made into rafts in the Lebanon mountains and floated down the coast from Tyre to Joppa. Many poets mentioned cedar in their poetry and songs as a symbol of strength and glory. *Numbers 19:6; 1 Kings 7;2-3; Psalms 29:5; 92:12; Ezekiel 31:3-9.*

CENTURION
(sen-TYUR-ee-uhn)

The commanding officer of one hundred foot soldiers, part of a cohort or division in the Roman army. His duty included the punishment of prisoners and the supervision of the executions. In NT stories centurions are mentioned more often than any other army officers. *Matthew 8:5-13; Mark 15:39, 44-45; Luke 7:2-10; 23:44-47; Acts 10:1; 21:31-32; 27:1.*

CENTURION

CHAFF

The useless dry husks of grain which were blown away from the good seed in the process of winnowing. Many Bible references use the word "chaff" as a figure of speech to indicate someone or something worthless. (See *Winnow*.) *Job 13:25; 21:18; Psalms 1:4; 35:5; 83:13; Isaiah 17:13; 29:5; 41:15; Jeremiah 13:24; Hosea 13:3; Zephaniah 2:1-2; Matthew 3:12; Luke 3:17.*

CHALDEANS
(kal-DEE-unhz)

The inhabitants of a region in south Babylonia between the Tigris and Euphrates Rivers. The term came to mean "Babylonians." They conquered the Assyrian Empire, and their kings ruled from the city of Babylon. Nebuchadnezzar was their greatest king (605–562 B.C.). Under him Judea was conquered, Jerusalem destroyed, and the Hebrews carried away into Babylonia (see 2 Kings 24:10-17). *Genesis 11:28; 2 Chronicles 36:17-21; Jeremiah 21:4; 32:4-5; and other places in Jeremiah; Ezekiel 23:23.*

CHAMPION

In the OT a mighty warrior. This word referred to a man who went into the space between two warring armies and as a representative of his army challenged someone from the other army to come out and fight in single combat. Goliath was called a champion. (See *Goliath*.) *1 Samuel 17:4-51.*

CHARIOT

A two-wheeled, horse-drawn vehicle used in war and for travel, especially by kings and officials. The use of swift horses and chariots of wood, wicker, or metal with a built-in case for carrying weapons changed the nature of war. They gave armies that used them a great advantage over foot soldiers. Chariots played an important part in establishing large empires like those of Assyria and Babylonia. The hilly land of Judah kept the Judeans from making good use of chariots in war, but King Solomon had hundreds and built chariot cities like Megiddo. *Genesis 41:43; 46:29; Exodus 14:5-9; 1 Kings 10:26; Acts 8:27-29, 38.*

CHERUB, CHERUBIM

(CHAIR-uhb, CHAIR-uh-bim)

In the OT the reference is to winged angelic creatures. Cherubim are often mentioned in the myths and folklore of the Canaanites. Some of the Canaanite figures have the bodies of animals and the heads of men. There were images of two cherubim on the ark of the covenant. What they looked like we do not know, though they were made of wood and covered with gold. They were placed on either side of the mercy seat, which represented the throne of God, and their outstretched wings touched above it. There were also cherubim embroidered on tapestries hung in the tabernacle and carved on doors of the tabernacle and carved on doors of the temple. *Genesis 3:24; Exodus 25:18-22; 2 Chronicles 3:7, 10-14; Psalms 80:1; 99:1; Isaiah 37:16; Ezekiel 10:1-20.*

CHILDREN OF GOD

The spiritual family of God. In the OT the Hebrews were often referred to as sons or children of God because of their special relation to God as God's chosen people (see Jeremiah 3:14, 22). In the NT a special spiritual relationship with God is still indicated by the term which is used for the followers of Jesus Christ, who are the new people of God. *John 1:12; 11:52; Romans 8:15-16; 9:8; Philippians 2:14-15; 1 John 3:1.*

CHINNERETH, SEA OF

(KIN-uh-reth)

See *Galilee, Sea of.*

CHORAZIN

(KOR-uh-zin)

In NT times a city of Galilee on the hills above Capernaum. One of the cities reproved by Jesus for its unbelief. *Matthew 11:21; Luke 10:13.*

CHRIST

(kriste)

Greek word meaning "the Anointed One," "the Messiah." A title given to the king expected by the Jews. In the NT it is the title most commonly applied to Jesus by his disciples. It soon became almost a name or surname for Jesus. *Mark 1:1; 8:29; Luke 2:26; John 1:41; 4:25; Acts 5:42; Romans 5:8; 6:3; and many other references.*

CHRISTIAN

(KRIS-chuhn)

A term referring to a follower of Jesus, meaning "Christ's man." It was probably used first by pagans or unbelievers when speaking of and belittling the followers of Jesus Christ. The word is used only three times in the Bible. *Acts 11:26; 26:28; 1 Peter 4:16.*

CHRONICLES, FIRST AND SECOND
(KRONuh-kuhlz)

Two books in the OT. The word means "history" or "events of the past." These books contain a history of Israel from Adam to Cyrus, king of Persia. The author, whose name is not known, is called the Chronicler. His purpose was to write about the Hebrews—their national achievements, their temple worship, and their kings. He records special events in the reigns of David and Solomon. *See the books themselves.*

CHURCH

In the NT a fellowship of believers in Jesus Christ gathered together for the purpose of worship, prayer, instruction, and fellowship. The word was used by Paul for a group or congregation in a local community. The first organized church in the NT was made up of the followers of Jesus in Jerusalem. Today "church" also refers to the whole group of believers in Jesus Christ from every land and continent, which is the church universal. *Acts 8:1; 9:31; 11:22, 26; 12:5; 1 Corinthians 1:2; 11:18; 14:4-5, 19, 28; Ephesians 1:22-23; 5:23; Colossians 1:18; 1 Timothy 3:15; Philemon 1:2.*

CIRCUMCISION
(sur-kuhm-SI-zhuhn)

The act of cutting off the foreskin of a baby boy. Among the Hebrews it was a religious ceremony performed on the eighth day after birth. This act dedicated the child and was a sign of the covenant between God and the Hebrews. In the early Christian church some of the leaders insisted that the non-Jews, who were known as Gentiles, be circumcised and obey all the laws of Moses. But Paul argued that this was unnecessary, and at the first church council in Jerusalem it was officially decided that Christians would not be required to obey the Jewish laws or to be circumcised. *Genesis 17:10-14; Exodus 12:48; Luke 2:21; Romans 2:25-29; 1 Corinthians 7:18-19; Galatians 5:2-3.*

CISTERN
(SIS-turn)

A pit dug in the earth and lined with a lime plaster for the storage of water. *2 Kings 18:31; Jeremiah 38:6-13.*

CISTERN

CITADEL
(SIT-eh-duhl)
A fortified building or stronghold within a city, sometimes attached to a palace or temple for the purpose of defense. The last citadel of the Jews in Jerusalem was the Tower of Antonia in Herod's temple. The Romans overran it in A.D. 70. *1 Kings 16:18; 2 Kings 15:25; Psalm 48:3, 13.*

CITIES OF REFUGE
(REF-yooj)
Six cities given to the Levites or priests in OT times to provide refuge for persons who had bloodguilt by accidentally killing someone. In these cities the refugee was safe from anyone wanting to get revenge. The fugitive could remain protected until a congregation judged him to see whether the killing was accidental or intentional. (See *Bloodguilt.*) *Numbers 35:6-14, 25-33; Joshua 20:1-9.*

CITY
In OT times a walled town, in contrast to a village which lay open. The walls served as protection from enemy attack, and people living in the surrounding farmland came inside in times of danger. Cities provided a market and had cisterns to provide water in times of seige. Cities were built on hills as a safeguard against surprise attack. Except in royal cities the streets were narrow and unpaved. *Numbers 13:17-20; Deuteronomy 3:5; 1 Kings 16:24.*

CLOAK
A square of cloth worn as an outer garment over a coat. It was used also by a traveler and by the poor as a bed cover. If borrowed, a cloak had to be returned by nightfall. *Deuteronomy 24:10-13; Matthew 5:40.*

COAT
A long tunic-like shirt usually made of linen and worn by men and women as an undergarment. Coats were sometimes referred to as robes with long sleeves. A coat of mail was a protective garment made of leather and metal and worn into battle over a cloth coat. *Leviticus 8:5-7; 1 Samuel 17:5; 2 Chronicles 26:14; Jeremiah 46:4; Luke 3:11; Acts 9:39.*

COHORT
(KOH-hort)
In NT times a part of the Roman army. A cohort consisted of six hundred men. These were usually posted in small forts on the frontiers. In Jerusalem the cohort was stationed in the Tower of Antonia north of the temple. *Acts 10:1; 21:31; 27:1.*

COLOSSIANS, LETTER TO THE
(kuh-LAH-shuhnz)
A letter written by Paul to the Christians of Colossae, a city in southwestern Asia Minor. Paul was a prisoner in Rome when he had news of false teachings in Colossae. He wrote to remind the people there of the Christian way of life. This letter makes up the twelfth book in the NT. *See the book itself.*

COLT

A young horse or ass. In the OT it is also a young camel. A colt which had never been ridden was brought by the disciples for Jesus to ride into Jerusalem. *Zechariah 9:9; Matthew 21:2-7; Mark 11:1-7.*

COMMANDMENT
(kuh-MAND-ment)

A law or order from someone in authority. In the Bible it is used most frequently for the laws of God found in the early OT books, especially the Ten Commandments, which form the core of the laws given to Moses. *Genesis 26:5; Exodus 24:12; Deuteronomy 11:22-23; Psalm 119:6; Matthew 5:19; 22:35-40; Mark 12:28-31.*

COMMONWEALTH
(KOM-uhn-welth)

A body of people making up a community. Paul used the term to indicate that a Christian is first of all a citizen of heaven and that his conduct and welfare are determined by this citizenship. *Ephesians 2:12; Philippians 3:20-21.*

COMMUNION
(kuh-MYOO-nyuhn)

A term meaning the act of sharing. It is important in the covenant relationship between God and God's people and indicates close friendship (see Exodus 25:8). In the NT a deeper relationship between God and humanity was established through Jesus Christ. This relationship is remembered in the sacrament of the Lord's Supper which is also called Communion. (See Matthew 26:26-29; Mark 14:22-25; Luke 22:14-20; 1 Corinthians 11:23-26.)

JESUS RIDING A COLT

CONCUBINE
(KON-kyoo-bine)

In OT times a slave girl or servant who belonged to a Hebrew family and bore children (see Exodus 21:7-10). Such a girl achieved certain honor if she had sons. *Genesis 22:24; 25:6; 1 Kings 11:3; and other references.*

CONDUIT
(KON-dwit)

A water channel or tunnel. One of these ancient water-supply channels was built in Jerusalem by King Hezekiah to bring water into the city. *2 Kings 18:17; 20:20; Isaiah 7:3; 36:2.*

51

CONFESSION
(kuhn-FE-shuhn)
An act in the worship of God in which a person humbly admits sins and asks for God's forgiveness. *Leviticus 26:40-42; Numbers 5:7; Psalm 32:5; Mark 1:5; 1 John 1:9.*

CONGREGATION
(kon-gruh-GAY-shuhn)
A gathering or assembly. A term used for all the Israelites encamped in the wilderness. It is also used for the assembly of people before God for worship or for judgment. *Exodus 12:3-6; 16:1-2; Leviticus 4:13-14; Joshua 22:16-18; Psalm 1:5; Acts 15:30; Hebrews 2:12.*

CONIAH
(kon-NIGH-uh)
See *Johoiachin.*

CONSECRATE
(KON-si-krate)
To set apart or dedicate an offering, a building, or a person for some sacred purpose. *Exodus 13:2; 1 Kings 9:3, 7; 2 Chronicles 29:31, 33; John 17:19; 1 Timothy 4:4-5.*

CONVOCATION, HOLY
(kon-vuh-KAY-shuhn)
A solemn assembly to fulfill a sacred obligation. In the OT this term was used when the people of Israel were summoned together for worship and for rest on the sabbaths and on feast days, especially the Day of Atonement. *Leviticus 23:2-4, 7-8, 21, 24, 27, 35-37; Numbers 28:18.*

COR
(kor)
In the OT a large measure for grain and oil. It contained about six bushels of dry material or sixty gallons of liquid. *1 Kings 5:11; 2 Chronicles 2:10; Ezekiel 45:14.*

CORIANDER SEED
(kor-i-AN-duhr)
A small, grey seed used as a seasoning in food, much the way poppy and sesame seeds are used on breads and cakes today. It is mentioned in the OT in describing manna, the food of the Israelites during their long journey out of Egypt. It comes from a plant of the carrot family. *Exodus 16:31; Numbers 11:7-9.*

CORINTH
(KOR-inth)
The chief commercial city on the Isthmus of Corinth in Greece and the capital of the Roman province of Achaia in NT times. Because of its location on the isthmus, which was only 3½ miles across at its narrowest point, ships from east and west were unloaded and the goods hauled across on land. Some of the smaller vessels were themselves dragged over. Paul preached here to the Jews and Greeks. *Acts 18:1; 19:1; 1 Corinthians 1:2; 2 Corinthians 1:1, 23; 2 Timothy 4:20.*

CORINTHIANS, FIRST AND SECOND LETTERS TO THE
(kuh-RIN-thee-uhnz)
The letters written by Paul to the

Christians at Corinth, now the seventh and eighth books in the NT. They are letters full of advice, admonition, and encouragement to the people in the church in that city. *See the books themselves.*

CORNELIUS
(kor-NEEL-yuhss)

A centurion of the Italian Cohort, stationed in Caesarea. Cornelius was a Gentile and not a Jew. However, he was a religious man, worshiping the God of the Hebrews and giving liberally to the poor. His dramatic vision and conversion to the Christian faith through the preaching of Peter is one of the great stories in the book of Acts. This event also taught Peter that all foods had been cleansed through the word of Jesus so that the old Jewish food laws were no longer needed. *Acts 10:1-48.*

CORNERSTONE
(KOR-nur-stone)

A stone at the corner of a building uniting two intersecting walls. NT writers often referred to Jesus as the cornerstone of the Christian life. *Job 38:6; Psalm 118:22; Matthew 21:42; Luke 20:17; Acts 4:11; 1 Peter 2:7.*

COUNCIL
(KOUN-suhl)

In the OT an assembly made up of men of authority. Their duty was to consider and direct the affairs of the community in government, law, and religion. The council was made up of the wise men and elders of Israel, who directed matters according to the laws of the Hebrews. There are several references in the OT to the council of God, made up of God himself and the heavenly beings. In NT times the term referred to local councils and to the high council in Jerusalem, the Sanhedrin. This powerful body made judgments under Jewish law, including cases in which the punishment was death. However, the Roman government kept the power of carrying out the execution in the hands of its own officials. This can be seen in the judgment against Jesus by the council and the necessity of having the Roman governor, Pilate, accept their verdict. (See Matthew 26:65-66; Mark 14:63-64; 15:1-15; John 19:7, 10-16). *2 Kings 9:5; 25:19; Job 15:8; Psalm 82:1; Jeremiah 23:18, 22; 52:25; Mark 15:43; Luke 23:50; John 11:47.*

PETER VISITS CORNELIUS

COVENANT
(KUH-vuh-nuhnt)

An agreement or solemn promise binding persons together in a firm relationship. It was of great importance in OT law and religion. "Covenant" was the word used for the special relationship which God had established between God and Israel. God was to be their God, and they were to be God's people. This was the meaning of the original covenant which God made with Abraham. The covenant was dramatically renewed through Moses at Mt. Sinai as the Israelites journeyed toward the Promised Land. Against this background the early Christians in the NT thought of their relationships to one another and to Jesus as a covenant binding them together. Jesus spoke of a new covenant. *Genesis 15:18; 17:1-11; 21:31-32; 26:28; Exodus 24:8; 1 Samuel 18:3; 2 Samuel 23:5; Job 41:4; Jeremiah 31:31-34; Ezekiel 17:13-14; Matthew 26:28; Mark 14:24; 1 Corinthians 11:25; 2 Corinthians 3:14; Hebrews 8:6-13; 10:29; 13:20-21.*

COVETOUS
(KUH-vi-chuhss)

A desire to have something that belongs to someone else or to have more than one already possesses. Throughout the Bible covetousness is considered sinful. In the NT especially, covetousness is considered a hindrance to true worship and faith in God. *Exodus 20:17; Luke 12:15; Romans 1:29; Ephesians 5:3; Colossians 3:5.*

CREATION

God's act of bringing the world and all of life into being. Two stories of creation are found at the very beginning of the Bible, reminding us that creation is the starting point of history. *Genesis 1:1–2:25; Mark 13:19; Ephesians 3:9; Revelation 4:11; 10:6.*

CHRISPUS
(KRIS-puhs)

A leader of the synagogue in Corinth. He and all his family became Christians after hearing Paul preach. They were among the few early believers whom Paul personally baptized. *Acts 18:8; 1 Corinthians 1:14-15.*

CROSS

A large stake set upright in the ground as an instrument of execution. Often a horizontal piece was attached either at the top to form a "T" or just below the top to make the type of cross that is most familiar. Jesus was put to death on a cross, and this event is described in all four Gospels. The Jews were unable to believe that the long-expected Messiah, or king, would die in so painful and humiliating a way. For pagans too it made no sense that one who claimed to be God would die so. In spite of all this the cross has become the most important symbol of the Christian faith. Also the word was used by Jesus to mean the suffering and death that humans must bear. (See *Crucifixion.*) *Matthew 10:38; 16:24; 27:32-50; Mark 8:34; 15:21-37; Luke 14:27; 23:26; 1 Corinthians 1:17-18; Galatians 6:12-14.*

CROWN

A headdress for a priest or king often made of rich material and decorated with designs or jewels. There were also simple metal headbands which served as crowns. The wreath placed on the head of a winner in Greek games was called a crown. *Exodus 29:6; 2 Chronicles 23:11; Psalm 21:3; Revelation 6:2; 14:14.*

CROWN OF THORNS

A circlet of thorny briers made by Roman soldiers and pushed down on Jesus' head as a part of their torture and mockery of him. They teased and taunted him with this make-believe crown. *Matthew 27:27-29; John 19:2-5.*

CROSS

CRUCIFIXION
(kroo-si-FICK-shun)

The act of putting a person to death by nailing or binding him to a cross or sometimes to a tree. It was a very slow death resulting from hunger, thirst, and exposure. It was a form of execution practiced by the Romans at the time of Jesus' arrest and trial. Jesus' crucifixion is described in the four Gospels. (See *Cross.*) *Matthew 27:22-54; Mark 15:15-39; Luke 23:1-49; John 19:1-30.*

CRUSE
(kroos)

A small pottery jug four to six inches high used to hold olive oil. Also called a jar and bowl. *1 Kings 17:12-16.*

CUBIT
(KYOO-bit)

A unit of measurement based on the length from the elbow to the tip of the middle finger—about eighteen inches. *Genesis 6:15; Exodus 25:10; 1 Samuel 17:4; Matthew 6:27.*

CUMMIN
(KYOO-min)

The caraway-like seeds of the cummin plant were much used in ancient times to season foods. The seeds were beaten off the stalks with a rod. *Isaiah 28:25-28; Matthew 23:23.*

CUPBEARER

In OT times an official who served wine to the king. He was obliged to test the wine by drinking it himself to make sure that it was not poisoned. He had to be a person whom the king trusted. *1 Kings 10:5; 2 Chronicles 9:4; Nehemiah 1:11–2:1.*

CURDS

A thickened milk food made by churning fresh milk in a goatskin containing the leftover clots from the previous churning. In OT times curds were a part of the ordinary diet. *Genesis 18:8; Deuteronomy 32:14; Judges 5:25; 2 Samuel 17:27-29; Proverbs 30:33; Isaiah 7:14-15, 21-22.*

CURTAIN OF THE TEMPLE

The curtain that separated the Most Holy Place from the rest of the temple. Only the high priest could go through the curtain into the Most Holy Place. The curtain was torn in two at the death of Jesus, opening for all this place of meeting between God and humanity. In the OT the curtain was called the veil (see *Veil of the Temple*). *Matthew 27:51; Mark 15:38; Luke 23:45; Hebrews 10:19-20.*

CUSTODIAN

(kuhs-TOH-di-an)
A slave who in Roman times had charge over a young boy, guarding him and taking him to school until he was sixteen. Paul used the term in a word picture to explain that the law had been the guardian or custodian of the Jews until Christ came. *Galatians 3:24-25.*

CYPRUS

(SYE-pruhss)
An island in the Mediterranean Sea off the coast of Syria. Cyprus was the home of Barnabas, an early Christian who traveled with Paul on his missionary journeys. *Isaiah 23:1, 12; Jeremiah 2:10; Ezekiel 27:6; Acts 4:36; 11:19-20; 13:4; 15:39; 21:3; 27:4.*

CYRENE

(sye-REEN)
A Greek city on the northern coast of Africa. A man from Cyrene named Simon carried Jesus' heavy cross to the place of the Crucifixion. *Matthew 27:32; Mark 15:21; Luke 23:26; Acts 2:10; 11:20; 13:1.*

CYRUS

(SYE-russ)
A Persian king, founder of the Persian Empire, who reigned from 550 to 529 B.C. After he captured Babylon in 539 B.C., Cyrus proclaimed himself "king of the world." From this position of power Cyrus ruled with a tolerance, understanding, and wisdom that were unusual for those times. He allowed the many people who had been captured and deported by the Babylonians to return to their homes and to restore their old religions. This policy included the Jews who were in exile in Babylonia. They went home to Jerusalem and began to rebuild the temple. His empire, even before taking Babylon, extended from India across Asia to the Aegean Sea. Cyrus captured Babylon by digging a ditch around the city and causing the Euphrates River to flow into the ditch. His army then marched up the dry river bed into the surprised city of Babylon. The city itself was not attacked. (See *Darius*.) *2 Chronicles 36:22-23; Ezra 1:1-8; 6:3-5; Isaiah 44:28–45:4; Daniel 1:21.*

DAGON
(DAY-gon)

A god worshiped by the Philistines in Gaza and in Ashdod, where there was a temple dedicated to Dagon. Very little is known about the nature of this god or the way in which he was worshiped. The name means "corn," and it seems likely that he was a god of vegetation. It is also known that Dagon was worshiped by other peoples of the Near East in ancient times. During a period of war between the Philistines and the Israelites, the Philistines captured the ark of the covenant. It was placed in the temple at Ashdod beside the god Dagon. While the ark was kept by the Philistines, they had so many misfortunes that they sent it back to the Israelites. *Judges 16:23-24; 1 Samuel 5:1-7; 1 Chronicles 10:10.*

DAMASCUS
(duh-MAS-kuhss)

The capital city of Syria. Damascus is a very ancient city and was important in OT times. Its importance continues down to the present. It was located where important military and commercial routes met. It was the capital of the Armenean kingdom at one time and a rival city of Jerusalem and Samaria. It was conquered by the Assyrians, the Babylonians, the Persians, and the Greeks. Damascus was also an important center for early Christians. It was on the road from Jerusalem to Damascus that Paul became a Christian. *Genesis 14:13-15; 2 Samuel 8:5-6; 1 Kings 11:24-25; 15:18-19; 19:15; 20:34; 2 Kings 8:7-9; 14:28; 16:10-13; Isaiah 7:8; 17:1-3; Acts 9:1-22; 26:19-20; Galatians 1:17.*

DAN
(dan)

One of the twelve sons of Jacob and the ancestor of the tribe of Danites. The tribe settled in an area in the extreme northern part of Canaan at the foot of Mt. Herman near the Jordan River and called the place Dan. In the OT the phrase "from Dan to Beersheba" (which was at the southern end of Canaan) meant the entire length of the land. The most famous Danite was Samson. *Exodus 1:1-4; Joshua 19:40-48; Judges 1:34; 1 Samuel 3:20; 1 Kings 4:25; 12:26-29; 2 Chronicles 16:4; 30:5.*

DANIEL
(DAN-yuhl)

Meaning "God has judged." The name of a heroic Jewish youth in exile in Babylon. (See *Daniel, Book of.*)

DANIEL, BOOK OF

An OT book by an unknown author who probably wrote it when the Jews were ruled by the Greeks about 166 B.C. The book tells of Daniel, a very wise and upright young Jew, and three other persons who were loyal to their faith in God though far from their homeland and in exile in Babylon, where they were persecuted. The stories of Daniel's visions were probably meant to give a message of hope to the Jewish people that in spite of their troubles they would be triumphant. The stories were in a kind of secret language that represented persons and situations at that time. The writer knew his Jewish readers would understand what he was trying to say. This form of writing is similar to the book of Revelation. It is called apocalyptic. *See the book itself.*

DARIC
(DAR-ik)

In the OT thick gold coin of Persia. It was named for Darius, a Persian emperor, and is the first coin mentioned in the Bible. *1 Chronicles 29:7; Ezra 2:69; 8:27; Nehemiah 7:70-72.*

PAUL ON THE ROAD TO DAMASCUS

DARIUS
(DAIR-ee-uhss)

1. King of Persia from 522 to 486 B.C., known as Darius the Great. He decreed that all interference with the Jews' attempt to rebuild the temple in Jerusalem be stopped and that they be allowed to continue the restoration. *Ezra 5:6–6:13; Nehemiah 12:22; Haggai 1:1-2.*

2. The book of Daniel tells of another Darius called Darius the Mede. *Daniel 5:31–6:28.*

DAVID
(DAY-vid)

The second and greatest king of Israel (from about 1000 to 965 B.C.). David was a shepherd boy living in Bethlehem when he was chosen to serve King Saul. His way of conducting himself soon made him a favorite at court. David is one of the most attractive personalities in the OT. He had many talents and used them with all his might. He was a gifted poet and musician and probably wrote some of the psalms. He was an excellent soldier, quick to realize what was needed in any military situation. He was also a man of inspiring courage. After Saul's death David became a great and powerful king, and proved to be as skilled in political affairs as he was in battle. David committed a great sin in taking Bathsheba while she was the wife of another man and having her husband killed. When the prophet Nathan accused King David to his face, the king repented with all his heart and asked God's forgiveness (see 2 Samuel 12:13). Under David's rule the kingdom of Israel reached its peak, and he was thought of ever after as their ideal king. The outstanding quality in David was his devotion to the Lord. *1 Samuel 16:1–1 Kings 2:11; 1 Chronicles 11:1–29:30; Jeremiah 33:15-17, 21; Ezekiel 37:24-25; Matthew 12:23; 22:42-45; Luke 1:32, 69; and other references (the name David appears nearly eight hundred times in the OT and around sixty in the NT).*

DAY
In OT times the period from sunrise to sunset with morning, noon, and night as the divisions of time. The sabbath was the only day with a name. Other days were counted by numbers. After the Babylonian exile the Hebrews divided the day into hours. *Psalm 55:10; Jeremiah 31:35; and other references.*

DAY OF THE LORD
The day when God will be fully revealed and will judge all the people. Many terms are used for this: Day of Judgment, Day of God, Day of the Lord, the Day, and others. There were many and varied ideas about this day. In the OT it was usually thought of as a day of vengeance on the enemies of Israel. Later the Hebrews came to understand that they also deserved judgment. Christians called Jesus "Lord," and in the NT "Day of the Lord" is understood to mean "Day of Christ." This refers to the expected second coming of Jesus Christ, who will exercise the judgment of God. *Joel 1:15; 2:31; Amos 5:18-20; Zephaniah 1:7; 2 Corinthians 1:14; Philippians 1:6, 10; 2:16; 2 Thessalonians 2:1-4; 2 Timothy 1:12.*

DAY'S JOURNEY
(JUR-nee)

The distance traveled from sunrise to sunset, about eighteen to twenty-five miles. In Bible times the measurement of distances was not exact. A day's journey depended on the nature of the ground traveled and the person doing the traveling. *Genesis 30:36; Exodus 3:18; Numbers 11:31; Jonah 3:3-4; Luke 2:44.*

DEACON
(DEE-kuhn)

Meaning "servant, attendant, minister." An officer in the early Christian church who probably had the responsibility for collecting and distributing the offerings of money or goods and of caring for the sick, the needy, and the elderly. *Philippians 1:1; 1 Timothy 3:8-13.*

DEACONESS
(DEE-kuhn-es)

Women in the early Christian church who assisted in the baptism of women, visited and bathed the sick, and called in pagan homes where there were Christian women. *Romans 16:1.*

DEACONESS

DEAD SEA

See *Salt Sea*.

DEBORAH

(DEB-uh-ruh)

One of the early "judges" of ancient Israel. She was a remarkable woman with great qualities of leadership. She was endowed with wisdom, and the people called her a prophetess. Deborah aroused the trives of Israel to fight the Canaanites, and a sense of unity and loyalty grew out of this common effort. Her achievements may be read in the poem called "The Song of Deborah." *Judges 4:1–5:31.*

DEBT

Something owed by one person to another. In the OT there are many rules and customs concerning debts. The older custom of the nomads was to lend to one another within a tribe without charging interest. However, there were violations of this rule, and the charge could become so high for a loan that the borrower's life was almost hopeless. Sometimes debtors had to sell themselves or their children into slavery to pay off their debts. OT laws stated that objects needed in daily living, such as a cloak or millstone, were not to be taken as a pledge for payment of debt unless they were returned to the owner as he needed them, and that people enslaved because of debts were to be freed periodically (see Exodus 22:25-27; Leviticus 25:35-37; Deuteronomy 23:19-20; 24:6, 10-13; 2 Kings 4:7). Jesus used these Jewish customs to illustrate his teachings. In the Lord's Prayer, "debts" is a figure of speech Jesus used for sins. Roman law permitted the imprisonment of debtors who could not pay. *1 Samuel 22:2; Nehemiah 10:31; Matthew 6;12; 18:23-35.*

DECAPOLIS

(de-KAP-uh-liss)

The word means "ten cities." These Greek cities in Palestine, located along or near chief trade routes and military highways, were founded by the followers of Alexander the Great. When the Roman army entered Palestine, these cities banded together to protect themselves and the trade routes and to promote the interests of Rome. In Jesus' time "Decapolis" was the name for the federation of the ten cities in a specific region southeast of the Sea of Galilee in the Roman province of Syria. *Matthew 4:25; Mark 5:20; 7:31.*

DECREE

In biblical use a declaration or proclamation usually in writing issued by a king and publicly read to the people to inform, instruct, or command them about what was to be done. *2 Chronicles 30:5-6; Ezra 5:13; Isaiah 10:1; Daniel 3:10; Luke 2:1; Acts 17:6-7.*

DEDICATION, FEAST OF

(ded-uh-KAY-shuhn)

A general term for a celebration in which something is set apart for a sacred purpose (see Numbers 7:10; 1 Kings 8:1-66; 2 Chronicles 7:9). In the Bible it referred specifically to the annual celebration commemorating the purification and rededication of the temple in 165 B.C. after the Greeks had defiled it by setting up an altar to pagan gods. This eight-day celebration is still kept by the Jews and is known as Hanukkah or the Feast of Lights. It falls in winter close to the Christmas season. *John 10:22-23.*

DEEP

A poetic term meaning ocean. This type of expression uses a quality of a thing, in this case, the deepness of the ocean, as a substitute word for the thing itself. *Genesis 7:11; Job 38:16; 41:31; Psalms 42:7; 104:6; 107:24-25.*

DEFILE

In OT usage to make persons, foods, places, or objects unclean in a religious sense so that they were unfit for a place in the community, especially in matters of worship. An important part of the duties of the OT priests was to judge between clean and unclean. It was also their duty to give instruction in the cleansing of whatever had been defiled. In the NT Jesus used the word in a deeper sense to mean that the words, thoughts, and actions of people may be ugly and unclean and that these defile them in the sight of God. *Leviticus 11:43; 2 Kings 23:13; Isaiah 59:3; Daniel 1:8; Matthew 15:10-20; Mark 7:15-23; Jude 1:8.*

DELILAH
(duh-LYE-luh)
In the OT story of Samson a woman who betrayed this hero of the Hebrew tribe of Dan to the Philistines. Pretending to have great affection for Samson, she persuaded him to tell her how he had such great strength. When she learned that his hair was the secret of his power, she cut it off while he was sleeping. He awoke to find the Philistines upon him. He was now no stronger than an ordinary man, and the Philistines captured him, put out his eyes, and imprisoned him. *Judges 16:4-22.*

DEMAS
(DEE-muhss)
One of Paul's co-workers in the early church. Later he gave up his work with Paul. *Colossians 4:14; 2 Timothy 4:10; Philemon 1:24.*

TEMPLE DEDICATION

DEMETRIUS

(duh-MEE-tree-uhss)

A silversmith at Ephesus who made and sold silver pieces that resembled the temple of the goddess Artemis. He complained that Paul's preaching of Christ was interfering with the sale of his shrines. He aroused the people against Paul, causing a riot through-out the city. *Acts 19:24-41.*

DEMON

(DEE-muhn)

In the OT a nameless god or spirit which might be friendly or unfriendly. When this word appears in the NT, it refers only to evil spirits who are the cause of all kinds of misfortunes—disease, insanity, accidents. Demons were also thought of as the messengers of Satan. The word also refers at times to pagan gods. *Deuteronomy 32:17; Psalm 106:37; Matthew 8:16; 9:33; 15:22; Luke 8:26-39; 11:14-15; John 10:20-21.*

DEMONIAC

(di-MOH-ni-ak)

In the NT one possessed by a demon. Such a condition may be associated with insanity and diseases of the mind. Demoniacs were among those healed by Jesus. *Matthew 8:28-34; Mark 5:15.*

DENARIUS (plural, DENARII)

(duh-NAIR-ee-uhss)

1. An ancient Roman silver coin, about the size of a dime. It was a common coin in Palestine during the time of Jesus. In Jesus' time it was the going rate for one day's wages for a soldier or a common laborer.

2. An ancient Roman coin valued at 25 silver denarii. *Matthew 18:28; 20:2, 9-10, 13; Mark 6:37; 14:5; Luke 10:35.*

DERBE

(DUR-bee)

A city in the central part of Southern Asia Minor in the Roman province of Galatia. It was twice visited by Paul, the first time with Barnabas. Here Paul and Barnabas made many disciples for Christ. *Acts 14:6, 20-21; 16:1; 20:4.*

DESTROYER, THE

A term used in the Bible for death or destruction or for the supernatural being that brings them. Sometimes Satan is referred to as the destroyer. *Exodus 12:23; Job 15:21; Isaiah 16:4; 21:2; Jeremiah 4:7; 48:8; 1 Corinthians 10:9-10; Hebrews 11:28.*

DEUTERONOMY

(dyoo-tuh-RON-uh-mee)

The fifth book in the OT. The name means "second law" because it states again the Ten Commandments that are found in Exodus. It was probably put together from various sources written at different periods of time. It is written in the form of a farewell address by Moses to the people he had led out of Egypt. The sermons of Moses urge the people to remember always God's deliverance of them, to keep his commandments, and to be faithful in the covenant. Parts of Deuteronomy are probably the book that was found when King Josiah ordered the temple to be repaired in 622 B.C. (see 2 Kings 22:8-13). *See the book itself.*

DEVIL

A term used when speaking of evil as if it were a person. One who leads people to sin and disturbs their relation with God. In the NT it often refers to Satan. *Matthew 4:1-11; Luke 4:1-13; 8:12; John 13:2; Acts 10:38; Ephesians 4:26-27; 6:11; 1 Timothy 3:6-7.*

DEVOTED

Things forbidden for common use. In the OT persons or things set apart for God were said to be "devoted." In warfare all men, beasts, and objects that were captured were "devoted" to God and were usually destroyed. Sometimes, however, precious metals captured in battle were taken to the sanctuary or holy place. Captured sheep might be used for burnt offerings to the Lord. *Leviticus 27:21, 28-29; Numbers 18:14; Deuteronomy 13:17; Joshua 6:18; 1 Samuel 15:21; 1 Kings 20:42; Ezekiel 44:29.*

DEVOUT
(di-VOUT)
In the OT the word means "righteous," that is, being free from wrong or sin. In the NT it means "godly" and "reverent," that is, devoted to God. *Isaiah 57:1; Acts 10:2.*

DILL

A kind of seed similar to caraway used for seasoning and for medicine. One tenth of all the seed stems and leaves that were harvested was given to the temple. This was called a tithe. *Isaiah 28:25, 27; Matthew 23:23.*

DISCIPLE
(duh-SYE-puhl)
A pupil or learner. One who accepts and follows a certain teaching or teacher. In the Bible we read of the disciples of Isaiah, or the Pharisees, and of John the Baptist, but the term is most familiar when used to indicate all those who followed Jesus and were called disciples. *Isaiah 8:16; Matthew 10:24-25; 11:1-3; 27:57; Mark 2:16, 18; 6:45; Luke 5:33; 6:13; John 1:35-37; 6:66-67; 9:27-28; Acts 6:1-2, 7; 9:10, 23-26, 36.*

DISCIPLINE
(DIS-i-plin)
In the Bible this term refers to training and instruction. It also means "correction" and "punishment." This usually refers to the training of a child, but it is also used to indicate God's discipline of people through fortune and misfortune. *Deuteronomy 8:5; Proverbs 12:1; 13:24; Ephesians 6:4.*

65

DISPERSION
(dis-PURH-shuhn)
A word used for the settlement of the Jewish people away from their own land after the time of the Assyrian and Babylonian exiles. They had been scattered, or dispersed, until they came to live in many cities of the Greek and Roman Empires and in parts of Asia and Africa. Wherever these people settled, they built their synagogues for prayer and study. The word "dispersion" is used sometimes today as a term for Jews who live outside Israel. *Nehemiah 1:9; Esther 3:8; Jeremiah 25:34; Ezekiel 36:19; Zephaniah 3:10; John 7:35; James 1:1; 1 Peter 1:1.*

DIVINATION
(DI-vuh-nay-shuhn)
Any attempt to communicate with supernatural powers or to foretell the future by the aid of such natural events as dreams, the position of the stars, cloud formations, unexpected storms, and the like. In the OT divination was also practiced with objects or situations especially arranged for the purpose like the shooting of arrows, casting of lots, or examining of the insides of sacrificed animals. Divination was forbidden in Israel, and the prohets preached against it. *Genesis 30:27; Numbers 22:7; 23:23; Deuteronomy 18:10; 1 Samuel 15:23; Jeremiah 14:14; Ezekiel 12:24; 21:21; Acts 16:16-18.*

DOMINION
(deh-MIN-yuhn)
Meaning "rule," "to have power over," "authority," "kinship." In the Bible the word is used to mean the supreme rule of God, humanity's rule over nature, or power gained by conquest. It is often used in songs of praise for God. *Genesis 1:26; Numbers 24:19; Judges 14:4; 1 Kings 4:24; Nehemiah 9:28; Job 25:2; Psalms 8:6; 19:13; 22:28; 72:8; 119:133; 1 Timothy 6:14-16; 1 Peter 4:11; 5:11; Jude 1:25; Revelation 1:6.*

DOOR, DOORKEEPER
An entrance and one who watches or guards it. In the Bible "door" may refer to a swinging door set in sockets, to a gate, to an opening in a wall, a cavelike tomb, or a sheepfold. A doorkeeper guarded the entrance of the temple and collected money from the people. In the psalms the word "door" is used in a poetic sense as a "door of my lips." Jesus also used the term as a figure of speech when he said he was the "door" of the sheep, for at that time a shepherd slept at the opening in the wall of the sheepfold to protect his sheep from danger. *1 Kings 14:27; Psalms 84:10; 141:3; Matthew 6:6; John 10:7-8.*

DORCAS
(DOR-kuhss)
A woman disciple in Joppa. She was also called Tabitha. Dorcas was known for her good deeds especially among widows, for whom she made clothes. When Dorcas died, the apostle Peter was called, and he raised her from the dead. This the first report of an apostle raising a person from the dead. *Acts 9:36-42.*

DOTHAN
(DOH-thuhn)

An ancient town located west of the Jordan River and southwest of the Sea of Galilee. In the OT story of Joseph he found his brothers keeping the sheep there. They put him into a well and later sold him to a caravan of Ishmaelites. The modern city of Tell Dotha stands where Dothan stood in Bible times. *Genesis 37:17; 2 Kings 6:13.*

DORCAS

DOVE

A small species of pigeon which was very plentiful in Palestine. The mournful cry of the dove, its way of flying, its habit of nesting in the rocks, and its gentleness and faithfulness to its mate made this bird a favorite. The Hebrew poets spoke of it often in their poetry. In the story of the Flood it was a dove which brought back an olive leaf to the ark. The dove was also used as a sacrificial offering in the temple. At the baptism of Jesus the Holy Spirit is said to have descended "like a dove." For this reason the dove has become a symbol of the Holy Spirit for Christians. *Genesis 8:8-12; Psalm 74:17; Song of Solomon 2:12; 4:1; Isaiah 59:11; Jeremiah 48:28; Matthew 3:16; 10:16; John 1:32.*

DOXOLOGY
(doks-OL-uh-ji)

A short hymn or summary of praise to God. In the Jewish services blessings or doxologies were recited or chanted at the end of hymns (see 1 Chronicles 16:36; Psalms 41:13; 72:18-19; 89:52; 106:48). Sometimes they are found at the beginning of a prayer (see Luke 1:68; 2 Corinthians 1:3; 1 Peter 1:3). Doxologies are a part of Christian worship.

DRAGON
(DRAG-uhn)

In the OT a sea monster frightening to look at and very strong, sometimes called Leviathan or Rahab. In the book of Revelation the word is used to represent Satan as a dragon seeking to destroy. The dragon is defeated by the archangel Michael. *Psalm 74:13; Isaiah 27:1; 51:9; Revelation 12:3–13:4; 20:2-3.*

Ee

EAGLE

Any of several large birds of prey of the falcon family. The eagle and the vulture are the largest birds mentioned in the Bible. The two types of eagles of Bible times were the golden eagle and the imperial eagle. Being birds of prey, they were considered unclean (see *Unclean, Uncleanness*). The OT writers were impressed by the sweep and speed of the eagle's flight. The eagle's long life, its majestic appearance, its lofty nesting places in the tallest trees or on craggy, hard-to-reach places in the mountains, its care for its young, and its awesome ways were used as figures of speech. *Psalm 103:5; Proverbs 23:4-5; 30:18-19; Jeremiah 4:13; 49:14-16.*

EARTH

Dry land, in biblical usage. In OT poetry the Hebrews often pictured the earth as a flat strip of land suspended over the ocean by pillars which mountains grounded into the seas. It was covered with a domelike canopy, or covering of sky, called the firmament. The stars showed through openings in the firmament, and the rain and snow came through windows in the firmament. Heaven was up above the firmament. There are many references to the four corners of the earth. *Exodus 20:4; Job 9:6-10; Psalms 24:1-2; 69:34; Isaiah 11:12.*

EARTHQUAKE

A shaking of the earth caused by volcanic activity or by movement of the earth's crust. The lands of the Bible are within an active earthquake zone.

The Jordan Valley of upper Galilee, the Samaritan territory near biblical Shechem, and the edge of the Judean mountains near Lydda, Jericho, and Tiberias were centers of these disturbances. Fault lines, or cracks in the earth's crust along which some shifting can be observed, run into the Jordan Valley on an angle from east and west creating a condition that causes the earth's surface to move. *1 Kings 19:9-14; Amos 1:1; Zechariah 14:5; Acts 16:25-26.*

EBAL, MOUNT

(EE-bawl)

A mountain north of and opposite to Mt. Gerizim near Jerusalem. Mt. Ebal and Mt. Gerizim near Jerusalem. Mt. Ebal and Mt. Gerizim together form the sides of an important east-west pass. After the Israelites had entered Canaan, Joshua led them in a ceremony confirming the covenant which they had made with God, agreeing to obey his commandments. For this covenant ceremony six tribes were stationed in front of Mt. Ebal and six in front of Mt. Gerizim. The ark of the covenant was placed between them. Those tribes standing before Mt. Ebal pronounced curses on all who would fail to keep the commandments. Those tribes standing before Mt. Gerizim announced the blessings that would come to those who served the Lord. Joshua also built an altar on Mt. Ebal. (See *Covenant; Gerizim, Mount.*) *Deuteronomy 11:29; 27:4-13; Joshua 8:30-33.*

EAGLE

EBED-MELECH

(e-bed-MEL-ek)

An Ethiopian servant in the court of King Zedekiah who rescued the prophet Jeremiah from a cistern. The title "ebed" means "slave" and was used to designate the class of court official. Here it is a proper name. *Jeremiah 38:7-13; 39:16.*

EBENEZER

(eb-uh-NEE-zur)

Meaning "stone of help." A place near Aphek northeast of Joppa where the Israelites fought two battles with the Philistines and where the ark was captured by them. Also the name of a stone or monument which was set up near Mizpah, northwest of the Dead Sea, to commemorate a victory over the Philistines. The stone was a reminder that: "Hitherto the Lord has helped us." This shows plainly how the Hebrews understood that the hand of God was in all their victories and defeats, in fact, in all of their life as a nation. *1 Samuel 4:1-11; 5:1; 7:12.*

ECCLESIASTES
(e-klee-zee-AS-teez)
Meaning "preacher," "speaker before an assembly." The pen name of the author and the name of his book, which is the twenty-first book of the OT. It was probably written during the time when the Jews were ruled by Greek kings about 250 B.C. Very little is known of the author, but he was a wise man and a philosopher. He explored and considered life and wrote down what he thought best for the man who wanted a good, satisfying life and one that was pleasing to God. His writings suggest that he wanted his readers to think of him as another Solomon. *See the book itself.*

EDICT
(EE-dikt)
A public proclamation or ruling written, sealed with the king's ring, and read aloud before all the people. An edict was always written, and this is the way it differs from a decree, which did not have to be written down although it usually was. (See *Decree.*) *Esther 8:8-10; 9:1, 13; Hebrews 11:23.*

EDOM
(EE-dom)
In the OT a country located southeast of Judah. Edom received its name, which means "the red region," because of its red rocks and soil. Another name for this territory was Seir (see Joshua 12:7). Esau, the brother of Jacob, was called Edom possibly because of his ruddy complexion or from the redness of the lentil porridge which Jacob sold to Esau in exchange for his birthright. *Genesis 25:30; 36:1; Numbers 20:14-21; Deuteronomy 2:2-8; 1 Samuel 14:47; 1 Kings 11:14-17; 22:47; 2 Kings 8:20-22; Isaiah 11:14; Ezekiel 35:1-15; Amos 1:6, 9, 11; 2:1.*

EDOMITES
(EE-duhm-ites)
The people of Edom. The Israelites and Edomites were constantly at war, and in the time of the kings nearly all of the Judean prophets preached against the Edomites for their slavery and cruelty. Just as the Israelites were identified with Jacob, the Edomites were identified with his twin brother Esau. *Genesis 36:9; Deuteronomy 23:7-8; 2 Kings 8:21.*

EGYPT
(EE-jipt)
A land on the southern coast of the Mediterranean Sea in northwest Africa. Egypt lies along the valley of the great Nile River and because of this was probably the most fertile land of the ancient world. One of the names for Egypt was the "Black Land" because her rich, river-valley soil was such a contrast to the red, barren soil of her neighbors. There is very little rain in Egypt. The yearly flood brings a constant supply of fresh, rich soil and enough water to be stored for the rest of the season. The soil was so precious that not an inch of it was wasted. Instead of cutting into it with roads, the people used the river and its branches for transportation. Even the villages were crowded into the smallest possible space, while the fields for farming spread out all

around them. For centuries Egypt was a rich and powerful nation. Egyptians had many contacts with the Hebrews, sometimes friendly and sometimes not. Abraham and later Jacob and all his family journeyed into Egypt to get food during times of famine, and this planted the Hebrews in Egypt. A hostile pharaoh later made them slaves. It was from Egypt that Moses led the Hebrew people into the land of Canaan. After the establishment of the kingdom of Israel there were treaties and trade with the Egyptians. The famous stone pyramids and other tombs of the Egyptians are monuments to their former greatness. *Genesis 12:10–13:1; 39:1; 41:1-57; 47:1-31; 2 Kings 23:29; 2 Chronicles 12:2-3; Matthew 2:13-15.*

EHUD
(EE-huhd)
The only left-handed man mentioned in the Bible. He killed Elgon, king of Moab, by wearing his dagger on his right thigh, but striking with his left hand. *Judges 3:14-22*

ELAH
(EE-leh)
King of the northern kingdom of Israel about 886 to 885 B.C. He was killed by Zimri in the revolt which brought the Omride family to the throne. *1 Kings 16:6-14.*

ELAH, VALLEY OF
(EE-lah)
A fertile and strategic valley to the west of Bethlehem where Saul and the Israelites camped before the battle with the Philistines. It was here that David killed Goliath and won the battle for Israel. *1 Samuel 17:2, 19; 21:9.*

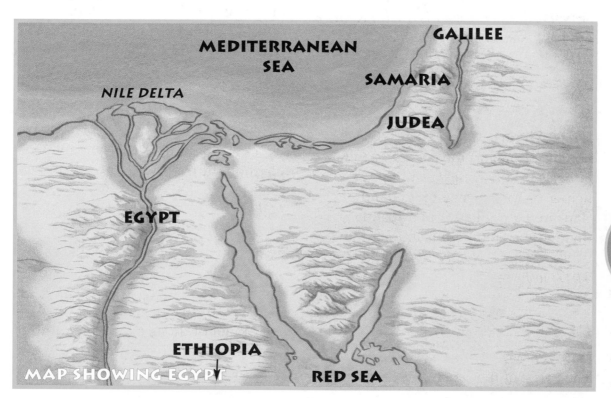

MAP SHOWING EGYPT

ELAM

(EE-luhm)

A mountainous country located east of the Tigris River at the north end of the Persian Gulf. The capital was Susa. The NT records the Elamites as among those present in Jerusalem on the day of Pentecost. Several men mentioned in the OT had the name Elam. *Ezra 4:9; Isaiah 21:2; Jeremiah 49:34-39; Acts 2:9.*

ELDER

In the OT a mature man, head of a family or tribe who had authority to judge in disputes or arguments and to give advice. The elders were the leaders in war. In NT times each synagogue and Jewish community had its council of elders. The most important council was the Sanhedrin in Jerusalem. Among the early Christians, elders presided over the churches and were associated with the apostles in governing the churches. *Genesis 25:23; Numbers 11:16-17; Ruth 4:2-12; 1 Samuel 15:30; Matthew 26:3; Acts 14:23; 15:2-4; 1 Timothy 5:17.*

ELEAZAR

(el-ee-AY-zur)

Son of Aaron and the successor to his father's priestly office as Moses' helper on the journey to the land of Canaan. Later Eleazar and Joshua divided the land by lots among the tribes of Israel. *Numbers 20:25-28; 34:17; Joshua 14:1.*

ELI

(EE-lye)

The priest of the sanctuary, or shrine, at Shiloh and judge of Israel for forty years. Eli trained the boy Samuel to help him in the work in the sanctuary. *1 Samuel 1:3–3:18; 1 Kings 2:27.*

ELIJAH

(ee-LYE-juh)

A prophet of the northern kingdom of Israel during the reign of Ahab in the ninth century B.C. Elijah opposed King Ahab and his wife Jezebel in their movement to establish the worship of Baal in Israel. Elijah is reported to have performed many miracles. He foretold a severe drought, warning King Ahab that it was a punishment from the Lord. At the end of the drought Elijah challenged 450 prophets of Baal to a great contest. The Baal prophets prepared a sacrifice but got no response from their god. Elijah also prepared a sacrifice, and at his prayer to the Lord, fire came from heaven and burned it. At the end of his life Elijah gave the cloak of his office to Elisha, who was to be his successor. The younger prophet witnessed the translation of Elijah, that is, his being taken up into heaven in a chariot of fire by a whirlwind. The memory of Elijah was so cherished by the Hebrews that in NT times many people thought Jesus was Elijah. *1 Kings 17:1–19:21; 21:17-29; 2 Kings 1:1–2:12; Malachi 4:5-6; Matthew 11:13-14; 16:13-14; 17:3-4, 10-13.*

ELISHA

(ee-LYE-shuh)

A prophet of the northern kingdom of Israel in the ninth century B.C. He was

ELIJAH AND THE PROPHETS OF BAAL

the disciple and successor of Elijah. He continued the task of Elijah in fighting against the worship of Baal. Many miracles are credited to Elisha including the healing of Naaman, commander of the Syrian army, who had leprosy; the reviving of a dead boy; and the feeding of a hundred men with twenty loaves of bread. He advised and attempted to guide the kings of Israel for fifty years. *2 Kings 2:1–13:21; Luke 4:27.*

ELIZABETH
(e-LIZ-uh-beth)
Mother of John the Baptist and a relative of Mary the mother of Jesus. *Luke 1:5-60.*

EMMAUS
(e-MAY-uhss)
A Judean town about seven miles from Jerusalem. Cleopas and another disciple who were friends set out to walk from Jerusalem to Emmaus a short while after the Crucifixion. They met the risen Jesus and though they did not recognize him, they walked along talking with him. They invited him to have supper with him, and when he blessed the bread and broke it, they realized that he was the risen Lord. *Luke 24:13-53.*

EN-ROGEL
(eh-ROH-gehl)
A spring near Jerusalem in the Kidron Valley. It marked the limit between the tribes of Benjamin and Judah. When David had to flee from Jerusalem during a revolt, two of his spies remained near En-rogel to gather information concerning the revolt. Also Adonijah, a son of David who hoped to get the throne instead of Solomon, had himself secretly crowned near this spring as David lay dying. *Joshua 15:7; 18:16; 2 Samuel 17:17; 1 Kings 1:9.*

ENROLLMENT
A public census, or counting of people, according to family position and tribe (see Numbers 1:2-3). In NT times Rome under Emperor Augustus Caesar required all families to return to their native cities to be enrolled for tax purposes. It was at the time of that enrollment that Jesus was born. *1 Chronicles 9:1; Luke 2:1-7.*

EPAPHRAS
(EP-uh-frass)
An early Christian who was a native of the city of Colossae. It was through Epaphras that the Colossians had come to know the Christian gospel. He preached in Colossae, Laodicea, and Hierapolis. He was a co-worker and close friend of Paul. The two men were in prison together in Rome. *Colossians 1:3-8; 4:12-13; Philemon 1:23.*

EPAPHRODITUS
(ee-PAF-roh-DYE-tuhss)
A friend and co-worker of Paul and a leader in the church at Philippi. He took a gift from that church to Paul in prison and stayed for a time to help him. *Philippians 2:25-30.*

EPHAH
(EE-fuh)
A measure for dry ingredients nearly equal to a bushel. *Leviticus 19:36; Ezekiel 45:10-11; Zechariah 5:5-11.*

EPHESIANS, LETTER TO THE
(e-fee-zhuhnz)
The tenth book in the NT. A letter addressed to the Christians in Ephesus about the plan of God to bring all people together in Christ. It explains the place of the church and Christians in the world. It may have been sent to churches in many other cities. It is not certain who wrote this letter, but it may well have been Paul. *See the book itself.*

EPHESUS
(EF-uh-suhss)
In NT times a large seaport city in the Roman province of Asia which is now Turkey. It was a commercial and religious center for the worship of the goddess Artemis. Paul lived for a time at Ephesus, teaching in the synagogue and in the hall of Tyranus. An outdoor theater may still be seen in the ruins of this old city. *Acts 18:19-21, 24; 19:1-10, 23-41; 20:16-21; 1 Corinthians 16:8-9; 1 Timothy 1:3-4; 2 Timothy 1:18; 4:12; Revelation 1:11; 2:1.*

EPHOD
(EF-od)
An OT name for the upper garment of plain linen worn by a priest. The high priest wore a more elaborate, embroidered ephod done in colors of gold, blue, crimson and purple. Also, it may have been an object carried by the priest when he was seeking direction from God. *Exodus 28:4, 28-29; 35:27; 39:1-22; Judges 17:5; 18:14, 17-18, 20; 1 Samuel 2:18; 14:3.*

EPHPHATHA
An aramaic word meaning "be opened." This was the word Jesus used when healing the deaf man. *Mark 7:31-35*

EPHRAIM
(EE-free-uhm)
A son of Joseph and brother of Manasseh. Though Ephraim was the younger, his good fortune and his landholdings in Palestine overshadowed his brother's. Originally

the name of a geographical area, "Ephraim" became the name of one of the twelve tribes of Israel. It also came to be a name for Israel after the territory of the northern kingdom had been reduced by war, first with Syria and then Assyria, until little more than the original Ephraimite territory remained. *Genesis 41:50-52; 46:20; 48:1-5, 13-22; 50:23; Numbers 1:32-33; Joshua 24:30; Judges 7:24; Hosea 4:17; 7:1; John 11:54.*

PHILIP AND THE ETHIOPIAN

EPHRATHAH

(EF-rah-thah)

A city in Judah, an ancient settlement that became a part of Bethlehem. Often the two names are combined—Bethlehem-Ephrathah. *Genesis 35:19; 48:7; Ruth 1:2; 1 Samuel 17:12; Micah 5:2.*

EPICUREANS

(ep-uh-KYUR-ee-uhnz)

In NT times the followers of a Greek philosopher named Epicurus who taught in Athens in the fourth century B.C. His philosophy was that happiness was the chief aim of life. The happy state could be reached without any belief in God or gods. He taught that religion disturbed or destroyed the contentment of people. *Acts 17:18.*

ESAU

(EE-saw)

A son of Isaac and Rebekah and elder twin brother of Jacob. His name means "red" and "hairy," indicating that Esau was a hairy, red-complexioned man. He loved the rugged outdoor life of a hunter. He sold his birthright to Jacob in exchange for some food once when he was very hungry. On another occasion Jacob deceived his father Isaac into bestowing upon him the blessing rightfully belonging to the older son. Esau was the ancestor of the Edomites as Jacob was of the Israelites. The unfriendly relations between the two nations through the years reflected this conflict between the brothers. (See *Edom.*) *Genesis 25:24-34; 27:1–28:9; 33:1-16; 1 Chronicles 1:34.*

ESTHER
(ES-tur)

A Jewish girl who was among the beautiful maidens chosen by the Persian king Ahasuerus to fill the place of the banished queen Vashti. She pleased the king so that he made her his queen. Haman, the prime minister, aroused the king against the Jews because of their religious beliefs and practices, which were different from any others in the kingdom. With great courage Esther approached the king and explained that his edict authorizing the destruction of the Jews would mean the end of her people. The king was persuaded, and Haman was executed on the gallows he had prepared for Esther's cousin Mordecai. (See *Esther, Book of.*)

ESTHER, BOOK OF

The OT book which tells the story of how Esther, the Jewish wife of a Persian king, saved the Jews from persecution. The book explains the festival of Purim, which is the annual Jewish observance of this deliverance. *See the book itself.*

ETERNAL LIFE

Life with God that is not destroyed by death and which can begin here and now. In the OT God was often referred to as the living God (see Deuteronomy 5:26; Joshua 3:10). This meant that God had the rule over death and could defeat it. The NT points to this victory over death in the crucifixion of Jesus Christ, in his rising again from the tomb, and in his offer of everlasting life to all those who believe in Christ. (See *Immortality, Resurrection.*) *Matthew 25:46; John 3:15-16; 6:39-40, 47-51, 54; Romans 6:22-23; 1 John 5:11-12.*

ETHIOPIA
(ee-thee-OH-pee-uh)

The ancient name of the African territory south of Egypt. In the Bible it is also called Cush. *2 Kings 19:9; Psalm 68:31; Isaiah 20:3-5; 45:14; Jeremiah 13:23; Acts 8:26-28.*

EUNICE

Mother of Timothy; praised for her faith and instruction of Timothy. *2 Timothy 1:5*

EUNUCH
(YOO-nik)

In Bible times a man servant whose male organs had been removed. Such men served in the women's quarters of the royal household. They were sometimes called "officers" and "captains." "Eunuch" is sometimes used to refer to men remaining unmarried by choice. *2 Kings 9:30-33; 20:18; Esther 2:3; Isaiah 39:7; 56:3-5; Jeremiah 38:7; 41:16; Matthew 19:12; Acts 8:27.*

EUPHRATES
(yoo-FRAY-teez)

The largest river in western Asia, originating in Armenia and emptying into the Persian Gulf. According to biblical tradition it was one of the four rivers into which the river that flowed from the garden of Eden divided. In Bible times the Euphrates formed the north boundary of the territories promised by God to Israel in God's covenant with Abraham. Because of its importance it was often called simply "the River." *Genesis 2:14; 15:18; Joshua 1:4; 1 Kings 4:24; 1 Chronicles 18:3.*

EVANGELIST
(ee-VAN-juh-list)
Meaning "one who announces good news." A title of early Christian missionaries and preachers of the gospel. It is used in a more limited way to indicate the authors of the NT gospels. *Acts 21:8; Ephesians 4:11; 2 Timothy 4:5.*

EVE
(eev)
In the Genesis stories of creation, the first woman, the wife given by God to Adam to be his companion and helper. She was the "woman" who listened to the serpent and ate the for-bidden fruit. She persuaded Adam to eat, and they were banished from the garden of Eden. *Genesis 3:1–4:2.*

EXILE, THE
(EK-sile)
The time in biblical history when the Babylonians conquered the country of Judah and the city of Jerusalem and carried many of the Jews away to live in Babylonia. The first of the exiles left their homes in 597 B.C. Other exiles went in 586 and 582 B.C. Many returned home in 538 B.C. when Cyrus, the Persian king, conquered Babylonia and permitted the exiles and prisoners of war to go home. The word "exile" is also used to refer to an individual's banishment from his home or country. Kings were sometimes banished to other lands because they were weak or poor rulers. *2 Samuel 15:19; 2 Chronicles 36:19-20; Ezra 6:16.*

THE JEWS GO INTO EXILE

77

EXODUS, BOOK OF
(EK-suh-duhss)

Meaning "a going out." The second book of the OT telling of the "going out" from Egypt by the Hebrew people under the leadership of Moses. It tells of the deliverance of the people from slavery and the long journey to the land of Canaan. *See the book itself.*

EXPIATION
(eks-pi-AY-shuhn)

An action of atonement that takes away a sin or "covers" it and thus restores a person to holiness and divine favor. (See *Atonement.*) *Numbers 35:33; Deuteronomy 32:43; Romans 3:23-25; Hebrews 2:17; 1 John 2:1-2; 4:10.*

EZEKIEL
(ee-ZEE-kee-uhl)

A prophet of the Babylonian exile. Ezekiel was the son of a priest and had grown up close to the temple in Jerusalem. He was carried to Babylonia in 597 B.C. There among the exiles Ezekiel had a vision of God and received the call to be a prophet to Israel. He preached to the Jews in exile and prepared them for the time when God would restore them to their own land. (See *Ezekiel, Book of.*)

EZEKIEL, BOOK OF

An OT book containing the prophecies and sermons of Ezekiel. The prophecies are in poetic language with much symbolism. One of Ezekiel's most important messages to the Jews was that being separated from their land and from the temple in Jerusalem did not separate them from God. *See the book itself.*

EZRA
(EZ-ruh)

A priest and scribe who led a group of Jewish exiles from Babylonia back to Jerusalem around the middle of the fifth century or the beginning of the fourth century B.C. In a royal decree King Artaxerxes gave Ezra great authority in supervising the rebuilding of Jerusalem. He made a great effort to restore the community life of the Jews according to the old Jewish law. (See *Ezra, Book of.*)

EZRA, BOOK OF

Originally the book of Ezra and the book of Nehemiah were a single book. The two books are a continuation of the books called Chronicles 1 and 2 and relate the history of the Jews from 536 to 432 B.C. The book of Ezra lists the exiles who returned to Jerusalem with Ezra and the temple vessels they brought with them. *See the book itself; Nehemiah 8:1–10:39.*

JOSEPH PREPARES FOR FAMINE

FABLE

A form of short story which teaches a lesson and in which plants and animals speak and act as persons do. A fable could not possibly happen, but it has some truth the reader or listener will find helpful. The Bible has two fables. Each tells some truth about a king. (See *Allegory, Myth, Parable.*) *Judges 9:8-15; 2 Kings 14:9.*

FACE

The front part of the head of people or animals. The face expresses most clearly the thoughts and feelings of a person. In the Bible such phrases as "to set one's face against" or "to hide one's face" express anger and displeasure. "Face" is used also as a figure of speech to suggest God's presence, as in "the Lord make his face to shine upon you." *Numbers 6:24-26; Psalm 27:8-9; and other references.*

FAIR HAVENS

(fair HAY-venz)
A harbor at the south side of the island of Crete where the Alexandrian ship Paul was sailing on to Rome stopped for awhile. Paul suggested remaining there for the winter. Against his advice the ship continued on and was shipwrecked. *Acts 27:6-12.*

FAITH

Faith, as used in the Bible, is belief in, trust in, and loyalty to God. It is the confident response humans make to the love, care, and seeking of God. Faith in God also came to mean faith in Jesus with the advent of the NT. Jesus gave the people a new understanding of God as father. Jesus charged humanity to respond in faith to the highest, the ultimate (especially in his crucifixion and resurrection). *2 Chronicles 19:9; Psalms 78:22; 116:10;*

Habakkuk 2:4; Matthew 21:22; Mark 2:5; 5:34; 11:22; Luke 7:9; 18:8; Acts 14:9; 20:21; 24:24; Romans 1:16-17; 4:13-22; 1 Corinthians 13:13; Galatians 2:16; Hebrews 11:1-31; 1 John 5:4.

FAMILY

A group of persons related to each other by kinship or marriage, usually living under the authority of the father. In early OT times families were very large— a man then was permitted to have more than one wife and to have children by more than one wife. The family group would consist of wives, children, grandparents, concubines, servants, and grown children with their own family circles. In later times it became the custom for a man to have only one wife. Among the Hebrews the family was a religious community which had a solemn duty to pass on the traditions of their worship, history, and knowledge of God. So close were these ties that the entire nation was thought of as the family of God. The community of Christian believers is also referred to as the family of God In the NT. *Genesis 37:1-2; Ruth 2:1-2; Psalm 22:27; Jeremiah 31:1; Acts 3:25.*

FAMINE

Scarcity of food caused by drought, insects, disease of the grain or cattle, war, and other disasters. *Genesis 12:10; 41:54-57; Job 5:20; Jeremiah 14:15-16; Acts 11:28.*

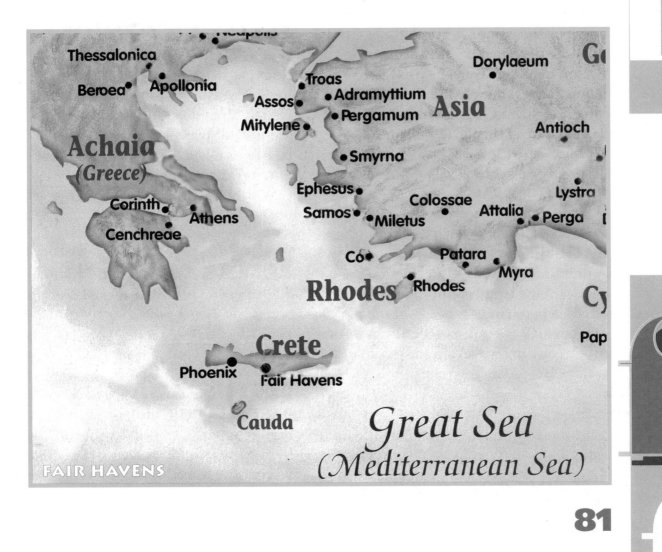

81

FAST

To go without food and water for a period of time as religious and moral discipline. In early OT times there was often public fasting to express personal grief or to express sorrow and alarm at a national disaster. Fasting was also an act of repentance for sin. After the Exile fast days were appointed at regular times of the year. In the NT Jesus emphasized that fasting should be done in sincerity and for the glory of God, not for praise. The early church used it as a discipline. *Judges 20:26; 2 Chronicles 20:3; Ezra 8:21-23; 9:5-6; Nehemiah 9:1; Matthew 4:2; 6:16-18; 9:14-15; Acts 13:2-3; 14:23.*

FATHER

The male head of a household, family, or tribe. The name was sometimes used as a title of respect for an ancestor or a person in authority. Jesus used the name in speaking of God to help people understand God's nature. *Genesis 28:13; Deuteronomy 5:16; 1 Samuel 24:8-11; Matthew 6:9, 14, 32; Luke 2:48-49; 6:36; Ephesians 5:19-20.*

FATHOM
(FATH-uhm)

A unit of measurement in NT times based on the length from the tip of one outstretched hand to the tip of the other, usually about six feet. It is a term used today in measuring the depth of water. *Acts 27:28.*

FATLING

A well-cared-for and well-fed animal, such as a cow or sheep, important for its use in Israel's sacrificial worship. *2 Samuel 6:13; 1 Kings 1:9, 25; Psalm 66:15; Isaiah 11:6.*

FEAR

Alarm, dread. In the Bible the term appears with many different meanings. The expressions "fear of God" and "fear of the Lord" also have the meanings of awe, reverence, respect, love, trust, and faith. This sort of fear is a recognition of God's holiness. *Deuteronomy 6:13; Joshua 24:14; 2 Samuel 23:3-4; 2 Chronicles 19:7; 26:5; Psalms 23:4; 33:8; 130:4; Acts 9:31; 1 Peter 2:17.*

FELIX, ANTONIUS
(FEE-liks, an-TOH-ni-ehs)

Roman governor of Judea from A.D. 52 to 60. He was governor when Paul last visited Jerusalem and was arrested there. Paul was brought to Caesarea to be tried by Felix. The governor kept him in prison for two years, hoping that Paul would pay to secure his release. *Acts 23:24–24:27.*

FESTAL GARMENT

Fine clothing worn on special days or occasions. *Genesis 45:22; Judges 14:12-13, 19; 2 Kings 5:5, 22-23.*

FESTUS, PORCIUS
(FEST-uhss, POR-shuhs)

Roman governor of Judea probably from A.D. 60 to 62. Successor to Felix. Festus was forced to send Paul to Rome for trial when Paul as a Roman citizen appealed to Caesar. Paul had already been in prison in Caesarea for two years. *Acts 24:27–26:32.*

FETTER

Anything that restrains a person's movements; a shackle. In Bible times fetters were made of wood, bronze, and iron. A prisoner's feet might be placed in fetters or shackles. The fetters were joined together by a rope and allowed him to take only short steps. A captive's hands were often placed in a fetter suspended from his neck by a rope. *Judges 16:21; Psalms 105:18; 149:8; Mark 5:4; Acts 16:25-26.*

PAUL AND SILAS IN FETTERS

FIG

Oblong fruit with sweet pulp from a tree native to southwestern Asia. Figs were an important item of food in Bible times. They were pressed into cakes, eaten fresh, or dried. Fig cakes were applied to the body for medication. The fig tree provided shade from the sun. Its leaves sewn together served as wrappings for fruits and vegetables taken to market. *Numbers 13:23; 20:5; Deuteronomy 8:8; 1 Samuel 25:18; 30:12; 2 Kings 20:7; Song of Solomon 2:13; Isaiah 28:4; 34:4; 38:21; Habakkuk 3:17-18; John 1:48-50; Revelation 6:13.*

FILLET

(FIL-et)

A metal band joining the tops of the pillars in the tabernacles. Hooks were probably fixed to the band by which the curtains were hung. *Exodus 27:10-11; 36:38; 38:10-12, 17, 19.*

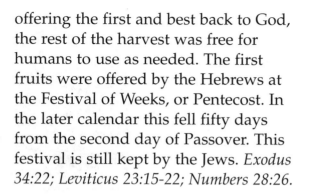

FINGER OF GOD

A figure of speech used in the Bible to indicate the power of God. *Exodus 8:19; 31:18; Deuteronomy 9:10; Psalm 8:3; Luke 11:20.*

FIRMAMENT
(FUR-muh-ment)

An OT word meaning "a strip of beaten metal." The Hebrews sometimes pictured the sky as a metallic sheet that separated the upper waters from the lower waters. (See *Earth; World.*) *Genesis 1:6-7; Psalms 19:1; 150:1.*

FIRST-BORN

In the OT the term is used mainly to mean the eldest son. The Hebrews gave a special place to the first-born son. He became the next head of the family or tribe, and was responsible for its welfare. He claimed the family blessing and received a double portion of the family inheritance (see *Birthright*). The term refers also to the sacrifice of first-born animals. In the NT the term is applied to Jesus and indicates his relationships to God. *Exodus 4:22-23; 13:11-15; Numbers 18:15-18; Deuteronomy 21:15-17; Luke 2:7; Romans 8:29; Colossians 1:15, 18; Hebrews 1:6.*

FIRST FRUITS

The sacrificial offering to God from the annual crop of vegetables, grain, and animals. The Hebrews were very conscious of the fact that their land was a gift of God; God was their landlord, so to speak. For this reason all the fruit of the earth belonged to God, but by offering the first and best back to God, the rest of the harvest was free for humans to use as needed. The first fruits were offered by the Hebrews at the Festival of Weeks, or Pentecost. In the later calendar this fell fifty days from the second day of Passover. This festival is still kept by the Jews. *Exodus 34:22; Leviticus 23:15-22; Numbers 28:26.*

FISH

Not much is found in the OT about fishing, although eating fish is mentioned several times (*Numbers 11:5*). In the NT fishing had become a major industry on the Sea of Galilee. Fish that were not eaten fresh were salted, pickled, or dried. Fish was quite cheap, making it a mainstay of the daily diet. Several of Jesus' followers were fishermen. *Mark 1:19-20; Matthew 13: 47-48.*

FLAGON
(FLAG-uhn)

A large pitcher of pottery or metal usually having a cover. Oil, wine, and other liquids were kept in flagons. *Exodus 25:29; 37:16; Numbers 4:7; Isaiah 22:24.*

FLASK

A small, bottle-like container for oil, water, perfume, or ointment. In ancient times flasks were made of pottery or alabaster; later they were made of glass. *2 Kings 9:1-3; Jeremiah 19:1, 10; Matthew 25:4; Luke 7:37.*

FLAX

The plant from which linen comes. In Bible times it was cultivated in Egypt and Canaan. The fibers of the plant are soaked, combed, and spun into linen thread, then woven into linen cloth and rope. *Exodus 9:31; Joshua 2:6; Judges 15:14; Proverbs 31:13; Isaiah 19:9; Ezekiel 40:3.*

FLESH

The soft, muscular part of the body. However, the word was used in the OT to refer to the whole human body. In this sense it means personhood or humanity. "Flesh" is often used to indicate weakness, especially in contrast to the spiritual part of humanity. The spiritual part is thought of as the seat of humanity's goodness. *Genesis 2:23; 2 Chronicles 32:8; Psalm 78:39; Matthew 26:41; John 1:14; 8:15; Galatians 5:16-24; 1 Peter 1:24-25.*

FLOG

To whip with a scourge, that is, a barbed whip. *Deuteronomy 25:2-3; Matthew 27:26; Acts 16:23.*

FOOTSTOOL

A footrest for a king's throne or steps leading to the throne. Solomon's throne had a footstool of gold. Some ancient kings had carvings on the steps or footstool, representing other peoples and nations. Thus, they felt they walked over their captives or enemies as they mounted the throne. In the Bible this word is often used as a symbol to represent the earth as God's footstool to show the dominion or authority of God as king and sovereign over all things. *1 Chronicles 28:2; 2 Chronicles 9:18; Psalms 99:5; 110:1; 132:7; Isaiah 66:1; Lamentations 2:1; Matthew 5:34-35; Acts 7:49.*

FORD

A place where a river is shallow enough to cross by wading. Until recent times fording was the most common way to cross rivers except in prosperous and well-traveled places where bridges were built. *Genesis 32:22; Joshua 2:7; Judges 3:28; 12:5-6; 1 Samuel 13:7; 2 Samuel 15:28; 17:16; 19:18; Isaiah 16:2.*

FLASK

85

FORGIVENESS
(for-GIV-nes)

The plainest meanings of forgiveness are the pardoning of an offender, the giving up of a claim to a debt, or the release from an obligation. In the relationship of humans to God, forgiveness is God's gracious taking away of the barriers which separate people from God. The central fact of the NT is that in the life and death of Jesus Christ the obstacles of humanity's sin and disobedience are removed for those who, believing in Christ, repent of their sins. Their guilt is wiped away, forgiven. In the relationship of persons, forgiveness is the pardoning of an offender. The person who has been wronged excuses the offender and counts the wrong as if it had not happened. *Genesis 50:17; Numbers 15:25-26; Psalm 130:4; Luke 3:3; 6:37; Acts 2:28; 10:43; Hebrews 9:22.*

FORUM OF APPIUS
(FOH-ruhm, AP-i-uhs)

A stopping place or station on the Appian Way between Puteoli and the city of Rome, where ships unloaded passengers and cargo. It was about forty-three miles, slightly more than a day's journey, from Rome; though because the road was good, the trip could be made in a day. Paul passed through this place on his way to prison in Rome. *Acts 28:15.*

FOUNDATION

The base on which a structure is erected. While foundations are often spoken of quite literally in the Bible to mean the base of the temple or other important building, many scripture passages use the term figuratively. Biblical writers speak of God laying the foundation of the world, of Christians laying for themselves a foundation for the coming age, and the church as having a foundation built on the "apostles and prophets, with Christ Jesus himself as the "chief cornerstone" (*Ephesians 2:20*). 1 Kings 5:17; Job 38:4; Psalm 102:25; John 17:24; 1 Timothy 6:19.

FOUNTAIN

A spring of water flowing from an opening in a hillside or valley. In the dry Bible lands a fountain was an important source of water. The presence of a fountain often determined the location of a village. Fountains were also mentioned in the OT in figures of speech for the power and wisdom of God as the source of life and refreshment. *Deuteronomy 33:28; Nehemiah 2:14; 3:15; Psalm 36:9; 68:26; Proverbs 13:14; 14:27; Ecclesiastes 12:6; Jeremiah 17:13; Joel 3:18.*

FRANKINCENSE
(FRANG-kin-senss)

A fragrant gum resin taken from the bark of a tree that grows in northern Arabia. The resin hardens into small, white chunks and beads that are easily ground into a powder. This powder was an important ingredient in incense and has a balsam-like odor when burned. Frankincense was used in many ways in the sacrificial worship of Israel. It was set with the bread of the presence before the Holy of Holies and was mixed with oil in the offerings of grain, vegetables, or fruit. It symbolized worship when given as a gift to the infant Jesus. *Exodus 30:34-38; Leviticus 2:1-2; 24:7; Isaiah 43:23; 60:6; Matthew 2:10-11.*

FRINGE

A cord or thread which ended in a kind of tassel sewn on the corners of an outer garment (see *Deuteronomy 22:12*). The fringe, or tassel, was to remind the Hebrews of the commandments of God. *Matthew 9:20; 14:36; 23:5; Mark 6:56; Luke 8:44.*

FRINGE

FRONTLET

A band worn on the forehead between the eyes at prayer times as a reminder of the commandments of God. It may occasionally have been thought of as being effective against certain kinds of evil. *Exodus 13:16; Deuteronomy 6:4-9; 11:18.*

FRUIT

A product of a plant or tree useful to humans. The word is used as a figure of speech in the Bible to mean the result of any specific action, good or evil. *Genesis 30:2; Psalm 104:13; 127:3; Proverbs 1:31; 12:14; 31:31; Isaiah 3:10; 13:18; 57:18; Jeremiah 17:10; Hosea 10:12-13; Amos 6:12; Matthew 3:10; 7:15-20; 21:43; Mark 4:20; Luke 1:42; Ephesians 5:9; Hebrews 12:11; 13:15.*

FULLER'S FIELD

A place outside the city of Jerusalem near the canal of the Upper Pool. Probably the location where cloth had once been "fulled." This process involved thickening and shrinking newly shorn wool or newly woven cloth. The natural oils were removed and the material cleaned and bleached. The worker who did this was called a "fuller." *2 Kings 18:17; Isaiah 7:3; 36:2.*

GABRIEL
(GAY-bree-uhl)
In the Bible, a messenger angel. The name means "man of God" or "God has shown himself mighty." Gabriel is specifically named in the NT as the messenger from God sent to announce the births of John the Baptist and of Jesus. *Daniel 8:16; 9:21; Luke 1:11-20; 26-38.*

GAD
(gad)
The seventh son of Jacob and the ancestor of the tribe of Gad, called Gadites. The territory of the Gadites was east of the Jordan River. *Genesis 35:26; Numbers 1:24-25; 1 Samuel 13:6-7; 1 Chronicles 5:11; 12:8-15.*

GAIUS
(GAY-uhss)
1. A Christian baptized by Paul in Corinth. Gaius made Paul welcome in his home there. At this time Paul wrote a letter to the Romans. *Romans 16:23; 1 Corinthians 1:14.*
2. Gaius of Macedonia was one of Paul's traveling companions who were arrested with Paul in Ephesus. *Acts 19:29.*
3. Gaius of Derbe is also mentioned as another traveling companion of Paul. Gaius of Macedonia and Gaius of Derbe may possibly have been the same person. *Acts 20:4.*
4. Another Gaius was a Christian leader to whom the third letter of John was addressed. *3 John 1:1.*

GALATIA

(guh-LAY-shuh)

In NT times a Roman province in central Asia Minor named for the Celtic (Gallic) tribe of the Galatians. It is now a part of Turkey. Important NT cities in Galatia were Derbe, Antioch of Pisidia, Iconium and Lystra. *Acts 16:6; 18:23; 1 Corinthians 16:1; Galatians 1:2; 2 Timothy 4:10; 1 Peter 1:1.*

GALATIANS, LETTER TO THE

(guh-LAY-shuhnz)

The ninth book of the NT. A letter written by Paul to "the churches of Galatia." In it Paul tells of his own conversion. He explains that Christians are not required to keep all the Jewish laws and regulations. Their faith in Christ makes them free to follow the law of love. He gives a description of the kind of goodness a Christian should practice. *See the book itself.*

GALILEE

(GAL-i-lee)

A small region in northern Palestine east of the Mediterranean Sea. In OT times its boundaries changed many times, and for centuries it was ruled by one nation after another. In 63 B.C. Galilee became a fixed area under Roman rule with Sepphoris and then Tiberias as the capital. It was bounded on the west by the Mediterranean Sea and on the east by the Sea of Galilee and the Jordan River. Oil, wine, fish, and grain were the common exports. Almost all Jesus' career lay within the borders of this tiny region. Galileans spoke with an accent different from that of Judeans. The modern state of Israel, established in 1948, includes all of Galilee. *Joshua 21:32; 1 Kings 9:11; 2 Kings 15:29; Isaiah 9:1; Matthew 2:22; 4:12-15; Mark 1:9, 28, 39; Luke 4:31; 17:11; John 4:43-47; 7:1, 41, 52; Acts 1:11; 9:31.*

GALILEE, SEA OF

A freshwater, heart-shaped, inland lake that empties into the Jordan River. It is about thirteen miles long and seven miles wide with an abundance of fish and birds. Almost surrounded by mountains, the lake reaches to a depth of two hundred feet. The surface of the lake is about six hundred feet below sea level. It has been called by several names during the period of Hebrew history— "Chinnereth," "Gennesaret," and "Tiberias." It is best known as the Sea of Galilee. Many persons and places associated with Jesus came from this area. Here fishing was an important means of making a living. *Numbers 34:11; Joshua 12:3; 13:27; Matthew 4:18; Mark 1:16; 7:31; Luke 5:1; John 6:1; 21:1.*

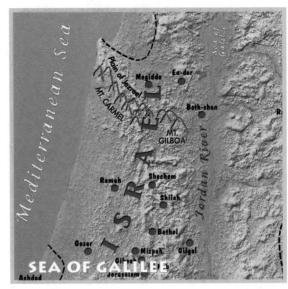

GALL

The juice of a bitter herb. The term is also used to describe or symbolize a feeling of bitterness. The gall offered to Jesus on the cross was made from the juice of the poppy added to sour wine. It was supposed to have the effect of easing pain. Jesus refused to take it. *Job 20:14; Lamentations 3:19; Matthew 27:34; Acts 8:23.*

GALLIO

(GAL-ee-oh)
Proconsul of Achaea about A.D. 52 with headquarters at Corinth. Paul was brought before him on the charge that faith in Christ was contrary to Roman law, but Gallio was unwilling to be the judge and dismissed the case. *Acts 18:12-17.*

GAMALIEL

(guh-MAY-lee-uhl)
A Pharisee, a famous interpreter of the Jewish law, and an honored member of the Sanhedrin in Jerusalem. He is said to have been Paul's teacher. He was a man of generous spirit, and he cautioned his fellow council members to be careful about how they opposed the apostles who preached and healed in the name of Jesus Christ. If their teaching were false it would fade away, he pointed out. If it were true the council would be working against God. *Acts 5:34-39; 22:3.*

GARRISON

A body of troops stationed for defense, usually at a frontier post. *1 Samuel 10:5; 13:3-4; 2 Samuel 8:6, 14; 23:14; 1 Chronicles 11:16; 18:13; 2 Chronicles 17:2.*

GASH

In the OT to cut oneself as a sign of mourning or as a part of the worship of pagan gods. *Jeremiah 41:5; 47:5; 48:37; Hosea 7:14.*

GATE

In the OT an opening in the wall of a city such walls were built so that the city could be well defended. There were usually an outer gate and an inner gate built at angles to the wall, with a lookout tower. Gates were closed at night. Near the gate was the center of interest in the town, and most business was carried on there. News was best gathered at the gate, and it was also the place of judgment. The elders sat between the outer and inner gates to judge cases brought to them. Just inside the gate was the busy marketplace. *Deuteronomy 21:19; Joshua 20:4; Ruth 4:1-2; 2 Samuel 18:24; 2 Kings 7:1, 18; Amos 5:10, 12, 15.*

GATH

(gath)
In the OT one of the five principal cities of the Philistines. It was nearer Judah than the others; therefore, now and again it came under Judah's control. It was an old city once inhabited by the Anakim, a race of giants. Goliath and other giant Philistine war-

riors came from Gath. David's lament "Tell it not in Gath" is often quoted in works of literature when mentioning some disastrous or regrettable event which might give one's enemies cause to rejoice. *Joshua 11:22; 13:3; 1 Samuel 5:8; 17:4, 52; 21:10-12; 27:2-4; 2 Samuel 1:20; 1 Chronicles 18:1; 20:6-8; 2 Chronicles 26:6; Micah 1:10.*

GAZA
(GAH-zuh)
An ancient city southeast of the Mediterranean Sea, located three miles from the seacoast of Philistia on the road to Egypt. It was a place of importance because it was on a trade route. Gaza was one of the five principal cities of the Philistines and fought against the Israelites. The prophet Amos condemned Gaza for its slave trade. *Genesis 10:19; Deuteronomy 2:23; Joshua 10:41; 11:22; 13:3; 15:47; Judges 1:18; 6:4; 16:1-2; 1 Samuel 6:17; Amos 1:6-7; Acts 8:26.*

GEBA
(GEE-buh)
A city on the northern boundary of the kingdom of Judah about six miles northeast of Jerusalem. Here Saul, Jonathan, and David fought the Philistines. After the Exile, Geba became the home of many Jews returning from Babylon. *Joshua 18:24; 21:17; Judges 20:33; 1 Samuel 13:3, 16; 14:5; 2 Samuel 5:25; 2 Kings 23:8; 1 Chronicles 6:60; 8:6; 2 Chronicles 16:6; Nehemiah 7:30; 11:31; 12:29.*

JESUS BEING OFFERED GALL

GEHENNA
(geh-HEN-uh)

Meaning "fiery hell." A valley south of Jerusalem called the valley of Hinnom (see *Hinnom, Valley of the Son of*) where in OT times in the pagan worship of Molech, children were passed through fire as a sacrifice. This was forbidden by Jewish law. Later and in NT times rubbish was burned there. So all through its history ill-smelling and disagreeable smokes had risen from this valley (see *2 Kings 23:10; 2 Chronicles 28:3; 33:6; Jeremiah 7:31; 19:5; 32:35*). By the first century B.C. the term Gehenna was being used to mean a place of fiery punishment after death—a hell of fire or lake of fire for those who did not repent (see *Matthew 5:22; 29-30; 10:28; 18:9; 23:15; Mark 9:43, 45, 47; Luke 12:5; James 3:6*).

GENEALOGY
(jee-nee-AL-uh-jee)

An orderly list of names recording the ancestry of individuals or the relation- ships of families, clans, tribes, or nations. In Bible times the purpose of this listing was to establish legal rights to property and to show which of the sons of a king or a priest would inherit the father's kingdom or priestly office. Early genealogies often included tradi- tions about the origin of the nations. In many cases the writers were inter- ested in telling of the people who had maintained a strong relationship with God. Some of the lists are not accurate because names were forgotten. Lacking some names, biblical writers often made an orderly division of gen- erations. Today a generation is esti- mated to be about thirty-three to forty years. *Genesis 10:32; 1 Chronicles 5:17; Ezra 2:62; 8:1; Nehemiah 7:5; Matthew 1:1-17; 1 Timothy 1:4; Titus 3:9.*

GENESIS
(JEN-uh-sis)

Meaning "beginning." This is the first book of the Bible, and it covers the time from the very first beginnings of history until the journey of the Israelites into Egypt. There are two divisions to the book of Genesis. The first eleven chapters contain some of the most noble and poetic images ever written. The stories of Adam and Eve in the Garden of Eden, the Great Flood, and the attempt to build the Tower of Babel suggest and symbolize the grandeur and mystery of creation in a way that has inspired and instructed readers for thousands of years. The rest of Genesis tells of God's dealing with a particular man, Abraham. There is the call of God to Abraham; the covenant between them; the birth of Isaac, Jacob, and the twelve sons of Jacob; the exile of Joseph into Egypt; and the reunion of the family with Joseph there. These stories trace the development of this family of Abraham into the people of Israel. The significance of the book of Genesis lies in the light it sheds on the relationship between God and his cre- ation before humanity rebelled. It indi- cates how God entered into history after God's creation had been dam- aged by the sinfulness of humanity. God did this through the Hebrew peo- ple, and the entire Bible focuses on them and the working out of God's purpose through them. *See the book itself.*

GENNESARET

(guh-NESS-uh-ret)

The name for the Sea of Galilee in NT times; also, a fruitful valley northwest of the Sea of Galilee. (See *Galilee, Sea of.*) *Mark 6:53; Luke 5:1.*

GENTILE

(JEN-tile)

NT word for a person who was not a Jew. In the plural it meant "nations" in general. *Matthew 5:47; 6:32; 10:5; Acts 11:1; Romans 3:29; 9:24.*

GENNESARET REGION

GERAH

(GEE-rah)

A small Hebrew weight, 1/20 of a shekel. *Exodus 30:13; Numbers 18:16; Ezekiel 45:12.*

GERIZIM, MOUNT

(GAIR-uh-zim)

A mountain in Canaan directly south of Mt. Ebal. The sides of this mountain and of Mt. Ebal form a pass, now an important east-west highway about forty miles from Jerusalem. Ancient Shechem lies at the eastern entrance to the narrow valley between the mountains. In this pass and from the sides of the two mountains the ceremony of covenant renewal was held (see *Ebal, Mount*). The modern name of Mt. Gerizim is Jebel et-Tor. The Samaritan woman whom Jesus met at the well mentioned to him that her ancestors worshiped on "this mountain," and she indicated Mt. Gerizim (see John 4:20). The small groups of Samaritans that remain today still celebrate the Passover on its summit. *Deuteronomy 11:29; 27:12; Joshua 8:33; Judges 9:7.*

GERSHOM

(GUR-shuhm)

The older son of Moses and Zipporah. He was born in Midian. Because Moses had escaped there from Egypt to save his life, he gave his son a name which meant, "I have been a sojourner in a foreign land." *Exodus 2:22; 18:3.*

GETHSEMANE

(geth-SEM-uh-nee)

Meaning "oil press." The site on the Mount of Olives outside Jerusalem where Jesus went to pray after the Last Supper with his disciples. It was in this place that he was betrayed by Judas. *Matthew 26:36; Mark 14:32.*

GIANTS

Humans of huge proportions. When a group of men were sent by Moses into Canaan to spy out the land and see what sort of place it was, they brought back the report that there were giants, "the descendants of Anak," in this land. The Hebrews may have thought that in addition to their enormous size and strength these huge men had some supernatural power. In any case they were afraid to enter Canaan (see *Numbers 13:23-30*). There were also some men among the Philistines who were unusually tall. Goliath is the most famous of these. *2 Samuel 21:16-22.*

GIBEAH

(GIB-ee-uh)

A city in the hill country north of Jerusalem. Its name meant "hill" or "height." It was the home of Saul, and it became his provincial capital after he was acclaimed the first king of Israel. Gibeah played an important part in Saul's struggles with the Philistines. Part of a fortress dating from the time of Saul has been uncovered there. (There are other places mentioned in the OT with the same name.) *Judges 19:12-16; 1 Samuel 10:26; 14:16; 22:6; Hosea 10:9.*

GIBEON

(GIB-ee-uhn)

An OT town six miles northwest of Jerusalem. Gibeon stood in the path of the victorious armies of Joshua as they invaded Canaan. The cities of Jericho and AI had already been overcome, and the people of Gibeon were very frightened even though their city was strong and the men mighty. They hatched a clever plan by which they could prevent Joshua's attacking them. Many years later some of the battles between the forces of King Saul and the men loyal to David were fought near Gibeon. This was also the place in which Solomon had his famous dream in which he asked God for wisdom to be a good king. Still later, Nehemiah mentioned that the men of Gibeon helped in rebuilding the walls of Jerusalem after the Hebrews had returned from their exile in Babylon. *Joshua 9:3–10:10; 1 Kings 3:4-14; 1 Chronicles 14:16; 16:39; 2 Chronicles 1:3; Nehemiah 3:7; Jeremiah 28:1; 41:12.*

GIDEON

(GID-ee-uhn)

An OT hero, also known as Jerubbaal, who was a judge called by God to lead the Israelites. At the time of his call Gideon was a farmer. The whole land was gripped with fear of the fierce Midianites, who would ride into the country on their swift camels and ruin or steal whatever they wanted. For this reason the people hid their animals and their food as best they could. Gideon was told by the angel of the Lord that he was to defeat the Midianites. His confidence and enthusiasm aroused the whole tribe of Manasseh, and Gideon set out with ten thousand men. However, God told him that not nearly that many were needed. After testing them, he picked three hundred of the best soldiers and took them only. They completely defeated the enemy. The grateful Israelites wanted to make Gideon their king, but he refused. *Judges 6:11–9:5, 16; Hebrews 11:32-34.*

GOLIATH

95

GILBOA, MOUNT

(gil-BOH-uh)

A ridge of limestone hills rising 1,737 feet above the Mediterranean Sea at the east end of the Valley of Jezreel. Because of its location it was often the scene of battles. King Saul chose this place to fight the Philistines. *1 Samuel 31:1; 8:2; Samuel 1:6, 21.*

GILEAD

(GIL-ee-uhd)

Grandson of Manasseh and ancestor of the tribe of Gilead. It is also the name of a territory of hills and valleys located to the east of Jordan, where grapes and olives were grown. *Genesis 37:25; Numbers 26:29-30; 27:1; Judges 5:17; 2 Kings 10:32-33.*

GILEAD, BALM OF

A soothing medicine and antiseptic made from the bark of an evergreen tree. This substance did not come from Gilead as the name suggests. Jeremiah's cry "Is there no balm in Gilead?" is often quoted today when one wishes relief from suffering. *Jeremiah 8:22; 46:11.*

GILGAL

(GIL-gal)

Meaning "circle of stones." Gilgal near Jericho was the site of the first encampment of the Israelites after crossing the Jordan River and entering Canaan. There they erect twelve memorial stones taken from the bed of the Jordan. Gilgal became the base city for the Israelites' military operations against the Canaanites. A great

sanctuary was built there. At Gilgal Saul was made king of Israel, and here he was rejected from the kingship. Gilgal is mentioned frequently in OT history, and there are several towns with this name. *Joshua 4:19-20; 1 Samuel 7:15-16; 11:14-15; Hosea 9:15; 12:11; Amos 4:4-5; Micah 6:5.*

GIRDLE

A shashlike piece of the high priest's clothing of fine embroidered linen. The belts, or sashes, worn by ordinary men and women were also called girdles. These were used to fasten in the long, flowing robes. Money pouches or weapons were carried in the girdle. In the case of messengers and travelers who wished to free their legs for easier movement, the robe was brought between the legs toward the front and tucked into the girdle. This was called "girding up the loins" (see 1 Kings 18:46; 2 Kings 4:29). *Exodus 39:29; 2 Kings 1:8; Proverbs 31:24; Isaiah 11:5; Matthew 3:4; Acts 21:11.*

GLASSY SEA

See *Sea of Glass.*

GLEANING

The practice of gathering or picking up what had been left behind or overlooked in the fields or orchards after harvesting. The Hebrew law provided that the privilege of gleaning be granted to the needy. *Leviticus 19:9-10; 23:22; Deuteronomy 24:19-21; Ruth 2:2-19.*

GLORY

Honor, praise, importance, and splendor. The word was chiefly used to describe the presence of God. In the Bible glory is sometimes connected with riches, bravery, uprightness, beauty, and similar qualities in people and the works of people. *Leviticus 9:23; 1 Samuel 4:22; Psalms 8:5; 49:16; 148:13; Isaiah 60:13; Jeremiah 2:11; Matthew 6:28-29; Luke 2:14, 29-32; John 8:54; Acts 7:2; Ephesians 3:16; Hebrews 2:9; Revelation 4:11.*

GOD (NAMES OF)

For the Hebrews every name represented the very selfhood of the person who bore it. It was the same for the holy name of God. God's name expressed God's power and holiness.

The very fact that God had revealed God's name to the Hebrews was a sign of God's special care for them. They regarded the divine name with great reverence. It was not to be used carelessly. Advice and prophecies given in the name of God had God's authority. Other ways of referring to God are: Lord (see *Holy One, Yahweh*), The Rock, Father, Savior, King, Judge, Shepherd, Creator, Redeemer, Maker, Almighty, and such descriptive expressions as the Living God, the Everlasting God, the First and the Last, the Ancient of Days, the God of our Fathers, the God of Abraham. *Genesis 17:1; 49:24-25; Exodus 3:13-15; 33:19; Isaiah 17:7; 33:22; 40:28; Jeremiah 3:19; Daniel 7:13; Matthew 6:6; Acts 4:24.*

GLEANING

GOD (NATURE OF)

To the Hebrews of the OT God was the living God who was the LORD, the ruler of their lives. The Hebrews did not ask, "Is there a God?" In the biblical accounts, the Hebrews never questioned the existence of God; they knew God because of what God had done for them. Their questions were: "What is God called? What is God like?" The OT reports the historical events in which the Hebrews were involved not as the acts of people so much as the acts of God. As the Hebrews lived out their special history as the people with whom God had made a covenant, or agreement, they found answers to their questions about God (see *Covenant*). In the NT God was revealed in Jesus Christ, and humanity's relationship with God was made richer because it could be experienced in a very personal way. It can be compared a relationship with an earthly parent or beloved friend.

GOLDSMITH

A worker in gold, a maker of jewelry and idols frequently referred to in the OT. Gold was probably the first metal known to humanity. *Nehemiah 3:8, 31-32; Isaiah 40:19; 41:7; 46:6; Jeremiah 10:9, 14; 51:17.*

GOLGOTHA
(GOHL-guh-thuh)

Meaning "skull." A place of execution probably outside the city wall of Jerusalem, where Jesus was crucified. The exact location is not certain. *Matthew 27:33-36; Mark 15:22; John 19:17-18.*

GOLIATH
(guh-LYE-uhth)

The Philistine champion and giant who defied the Israelite army. In spite of Goliath's huge size and heavy armor the boy David accepted the challenge to fight him and went out to meet him with only a slingshot. He shot a small round stone that struck the forehead of the giant, and Goliath fell dead. *1 Samuel 17:4-11, 23-49; 21:9; 22:10.*

GOMER
(GOH-mur)

The wife of the prophet Hosea who was unfaithful to him. Hosea forgave her and took her back into his home. He used this sad experience in his prophecies about Israel. The Hebrews were behaving toward God like an unfaithful wife, Hosea pointed out, but God would forgive them if they would repent. *Hosea 1:3.*

GOMORRAH
(guh-MOR-uh)

An OT city usually mentioned together with Sodom. The two cities "in the Valley" were noted for their wickedness. Abraham pleaded with God not to destroy those cities if as many as ten good men could be found there. But according to the story there were not ten. It is thought that these cities may be buried under the waters at the southern end of the Dead Sea. *Genesis 18:20-33; 19:24-29; Isaiah 1:9; Jeremiah 49:18; Matthew 10:15.*

GOPHER WOOD
(GOH-fehr)
A material, probably cypress, from which Noah was instructed to make the ark. *Genesis 6:14.*

GOSHEN
(GOH-shin)
1. An area of Egypt probably in the northeastern part of the Nile delta. It was occupied by the Israelites from the time of Joseph to the Exodus. *Genesis 46:28–47:6; Exodus 8:22.* The same name refers to a hill country in Canaan and a town in Judah. *Joshua 10:41; 11:16; 15:51.*

GOSPEL
(GOS-puhl)
God's announcement of the good news that Jesus Christ is the Son of God. This new announcement was made in the same style as the message of the OT, through historical facts. The words and actions of Jesus—his birth, loving deeds, suffering, death, and rising from the dead— have fulfilled the plan of God. It is a plan in which all humans can have a part. These deeds of Christ accomplished salvation. This means that those who believe in Jesus and his works are saved from the worst results of their own sinfulness and weakness and

GOVERNOR

may enjoy the benefit of Jesus' goodness and righteousness. "Gospel" is also the name given each of the first four books of the NT. In Matthew, Mark, Luke, and John we find accounts of the life of Jesus and the facts that make up the good news. *Matthew 4:23; 24:14; Mark 1:1; 8:35; 10:29-30; Acts 8:40; Romans 1:1-4; Philippians 1:12; 1 Thessalonians 2:9.*

GOVERNOR
In the OT a ruler appointed by a king to govern a specific territory or province. He governed by authority of the king, not in his own right. Joseph was a governor in Egypt. The king of Babylon left a governor named Gedaliah to rule Judah after the Babylonians had conquered it. In the NT these officials were appointed by the Roman emperor and had authority to give the sentence of death or to free a prisoner. Other Roman names for governor are proconsul, procurator, prefect, and legate. *Genesis 42:6; Ezra 2:63; 5:3, 14; Nehemiah 2:7; 5:14; Jeremiah 40:5; 51:23; Haggai 1:1; Matthew 10:18; Mark 13:9; Luke 2:2; 3:1; Acts 7:10.*

GRACE

God's great love for humanity which cannot be earned, but which is offered by God as a free gift. In the OT a similar Hebrew word is translated "steadfast love" (see *Psalm 136:1-26*). In the NT the grace of God is one of the most distinctive features of the Christian gospel. It is seen as divine power flowing through Jesus Christ into the lives of those who believe in him. This grace makes it possible for persons to think, act, and speak according to God's will. *Romans 5:15; 1 Corinthians 15:10; 2 Corinthians 6:1; 8:1; 9:14; Ephesians 3:7; 2 Thessalonians 1:12; 1 Peter 1:10, 13; 5:10; and other references.*

GRAVEN IMAGE

An image carved from stone, metal, or wood. These idols were used in ancient times to represent a deity, or god. The Ten Commandments forbade the Hebrews to make such things. *Exodus 20:4; Leviticus 26:1; Deuteronomy 4:23, 25; 5:8; 7:5; 12:3; 27:15; Judges 17:3-4; 2 Kings 21:7; 2 Chronicles 34:3-4; Isaiah 10:10-11; 30:22; Jeremiah 8:19.*

GREAT SEA

The name by which the Mediterrnean Sea was known in Bible lands in ancient times. It was also referred to as the "western sea" and "the sea." The Mediterranean Sea is an inland ocean more than two thousand miles long, stretching from Gibralter to Lebanon between the continents of Europe and Africa. Its width varies from one hundred to six hundred miles. *Numbers 34:6; Joshua 1:4; Ezekiel 47:10.*

GREECE

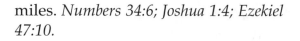

(greess)

In Bible times a land which occupied the southern end of the Balkan Peninsula and also included western Asia Minor and the islands of the Aegean Sea. There were also Greek settlements in southern Italy. The Greeks ruled their known world from the fourth to the first century B.C. Their arts, customs, literature, government, and religion had much to give to the Roman civilization that followed. While Greece was the dominant world power, its influence was spread very wide. The Greek language was the one most widely used. The OT was translated into Greek. At first the NT was written in common, everyday Greek known as Koine. The Greek language version of both Testaments was the official Bible among early Christians. Some of the earliest Christian churches were started in Greece. The name "Hellenists" was given to Jews who adopted Greek manners and lived among the Greeks. *Mark 7:26; John 7:35; 19:20; Acts 11:20; 14:1; 16:1, 3; 17:4, 12; 20:2; 21:37; Romans 1:14, 16; 10:12; 1 Corinthians 1:22-24; Galatians 2:3; 3:28; Colossians 3:11.*

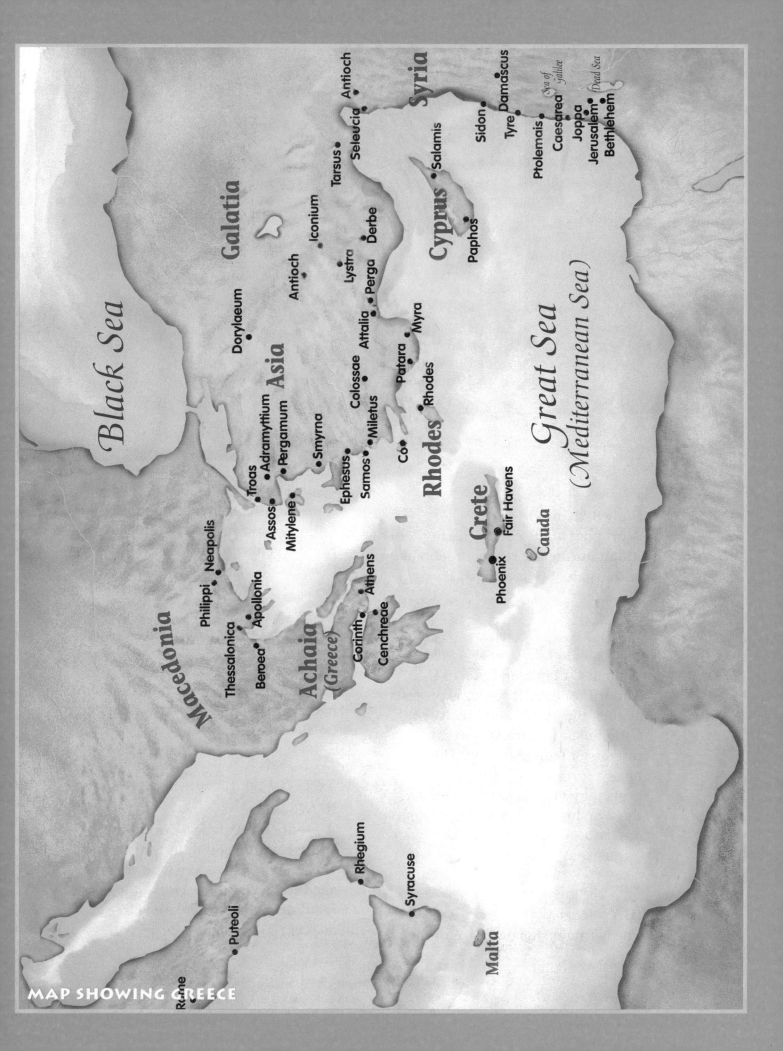

Black Sea

Galatia

Asia

Macedonia

Achaia
(Greece)

Syria

Cyprus

Rhodes

Crete

Great Sea
(Mediterranean Sea)

Antioch
Tarsus •
• Seleucia

Salamis
•

Paphos
•

Sidon •
Tyre • Damascus
•

Sea of
Galilee   Dead Sea

Ptolemais •
Caesarea •
Joppa •
Jerusalem • Bethlehem

Dorylaeum
•

Iconium
•

Antioch
•

Derbe
•

Lystra
•
Perga •
Attalia •

Myra
•

Patara •

Rhodes •

Adramyttium •
Pergamum •
Smyrna •

Colossae •

Troas •

Ephesus •
Samos • Miletus •

Co •

Assos •
Mitylene •

Neapolis •
Philippi •
Thessalonica •
Beroea • Apollonia •

Athens •
Corinth •
Cenchreae •

Fair Havens
•
Phoenix
•

Cauda

Rhegium •
Syracuse •

Puteoli •

Malta

Rome •

HABAKKUK
(huh-BAK-uhk)
A prophet of the southern kingdom of Judah during the reigns of Jehoiakim and Josiah. (See *Habakkuk, Book of.*)

HABAKKUK, BOOK OF
A small OT book and one of the Minor Prophets. It contains protests against the power and cruelty of the Babylonian Empire. It also contains prayers of faith and trust. The prayers have a form about them which suggests they may have been chanted by the worshipers on days of penitence. *See the book itself.*

HADES
(HAY-deez)
The NT name for the place of the dead. The word "Hades" was adopted from the Greeks, who thought of the underground regions as a place of punishment for evildoers. (See *Gehenna.*) *Matthew 11:23; Luke 16:23; Acts 2:27, 31; Revelation 20:13-14.*

HAGAR
(HAY-gar)
Servant of Sarah by whom Abraham had a son, Ishmael. *Genesis 16:1-16; Galatians 4:24-25.*

HAGGAI
(HAG-eye)
A prophet in Babylon during the Exile. He returned to Jerusalem and was one of the leaders who encouraged the Jews to undertake the task of rebuilding the temple. (see *Haggai, Book of.*)

HAGGAI, BOOK OF

The tenth in the series of twelve short prophetic books that come at the end of the OT. It is a collection of prophecies by Haggai and gives an account of their effect in rallying the people to rebuild the ruined temple. *See the book itself.*

HALF-SHEKEL TAX

(HAF-shek-ehl)

See *Money-changers.*

HALLEL

(HAL-uhl)

A song of praise to the Lord. The Hebrew word means "praise." It was one of the duties of the Levites (*the choirmasters of OT times, see 2 Chronicles 7:6; Ezra 3:11*) to praise the Lord. Psalms 120–36 were called the Great Hallel. Psalms 113–18, called the Egyptian Hallel, were used as Passover in homes, the temple, and synagogues.

HALLEL

HALLELUJAH

(HAL-eh-LOO-yuh)

A Hebrew word meaning "praise the Lord." It was a form of doxology used mainly in the psalms (see *Psalm 104:35; 106:1*); *Revelation 19:1, 3-4, 6.*

HALLOW

To make holy, to set apart, to treat with reverence. In ancient Israel a place in which God's presence had been experienced was often set apart for worship and as a memorial of the event. Anything that is separated from ordinary use and reserved for the service of God is said to be hallowed. Among things that were especially hallowed in Israel were God's name (see *God, Names of*), the sabbath, and the temple. *Exodus 20:11; Leviticus 16:19; 22:32; 25:10; Ezekiel 20:20; Matthew 6:9; Luke 11:2.*

HAM

(ham)

Youngest of Noah's three sons. According to Genesis the nations of the world are descended from the sons of Noah. Ham was said to be the ancestor of the Egyptians and North Africans. The name is used in referring to Egypt in some of the poetry of Psalms. *Genesis 5:32; 6:10; 9:18; 10:1, 6, 20; 1 Chronicles 1:4, 8; Psalms 105:23, 27; 106:22.*

HAMAN

(HAY-min)

Prime minister of the Persian king Ahasuerus. He plotted to have all the Jews in Persia killed because Mordecai, a Jew and the cousin of Esther, would not bow down to him. *Esther 3:1–7:10.*

HAMATH
(HAY-muhth)
A town on the Orontes River north of Damascus in Syria. For long periods Hamath was the center of an independent kingdom to the north of the Israelite kingdom. The phrase "entrance of Hamath" might refer to Israel's northern border. *Numbers 13:21; 34:8; Joshua 13:5; 2 Kings 14:25, 28; 19:13; Jeremiah 52:27; Ezekiel 47:15; 48:1; Amos 6:14.*

HANDBREADTH
A measure based on the width of the hand at the base of the fingers, about three inches. *Exodus 25:25; 37:12; 1 Kings 7:26; 2 Chronicles 4:5; Psalm 39:5; Ezekiel 40:5.*

HANNAH
(HAN-uh)
Wife of Elkanah and mother of Samuel. Hannah and her husband waited many years for a child. Hannah prayed for a son and promised to dedicate him to the service of God. A son, Samuel, was born to her. As soon as he was old enough she took him to serve in the sanctuary in Shiloh. Samuel grew up to be one of the great judges and prophets of Israel. *1 Samuel 1:1–2:11.*

HARAN
(HAY-run)
1. Brother of Abraham and father of Lot. *Genesis 11:26-31.*
2. Also a city of northern Mesopotamia (now Turkey) where Abraham settled for a time after leaving Ur and before going on to Canaan. The wife of Isaac came from Haran, and this was the place where Jacob went to be safe after he had tricked his brother out of his birthright and blessing. Jacob's wives also came from Haran. It was an important trade city for caravans. Here archaeologists have found the ruins of a temple dedicated to a moon god, a library, a statue of a king with his name carved on his shoulder, and the kings' palace. *Genesis 12:4-5; 27:43; 28:10; 29:4; 2 Kings 19:12; Ezekiel 27:23; Acts 7:2, 4.*

HARLOT
(HAR-luht)
A woman who offers her body to men for money. The OT often uses the word "harlot" as a figure of speech, such as "playing the harlot," to describe those in Israel who had forsaken God and turned to the worship of other gods. *Genesis 34:31; Exodus 34:15-16; Numbers 25:1-2; Joshua 2:1; Judges 2:17; Jeremiah 3:3, 6.*

HARP
A stringed musical instrument small enough to be carried. It was used alone, with other instruments, with singing in processions, or in the worship of the temple. It was also used sometimes to go before the army as they marched to battle. (See *Musical Instruments.*) *1 Samuel 10:5; 2 Chronicles 20:28; Psalms 71:22; 150:3; Isaiah 5:12; Amos 6:5; 1 Corinthians 14:7.*

HARVEST

The gathering of ripe crops. In Bible lands the barley harvest came in April or May; the wheat harvest, in May or June; summer fruits (figs, grapes, pomegranates) ripened in August or September; olives, in September and November. *Leviticus 19:9-10; Deuteronomy 24:19-22; 1 Samuel 6:13; Isaiah 17:5-6; Matthew 9:37-38.*

HAZAEL
(HAY-zey-el)

A king of Damascus who had once been a servant of the king and had seized the throne by murdering his master. He was a mighty warrior, a builder, and a powerful king from about 841 to about 798 B.C. He frequently invaded the kingdoms of Israel and Judah. His attacks were seen by the prophet Elisha as the wrath of God turned against the Hebrews because of their sins. He once approached Jerusalem but was bribed by King Joash to stay away. To get the treasure to pay the bribe to Hazael, Joash stripped his own palace and the temple. *1 Kings 19:15; 2 Kings 8:13-15, 28-29; 10:32; 12:17-18; 13:3, 22, 24; Amos 1:3-4.*

HAZOR
(HAY-zor)

A city in Galilee about ten miles north of the Sea of Galilee. Hazor has been destroyed and rebuilt many times throughout history. Because of this there is a huge mound containing the ruins of the many cities. These were uncovered by an Israeli archaeologist in 1955–56. A Canaanite royal city was found on the bottom layer. In the late thirteenth century B.C. Joshua conquered and destroyed Hazor. King Solomon rebuilt and fortified the city as did Ahab. In 732 B.C. the city was completely destroyed when Tiglath-pileser III of Assyria captured it and took the people into captivity. *Joshua 11:1-5, 10-13; 12:19; 1 Kings 9:15; 2 Kings 15:29.*

HANNAH AND SAMUEL

HEAP OF STONES

A pile of stones set up in OT times to help people remember an important event connected with a place, This is similar to the way people set up monuments today (see *Gilgal.*) A heap of stones was also made as a witness to an agreement. The phrase was sometimes used to indcate ruin or collapse as when some disaster destroyed an altar, a house, or a city, leaving it a "heap of stones." *Genesis 31:44-52; Joshua 7:26; 8:29; 2 Samuel 18:17.*

HEAVEN

This word is used in two ways in the Bible. The first and most important meaning is the place where God dwells. It is also used to refer to the sky. There were many figures of speech for this heaven. It was referred to as having "windows" to let the rain through and was called a "tent", a "curtain", a "mirror", and the "firmament". (See *Earth..*) *Genesis 1:6-8; 7:11; 8:2; 1 Kings 8:30; 1 Chronicles 27:23; Job 16:19; 22:12-14; 38:37; Psalms 19:1; 104:2; Isaiah 66:1; Jeremiah 10:2; 51:9; Daniel 2:28; 4:13, 15; Matthew 6:9, 20; Mark 1:10; 10:21; 12:25; John 6:32; Acts 1:11.*

HEBREW

(HEE-broo)

1. The ancient language of the Jews. Most of the books of the OT were written in the Hebrew language. A modern form of Hebrew is the common language of the country of Israel today.
2. "Hebrew" is also used to refer to the people descended from Abraham. The word is probably related to the name "Eber," one of Abraham's ancestors. "Hebrews" was used by the Israelites to refer to themselves, and it was also used by foreigners. *Genesis 14:13; 39:14; Exodus 1:15-16, 19; 2:11; Deuteronomy 15:12; John 20:16; Acts 22:2; Philippians 3:4-6.*

HEBREWS, LETTER TO THE

The nineteenth book of the NT, probably written at the end of the first century. Though called a letter, it is more like a sermon or lecture. The author is unknown. The title "To the Hebrews" indicates the first readers may have been Jewish (Hebrew) Christians. The author used the OT to prove that the religion of the covenant between God and the Hebrews is continued and fulfilled in Jesus Christ. *See the book itself.*

HEBRON

(HEE-bruhn)

A Canaanite royal city in the hill country of Judah, about ninetten miles south of Jerusalem. It was founded about the middle of the fourteenth century B.C. It was conquered and destroyed by the Israelites but later rebuilt. It was David's capital during the first years of his reign. Today Hebron is still an important city in the Near East. *Genesis 13:18; Joshua 10:36; 20:7; 1 Kings 2:11; 2 Chronicles 11:5-10.*

HELL

The NT name for the place under the earth for the punishment of the dead. (See *Gehenna, Hades, Sheol.*) *Matthew 5:22; James 3:6.*

HELLENISTS

(HEL-en-ists)
In the NT, Greek-speaking Jews and Jewish Christians, usually living in Greek-speaking countries. *Acts 6:1; 9:29.*

HERALD

An officer making public proclamations for the nation or the ruler, or one who bears ceremonial messages between countries or between royal persons. *Isaiah 40:9; 41:27; Daniel 3:4-6; 2 Peter 2:5.*

HERESY

(HER-uh-see)
A Greek term which meant a school or sect holding a special doctrine. As soon as the church was established in NT times, the term came to be used to denote wrong beliefs held by some people within the Christian church. In the NT the word is only used once, but the presence of heresy is implied many times by such words as "divisions," "dissensions," and "factions." *2 Peter 2:1.*

HERITAGE

The accumulation of material possessions. For Hebrews and for Christians the knowledge of God passed down from one generation to another is their special heritage. *2 Kings 21:14; Job 20:29; Psalms 94:14; 119:111; Jeremiah 3:18-19; Revelation 21:7.*

HERALD

HERMES

(HUR-meez)

A Greek god. He was a master thief and clever player of tricks. He was also the god of eloquence, or good speech, and served as the herald of the gods. When Paul was preaching in Lystra, the people thought he must be Hermes because of his impressive speech. There was a person with this name in the early church in Rome. *Acts 14:12; Romans 16:14.*

HERMON, MOUNT

(HUR-muhn)

A mountain in the southern end of the Lebanon mountain range. Rising over nine thousand feet, its snow-capped peak can be seen for many miles. Mt. Hermon was always considered a sacred mountain, partly because of this majestic aspect. In ancient times a local Baal probably was worshiped there (see *Judges 3:3*). *Deuteronomy 3:8-9; 4:48; Joshua 11:16-17; 1 Chronicles 5:23; Psalm 42:6.*

HEROD

(HAIR-uhd)

The name of a powerful family which ruled Jewish Palestine under the Roman Empire from 37 B.C. to A.D. 70. They were Idumeans (Edomites) who had become Jews and were not liked by the people of Palestine. Several of the Herods figured prominently in the NT.

1. Herod the Great was king when Jesus was born but died very soon afterward. *Matthew 2:3; 13-16; 19-23; Luke 1:5.*
2. His son, Herod Antipas, had John the Baptist beheaded. It was to this Herod that Jesus was brought for trial after his arrest. *Matthew 14:1-2; Mark 6:14-26; Luke 3:1, 19-20; 9:7-9; 23:7-16.*
3. Herod Agrippa, a grandson of Herod the Great, persecuted the apostles and the Christians in Jerusalem. *Acts 4:27; 12:1-3; 13:1.*

HERODIANS

(huh-ROH-dee-uhnz)

Jews in the NT who supported the dynasty of Herod. They are mentioned as opponents of Jesus. *Matthew 22:16; Mark 3:6; 12:13.*

HERODIAS

(huh-ROH-dee-uhss)

Wife of King Herod Antipas. She had first been the wife of Antipas' half brother. John the Baptist criticized this marriage, and Salome, the daughter of Herodias, after pleasing the king with her dancing, demanded and got the head of John. *Mark 6:14-29.*

HEWERS OF WOOD

One of the lowest classes of servants in the OT. They were the gatherers of firewood—an endless, dull task. The term has come to be used for persons of dull mind who can do nothing but the tiresome and menial jobs. (See *Gibeon.*) *Detueronomy 29:11; Joshua 9:21, 23, 27.*

HEZEKIAH

(hez-uh-KYE-uh)

King of Judah from about 716 to 687 B.C.; son and successor of Ahaz.

Hezekiah was twenty-five when he became king at a critical time in Judah's history. The nation had been weakened by wars, and the annual payments of tribute to Assyria had become a burden. The people had rejected God and turned to idols. Hezekiah, influenced by Isaiah the prophet, realized the urgent need for reform. In his first year he removed the high places and destroyed the idols. He reopened and purified the temple and restored the true worship of God. He strengthened the defenses of Jesus and brought water from near-by into the city by means of a tunnel so that the city would have water during siege. In later generations he was remembered as an able, vigorous and godly man. *2 Kings 18:1–20:21; 2 Chronicels 29:1–32:33; Isaiah 36:1–39:8; Jeremiah 26:18-19; Matthew 1:9-10.*

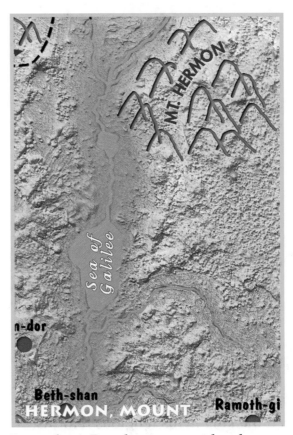

HIGH PLACE

A religious place of sacrifice, worship, and festival. High places, usually on hilltops, were first used by the Canaanites as places to worship their gods. The Israelites were commanded by God to destroy the high places when they entered Canaan. However, they did not obey and frequently joined in the Canaanite worship associated with great trees and green groves. Sometimes the Israelites took over a Canaanite high place for the worship of God. These places often had buildings of various kinds: raised platforms, halls, altars, and stone pillars. An Israelite sanctuary was a place set apart for the worship of God. An example of this is the tabernacle in the desert and later the temple at Jerusalem. But there were other less important sanctuaries built by people like Abraham, Jacob, and David in places where they had experienced a special sense of God's presence. Later in the NT the word "sanctuary" came to be used by Christians to mean the holy place set apart for the worship of God by the people. *Exodus 15:17; Numbers 33:50-52; Joshua 24:26; 1 Samuel 9:12; 1 Kings 3:2; 12:31; 2 Kings 17:32; 18:4; 23:8-9; 2 Chronicles 33:3, 17; Psalm 78:58; Hebrews 8:2, 5; 9:1, 24.*

HIGH PRIEST

Chief of the priests in the temple at Jerusalem. He acted as the representative of the people before God. (See *Priests and Levites.*) *Numbers 35:25, 28; 2 Kings 22:4, 8; Haggai 1:1, 12, 14; Matthew 26:57-66; Mark 14:53-54; John 11:49-52.*

HIGHWAY

The exact meaning is a road built up higher than the land on either side. But it is also used as a figure of speech for the route of returning exiles and to describe an upright way of living. *Numbers 20:17; Psalm 84:5; Proverbs 15:19; 16:17; Isaiah 35:8; 40:3; 49:11.*

HILKIAH

(hil-KYE-uh)

A high priest during the reign of King Josiah (about 641 to 609 B.C.). While the temple was being repaired, Hilkiah discovered the scrolls of the Book of the Law (which is Deuteronomy). These were taken and read to the king. Later, Hilkiah assisted the king in his religious reforms. Other persons in the OT have the same name. *2 Kings 22:4-14; 1 Chronicles 6:13; 2 Chronicles 34:9-22; 35:8.*

HIN

A liquid measure about equal to an American gallon. *Exodus 29:40; 30:24; Ezekiel 4:11.*

HINNOM, VALLEY OF THE SON OF

(HIN-uhm)

A deep valley south of Jerusalem that marked the boundary between the tribes of Benjamin and Judah. It was the center of worship of foreign gods where children were sacrificed by fire in honor of Baal and Molech. (See *Gehenna.*) *Joshua 18:16; 2 Kings 23:10; 2 Chronicles 28:3; Jeremiah 2:23; 19:2, 5-6; 32:35.*

HIRAM

(HYE-ruhm)

Also Huram. King of Tyre, 986 to 935 B.C. He enjoyed friendship and brisk trade relations with David and Solomon. These relations may have been based on a mutual need. Israel needed skilled workmen and raw materials for its building program, which included the temple, and Phoenicia needed agricultural products and olive oil. Hiram helped Solomon in his commercial enterprises by supplying ships and seamen for the merchant fleet. He probably received a share of the profits from these voyages. Later Solomon was so much in debt for these goods he was forced to sell twenty cities of Galilee to Hiram. *Hiram—2 Samuel 5:11; 1 Kings 5:1-12; 9:10-14, 26-28; 10:11, 22; Huram—2 Chronicles 2:1-16; 8:17-18; 9:10, 21.*

HIRELING

A servant or other worker paid wages. *Job 7:1-2; Malachi 3:5; John 10:12-13.*

HITTITES

(HIT-ites)

A people of the ancient Near East who lived in the territory that is now Turkey. Probably some Hittites were living in Canaan before the coming of the Israelites. Several names of individuals with a Hittite background are mentioned in the OT. It is almost certain that the Hittites first discovered the art of smelting and working iron. *Genesis 15:18-21; 23:3-20; 25:9-10; 26:34; 36:2; Exodus 3:8; Deuteronomy 7:1; Joshua 1:4; Judges 1:26; 1 Samuel 26:6; 2 Samuel 11:3,*

6; 12:9-10; 23:39; 1 Kings 10:29; 11:1; 15:5; 2 Kings 7:6.

HIVITES

(HIV-ites)
People living in Canaan before the coming of the Israelites. The name is usually given in the OT list of nations conquered and sent out of the land by the Israelites. Hivite settlements were along the way between Sidon, Beersheba, and Mt. Lebanon, and at the foot of Mt. Hermon. *Genesis 34:2; Exodus 3:8, 17; 23:23-33; Deuteronomy 7:1; 20:17; Joshua 3:10; Judges 3:3, 5:2; Samuel 24:7; 1 Kings 9:20-21; Isaiah 17:9.*

HOBAB

(HOH-bab)
One of the names for the father-in-law of Moses. He is also identified as Jethro and Reuel. *Numbers 10:29; Judges 4:11.*

HOLINESS

More than any other term, "holiness" suggests the nature of God. It does not indicate some quality of God but rather God's complete being. The idea of holiness includes some sense of a tremendous and mysterious energy that is beyond and above humankind. The Hebrews of the OT were very much aware of this power; they sensed the presence of God, God's holy love, in the events of their history, in the lives of certain people, and also in the natural world. (It is interesting to note that in the religion of Israel nature worship had no place and there is no word for

"nature" in the OT. See *Holy One.*) *Exodus 15:11; Psalm 93:5; Amos 4:2; Luke 15:11; Psalm 93:5; Amos 4:2; Luke 1:75; 2 Corinthians 7:1; Ephesians 4:24; 1 Thessalonians 3:13; Hebrews 12:10.*

HOLY OF HOLIES

Sometimes called the most holy place (see Exodus 26:33-34). The innermost room of the temple, the place of the presence of God. The high priest entered the Holy of Holies only on the Day of Atonement. In Solomon's temple it contained the ark and cherubim, but after the Jews returned from their exile in Babylon this room was left empty in later temples. *Hebrews 9:3-5.*

HOLY ONE

In the OT a name for God which emphasizes that God *is* absolute holiness and the source of holiness in all other things. In the NT "Holy One" referred to the Messiah, the one who would appear on earth among people and who would be holy as God is holy. (See *Holiness, Messiah.*) *2 Kings 19:22; Psalm 71:22; 78:41; 89:18; Isaiah 5:19; 30:11-15; and many other places in Isaiah; Mark 1:24; Luke 4:34; Acts 3:14.*

HOLY PLACE

In the tent of meeting, the courts with the inner and outer rooms of the tabernacle; in the temple, the rooms and the surrounding courts. *Exodus 26:33; 28:29; 29:31; 39:1; 40:9; Leviticus 6:24-26.*

HOLY SPIRIT

The mysterious power of God. Sometimes called the Spirit or the Spirit of the Lord. In the OT this power, or spirit, was given to certain powers as a revelation which gave them strength, courage, wisdom, and the knowledge of God's will. In the NT the Holy Spirit is brought through Jesus Christ to be personally present to guide, comfort, and strengthen those who believe in Christ. Spirit of the Lord—*Judges 14:6; 1 Samuel 16:13; Isaiah 11:2;* Holy Spirit—*Matthew 3:11; Luke 2:25-32; 4:1; John 14:25-26; Acts 1:5; 2:1-4; 4:8, 31; 9:31; 10:38; 2 Corinthians 13:14; Ephesians 1:13-14.*

HOMER

An ancient Hebrew measure for dry materials. It was probably the load that a donkey could carry, ten bushels, more or less. *Numbers 11:32; Isaiah 5:10; Ezekiel 45:11.*

HOOPOE
(HOO-poo)

A bird that is related to the kingfishers and has a head crest and a long, thin, curved bill. It was a summer visitor in Palestine. The hoopoe was classed as an unclean bird and could not be eaten because it searched for grubs and small insects in dung hills and other repulsive places. *Leviticus 11:19; Deuteronomy 14:18.*

HOREB, MOUNT
(HOR-eb)

Another name for Mt. Sinai, the place near the wilderness where the Israelites camped on their journey to Canaan. *Exodus 3:1; Deuteronomy 1:2; 5:2; 2 Chronicles 5:10; Psalm 106:19.*

HORSE

A domesticated animal. In Bible times the horse was chiefly used in war. Warhorses with chariots were used by the Egyptians, Canaanites, Assyrians, Medes, and Chaldeans. Joseph rode in a horse-drawn chariot. Solomon kept enough horses for a hundred chariots. *Exodus 14:9, 23; 1 Kings 10:26-29; Psalm 33:17; Nahum 3:1-3.*

HOSANNA
(hoh-ZAN-uh)

A term meaning "Save us, we beseech thee" (see Psalm 118:25). During the Feast of Tabernacles this verse was sung each day by the priests as they marched in procession around the altar while the congregation waved branches of myrtle, branches of willow, and a palm leaf. At Jesus' triumphal entry into Jerusalem the people greeted him by waving branches and singing "Hosanna." *Matthew 21:9; Mark 11:9-10; John 12:13.*

HOSEA
(hoh-ZAY-uh)

A prophet in Israel in the eighth century B.C. and the only one of the writing prophets who had his home in the northern kingdom. There were other prophets in Israel, but they were generally unreliable and had seen better days. Hosea criticized them and also the priests for their failure in leading the people, for giving them poor advice, and for their ignorance of the true nature of God. He accused them of guiding the people into pagan worship rather than into the true faith. (See *Hosea, Book of.*)

HOSPITALITY

Entertainment of a stranger or guest. Throughout the ancient Mediterranean world it was a sacred duty to entertain strangers. The Hebrews also held this view (see *Genesis 18:1-8; 19:1-11*). Jesus depended upon hospitality for his food and lodging wherever he went (see *Luke 9:58; 11:37*). When the apostles were sent out, they were told to rely on hospitality (see *Luke 10:7*). This practice among the early Christians bound them together. *Romans 12:13; 1 Timothy 5:10; Hebrews 13:2; 1 Peter 4:9.*

HOSTS, HOST OF HEAVEN

"Host" in military use means a body of men organized for war. The host of heaven includes the sun, moon, stars, and particularly angels. These forces are at God's command in carrying out his purpose for the world. In the OT the God of Israel is frequently called "God of hosts." *Exodus 7:4; 12:17; 14:17; Numbers 10:28; Deuteronomy 4:19; 17:3; 1 Samuel 17:46; 1 Kings 22:19; 2 Kings 21:3-5; Psalms 89:8; 103:21; Isaiah 1:9; and other places in Isaiah; Jeremiah 10:16; and other places in Jeremiah; Amos 5:27; Luke 2:13.*

HORSE

HOUSE OF GOD

The place of Jacob's dream. When he awoke, he took the stone he had used for a pillow and set it up for a pillar. He poured oil on the top of the stone and called the place where he was Bethel, which means House of God. See also: Bethel. *Genesis 28:1-5, 10-22.*

HOUSEHOLD OF GOD

A group of believers or the members of the church. *Ephesians 2:19; 1 Timothy 3:15; 1 Peter 4:17.*

HOUSEHOLDER

In the NT a house steward or master of the house. *Matthew 13:27; 20:1; Mark 14:14.*

HULDAH

(HUHL-duh)

A prophetess, the wife of Shallum. She was consulted by King Josiah after the Book of the Law had been found in the temple. It was very unusual for a woman to act as prophet. *2 Kings 22:14; 2 Chronicles 34:22.*

HURAM

(HUR-uhm)

See *Hiram*.

HYMNS

(himz)

Songs of praise. The earliest Christians continued to use the psalms and religious songs of Judaism. The hymn sung at the conclusion of the Last Supper was probably the Hallel, or Psalm 113–118, that was sung at the celebration of the chief Jewish festivals. In the NT there are many references to the use of songs in the churches' worship. *Matthew 26:30; Mark 14:26; Acts 16:25; 1 Corinthians 14:26; Ephesians 5:19; Colossians 3:16.*

HYPOCRISY, HYPOCRITE

(hi-PAH-kri-see, HIP-eh-krit)

From a Greek word meaning the act of playing a part and one who plays a part. In the NT Jesus used the word to condemn those who were so firmly convinced of their own goodness that they were blind to their faults. *Matthew 6:2, 16; 23:13-15; Mark 7:6-7; Luke 6:42; 13:15.*

HYSSOP

(HISS-uhp)

A small bushy plant, probably the Syrian variety of the herb marjoram. It was used like a brush by the Hebrews for sprinkling in cleansing ceremonies. Its use began at the Passover. A bunch of hyssop was used for marking the doorway with streaks of blood from the sacrificial lamb. *Exodus 12:22;* *Leviticus 14:4; Numbers 19:6; 1 Kings 4:33; Psalm 51:7; John 19:29; Hebrews 9:19.*

HULDAH READING THE SCROLL

ICONIUM
(eye-KOH-nee-uhm)
In NT times a city in south central Asia Minor in the Roman province of Galatia. Iconium was visited by Paul and Barnabas on their first missionary journey. Today it is called Konya and it is the country of Turkey. *Acts 13:15–14:7, 19; 16:2; 2 Timothy 3:10-11.*

IDOL
(EYE-duhl)
Usually an image of a god made of wood, stone, or metal; but it may be any other symbol of the supernatural that is an object of worship. *Deuteronomy 29:16-17; 1 Chronicles 16:26; Psalm 96:5; Isaiah 44:9-17; Jeremiah 50:38; Acts 7:41; 17:16; 1 Corinthians 8:1-7; 10:7; 1 Thessalonians 1:9; 1 John 5:21.*

IDUMEA
(id-yoo-MEE-uh)
In NT times the region south of Judea occupied by Edomites. In OT times it was known as Edom or Seir. *Mark 3:7-8.*

IMMORTALITY
This word which means neverending life is not found in the OT and is found only five times in the NT. The belief that God is an eternal (ever living) God is assumed throughout the OT. There were varied ideas in Judaism about humankind's life after death, but no one idea was accepted by all Jews. In the NT the death and resurrection of Jesus Christ signal a strong new hope of everlasting life for those who believe in him. Death is a fact for humanity, but the NT mentions a life for people after death, a life near God, many times. The biblical writers imagined what this might be like, but there is no complete picture. (See *Eternal Life, Resurrection.*)

Romans 2:7; 1 Corinthians 15:53-54; 1 Timothy 6:15-16; 2 Timothy 1:8-10.

INCENSE

A mixture of gums and spices made into a powder and burned so that the fragrance of the smoke would rise in the air as an offering to God or to the "gods." In the OT the powder was burned on an incense altar. The offering of incense was a very sacred ceremony wherever mentioned in the OT. In both the OT and the NT the offering of incense was symbolic of the prayers offered by the people. *Exodus 30:1, 7-9, 34-38; 1 Kings 9:25; Psalm 141:2; Hosea 11:1-2; Luke 1:8-10.*

INGATHERING, FEAST OF

See *Booths, Feast of.*

INHERITANCE

A possession handed down from the past. In the Bible the word refers to material possessions, such as land, cattle, wealth, and possessions given by God. In the NT the word more often refers to spiritual gifts from God, such as eternal life, or the kingdom of God. (See *Heritage.*) *Leviticus 27:24; Numbers 36:7; Deuteronomy 10:9; 19:14; Psalm 105:11; Proverbs 13:22; 17:2; Ezekiel 46:16-18; Luke 10:25; 12:13-21; Acts 20:32; Colossians 1:11-12, 3:23-24.*

INIQUITY

(in-IK-wi-tee)
Another word for sin. It is any action that separates people from God or

destroys a person's relationship with another person as well as with God. (See *Sin, Transgression, Trespass.*) *Leviticus 26:39; 2 Samuel 24:10; Psalm 51:9-12; Isaiah 40:1-2; Ezekiel 18:19-22; Matthew 23:28.*

INK

In Bible times writing fluid made from soot or lampblack mixed with gum resin. Red ink was made by using red iron oxide as a substitute for the soot. The ink was probably dried into cakes and moistened when needed. Most of the scribes carried cakes of red and black ink with them. Writing was done on flat clay tablets and on pieces of broken pottery as well as on parchment, leather, and paper. *Jeremiah 36:18; 2 Corinthians 3:3; 2 John 1:12; 3 John 1:13.*

INN

A shelter for travelers and their animals. It was used like the hotels and motels of today. In most inns the guests brought their own bedding and food. Some inns were merely a village guest house where travelers could spend the night. Others had a square, walled-in place for the travelers to sleep and eat. *Luke 2:4-7; 10:33-35.*

INQUIRE OF GOD

To seek the will of God before acting or making a commitment. In early OT times God was consulted through seers, priests, and prophets. They asked for help in matters of personal and public welfare and before people went into battle. Many different methods were used. The priest tried to find God's will by using the sacred lots, Urim and Thummim (probably stones or sticks of uneven length), or by making a sacrifice. Prophets sometimes reported help through dreams. The people prayed more and more directly to God for guidance after the time of the establishment of synagogues during the Exile. By NT times prayer was the chief means of inquiring of God to find his will. *Exodus 18:15-23; 1 Samuel 9:9; 2 Chronicles 18:4-7; Psalm 27:4.*

IOTA

(eye-OH-tuh)

The ninth and the smallest letter of the Greek alphabet. The term is used to mean something very small. *Matthew 5:18.*

IRON, IRONSMITH

A silver-white metallic mineral substance found in ore. An ironsmith is one who works in iron, both smelting the ore and casting the finished pieces. Iron is the most abundant and cheapest of the hard metals. In ancient times, however, the use of iron spread slowly beause it was difficult to work with. The metal had to be heated, and that required great amounts of fuel. The Canaanites and Philistines were using iron when the Hebrews came to

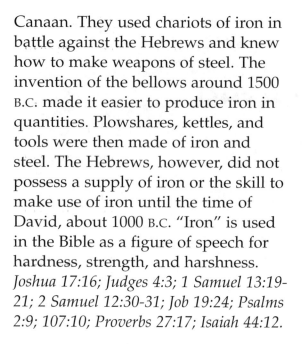

Canaan. They used chariots of iron in battle against the Hebrews and knew how to make weapons of steel. The invention of the bellows around 1500 B.C. made it easier to produce iron in quantities. Plowshares, kettles, and tools were then made of iron and steel. The Hebrews, however, did not possess a supply of iron or the skill to make use of iron until the time of David, about 1000 B.C. "Iron" is used in the Bible as a figure of speech for hardness, strength, and harshness. *Joshua 17:16; Judges 4:3; 1 Samuel 13:19-21; 2 Samuel 12:30-31; Job 19:24; Psalms 2:9; 107:10; Proverbs 27:17; Isaiah 44:12.*

ISAAC

(EYE-zik)

Meaning "he laughs." The son which God promised Abraham and Sarah. He was born to them in their old age. The boy Isaac and his father shared a deep faith in each other and in God. Their faith and obedience were tested when Abraham was commanded to return Isaac to God by sacrificing him, in the story of Issac's "sacrifice". Both the father and the son sadly consented to do this. At the moment when Abraham was about to kill his son, he was interrupted by the voice of God renewing the promise to Abraham on which the Hebrew covenant faith was based. Isaac married Rebekah when he was forty years old and became the father of Jacob and Esau. Abraham, Isaac, and Jacob are known as patriarchs, or fathers, of the Hebrew people. *Genesis 17:15-21; 21:1-12; 22:1-14; 24:62-67; 25:11, 20, 26; 26:6, 12-26; 27:1-40; 35:27-29; 49:31.*

ISAIAH
(eye-ZAY-uh)

A prophet in the southern kingdom of Judah, born about 760 B.C. His name meant "God has saved." Isaiah became a man of action, fearless and frank, after he received his call from God to be a prophet. He came from an important family, and rulers listened to his advice even though it was unpleasant. Isaiah condemned the religious and social evils of his time and denounced injustice and greed. He opposed all alliances with foreign powers and urged the people to put their trust in God. He looked forward to the coming of an ideal king who would "reign in righteousness" and "rule with justice." He was the first of the major prophets. His ministry lasted about forty years (742–701 B.C.). (See *Isaiah, Book of.*)

ISAAC

ISAIAH, BOOK OF

The first book of a major prophet in the OT. The book contains the prophecies of Isaiah (chapters 1–39) and of his followers (chapters 40–66). These are set down in poetic form. One of the most important things emphasized in the book is the holiness of God. There is also some history in the book. *See the book itself.*

ISHBOSHETH
(ish-BOH-sheth)

A son of King Saul, he ruled the northern tribes of Israel for about two years after his father's death (about 1000 B.C.). He struggled unsuccessfully with David for the leadership of all the tribes. Ishbosheth was murdered by two of his own men, a deed condemned by David even though it meant the last block to David's complete control of the land was removed. *2 Samuel 2:1–4:12.*

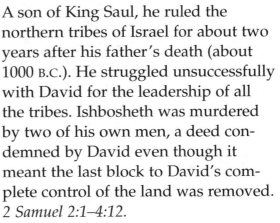

ISHMAEL
(ISH-may-el)

Son of Abraham by the serving woman Hagar; older half brother of Isaac. Jealous for her own son Isaac and annoyed by the behavior of her servant, Sarah forced Abraham to send Hagar and Ishmael into the wilderness of Paran. Later Ishmael married and had twelve sons. *Genesis 16:11; 5-16; 17:15-21; 25:9, 12-18.*

ISHMAELITES
(ISH-may-el-ites)

In the OT the name of wandering caravan traders, tent dwellers, and camel herders who dwelt in settlements or camps in the desert of northern Arabia. The Ishmaelites traced their descent from their ancestor Ishmael, the son of Abraham and Hagar. Today a person who roams about and does not seem to settle down in any one place is sometimes called an Ishmaelite. *Genesis 37:25-28; 39:1; Judges 8:24; 1 Chronicles 2:17; 27:30; Psalm 83:6.*

ISLAND, ISLE

Land completely surrounded by water. Islands located in the Mediterranean Sea are those referred to when islands are mentioned in the Bible. *Psalm 72:10; Isaiah 40:15; 42:15; Ezekiel 26:18; Acts 13:4, 6; 27:16; 28:11.*

ISRAEL
(IZ-ree-uhl)

A name given to Jacob after his vision of God (see *Jacob*). It later came to refer to the descendants of Jacob. The history of Israel probably began with the time of Jacob. Abraham, Isaac, and Jacob were the earliest ancestors of the Israelites. They are known as the patriarchs. Jacob's twelve sons became the leaders of the twelve tribes of Israel. The name "Israel" is used for the people as a whole or for their land, in the Exodus from Egypt, their desert wanderings, and their entrance into Canaan in the stories of their Egyptian slavery. This was also the name of the kingdom under Saul, David, and Solomon. With the death of Solomon the kingdom divided into two parts, the north and south. The northern kingdom continued to be called Israel. The southern kingdom became Judah. Israel, the northern kingdom, lasted about two centuries, until 722 B.C. It was overthrown by Assyria, and its people were taken into captivity. A century and a half later in 586 B.C. Judah, the southern kingdom, came to an end. There was no land called Israel for 2,670 years. The Israelites became a people instead of a nation. The idea that they were God's people always remained with them. An independent Jewish state was formed on May 14, 1948, at the eastern end of the Mediterranean Sea. It once more took the ancient name Israel. *Genesis 32:22-28; 35:9-12; 46:29-30; Exodus 1:7-14; 12:40; Deuteronomy 6:3-4; Judges 6:2-3; 2 Samuel 2:9-10; 1 Kings 6:1; 11:42; 12:12-20; 2 Kings 17:1, 21-23; 2 Chronicles 7:3; Isaiah 1:3; 5:7; Luke 1:68-79; John 1:47, 49; Acts 2:22; and other references.*

ASSYRIA

•HARAN

SYRIA

GREAT
SEA

PHOENICIA

SIDON •

• MT HERMON

TYRE •   • DAMASCUS

MT CARMEL •   SEA OF GALILEE
MEGIDDO • • JEZREEL

ISRAEL

TIRZAH •
SAMARIA •
SHECHEM •

SHILOH •

BETHEL •
ANATHOTH •

ARABIAN
DESERT

JERUSALEM •   SEA OF SALT
BETHLEHEM •
TEKOA •
GAZA •
HEBRON •

JUDAH   MOAB

PHILISTIA

MAP SHOWING ISRAEL

EDOM

ISRAELITES

(IZ-ree-uhl-ites)

The people descended from Israel and heirs of the spiritual gifts and historical purpose of God's chosen people.

ISSACHER

(ISS-uh-kar)

A son of Jacob and Leah and the ancestor of one of the twelve tribes of Israel whose territory was between Mt. Tabor and the southern end of the Sea of Galilee. *Genesis 30:18; Numbers 1:28-29; Judges 5:15; 1 Chronicles 12:40; 2 Chronicles 30:18.*

IVORY

A hard, creamy-white, bonelike substance forming the tusks of elephants. It is mentioned in the Bible as a sign of wealth and luxury. Ivory was carved for inlaid decorations on thrones, beds, houses, and possibly decks of ships. The tribute, or tax, was often paid in ivory-inlaid pieces. *1 Kings 10:18, 22; 22:39; 2 Chronicles 9:17; Psalm 45:8; Ezekiel 27:6, 15; Amos 3:15; 6:4.*

JABBOK
(JAB-ok)

A stream about fifty miles long which empties into the Jordan River fifteen miles north of the Dead Sea. The waters of the Jabbok flow steadily downhill through an ever-deepening canyon, so that its current is swift and strong. In Bible times it was the boundary between the Amorites and the Ammonites. Returning to be reconciled with his brother Esau, Jacob forded the Jabbok. It was near this stream that he had his encounter with God and received a blessing and a new name Israel. *Genesis 32:22-30; Numbers 22:1, 24; Deuteronomy 2:37; Joshua 12:2; Judges 11:13, 22.*

JACOB
(JAY-kuhb)

Son of Isaac and Rebekah and younger twin brother of Esau. Jacob became head of the family by bargaining for his older brother's birthright. Through a trick he obtained his father's blessing that was meant for Esau. After this Jacob fled from his home and went to Haran. On the way there he had an unusual vision in which he saw God and received the covenant promise which had first been given to Abraham. He, Jacob, was to become the father of a nation (Israel) and to inherit the land of Canaan. The twelve sons born to him while he lived in exile with his uncle Laban became the ancestors of the twelve tribes of Israel. After a period of years Jacob returned to Palestine. He now had his large family and was very wealthy. On his way to meet Esau and make peace with him, Jacob received the name Israel. In all of his wrongdoing Jacob felt that God was with him, calling him back to his true self. Jacob is linked with Abraham and Isaac as one of the great patriarchs. In the Bible the name Jacob, as well as Israel, is used to refer to the Hebrew nation. (See *Israel.*) *Genesis 25:21–49:33; Exodus 19:3; 2 Kings 13:23; Psalm 46:7; Isaiah 41:8-9; 44:1-2, 21; 48:20; Mark 12:26; Luke 1:33; Acts 3:13; 7:46; Hebrews 11:9.*

JACOB'S WELL

The well where Jesus met the Samaritan woman. It was near Sychar in Samaria. Today there is a Greek Orthodox church standing near the spot. *John 4:3-6.*

JAMES
(jaymz)

1. James, one of the twelve apostles, was the son of Zebedee and a brother of John. He was a fisherman by trade but left this prosperous business to become one of the first followers of Jesus. He was put to death by King Herod during the persecution of the Christians in Jerusalem about A.D. 43. *Matthew 4:21-22; 10:2; 17:1; Mark 1:9, 29; 3:17; 9:2; 10:35, 41; 13:3; Luke 5:10; 6:14; 8:51; 9:28; Acts 1:13; 12:1-2.*

2. James, the son of Alphaeus, was also a disciple of Jesus. This may be the same James listed as "James the son of Mary." This woman was present at the Crucifixion. *Matthew 27:56; Mark 3:18; 15:40; 16:1; Luke 6:15; 24:10; Acts 1:13.*

3. James, the brother of Jesus, was not at first a disciple, but after the Resurrection he became a believer and an important leader in the church at Jerusalem. *Matthew 13:55; Mark 6:3; Acts 12:17; 15:13; 21:18; 1 Corinthians 15:7; Galatians 1:19, 2:9, 12.*

JAMES, LETTER OF

The twentieth book in the NT. It is really a sermon in the form of a letter addressed to Christians everywhere. It describes the way a Christian must make faith and love work in everyday living. *See the book itself.*

JAPHETH
(JAY-fith)

A son of Noah. He was called the ancestor of the ancient people who lived to the north and west of the Hebrews. These people in Asia Minor

ESAU FORGIVES JACOB

in the region of the Aegean, Black, and Caspian seas are known as the Indo-European family of nations. *Genesis 5:32; 6:10; 7:13; 9:18-19; 10:1-5.*

JASHAR, BOOK OF
(JAY-shuhr)
An ancient written document, containing songs and poetry, which is now lost. It must have been well known among the Hebrews, for it is mentioned several times in the OT. The short poem of Solomon (*1 Kings 8:12-13*) is thought to be a quotation from this book. *Joshua 10:12-13; 2 Samuel 1:17-27.`

JEALOUSY
In the Bible this word has two very different meanings. It can mean the intense hatred and suspicion that grows out of envy and greed. It has another meaning that is something like "zeal." This type of jealousy is the single-minded devotion of humanity to God. God is also said to be jealous, and this means that God demands complete obedience and loyalty on the part of God's people. *Genesis 37:11; Deuteronomy 4:24; 5:9; 6:15; 1 Kings 19:10, 14; Galatians 5:19-20; James 3:14-16.*

JEBUSITES

(JEB-yoo-sites)

The name of a clan also called Jebus. The Jebusites occupied Jerusalem before David captured the city. *Joshua 18:16, 28; Judges 19:10-11; 1 Chronicles 11:4-9.*

JECONIAH, JECHO-NIAH

(jek-eh-NIGH-eh)

See *Jehoiachin.*

JEHOAHAZ

(juh-HOH-uh-haz)

Meaning "God has taken hold of." Name of three OT kings.

1. Jehoahaz, the son of Joram, was king of Judah about 841 B.C. His name is sometimes written Ahaziah. Jehoahaz was greatly influenced by his mother Athaliah, who was a cruel and cold-blooded Baal worshiper. .At her son's death she seized the throne. *2 Chronicles 21:17; 22:1-10.*

2. Jehoahaz, the son of Jehu, was king of Israel from about 814 to 798 B.C. During his reign Syria overcame Israel and forced the nation to pay tribute. *2 Kings 13:1-9.*

3. Jehoahaz, the son of Josiah, was king of Judah about 609 B.C. He was also called Shallum. This Jehoahaz had reigned in Jerusalem for three months when he was taken to Egypt in captivity by Phaeaoh Neco. *2 Kings 23:31-34; 1 Chronicles 3:15; 2 Chronicles 36:2-4; Jeremiah 22:10-12.*

JEHOASH

(juh-HO-ash)

See *Joash* (1).

JEHOIACHIN

(juh-Hoi-uh-kin)

Also called Jeconiah, Coniah, and Jechoniah. He was the son and successor of Jehoiakim and king of Judah (598–597 B.C.) in the time of the prophet Jeremiah. After a reign of only three months he surrendered to Nebuchadnezzar, king of Babylon, and was taken into exile. *2 Kings 24:8-17; 25:27-30; 1 Chronicles 3:16-17; Esther 2:6; Jeremiah 22:24-30; 24:1; 28:4; 52:31-34; Ezekiel 1:2; Matthew 1:11-12.*

JEHOIADA

(juh-HOI-uh-duh)

High priest in Jerusalem in the ninth century B.C. He led the revolt that overthrew Queen Athaliah of Judah and the Baal worship that she supported. He helped to establish the seven-year-old King Joash (Jehoash) on the throne about 837 B.C. and apparently governed for him until Joash was old enough to govern the kingdom himself. Jehoiada inspired Joash to have the temple repaired. *2 Kings 11:4–12:16; 2 Chronicles 22:10–24:27.*

JEHOIAKIM

(juh-HOI-uh-kim)

Son of Josiah and brother of Jehoahaz. He was king of Judah from about 609 to 598 B.C. In the time of the prophet Jeremiah he succeeded to the throne when Jehoahaz was taken into Egypt.

Jehoiakim was the throne name given the new king by Phaeaoh Neco. His given name was Elkakim. Later Jehoiakim became subject to King Nebuchadnezzar of Babylon. After three years of paying tribute he ignored the advice of Jeremiah and rebelled against Nebuchadnezzar. This cost the king his life. *2 Kings 23:34–24:6; 1 Chronicles 3:15-16; 2 Chronicles 36:4-8; Jeremiah 26:1-23; 46:2.*

JEHORAM
(juh-HOR-uhm)
See *Joram.*

JEHOSHAPHAT
(juh-HOH-shuh-fat)
Several persons had this name.
1. A priest who blew a trumpet before the ark when the ark was brought to Jerusalem. *1 Chronicles 15:24.*
2. A record keeper in the reigns of David and Solomon. *2 Samuel 8:16; 20:24; 1 Kings 4:3; 1 Chronicles 18:15.*
3. An officer in Solomon's government. *1 Kings 4:17.*
4. The son of Asa who reigned as king of Judah from about 870 to 848 B.C. He ended the warfare between the kingdoms of Israel and Judah. He was an able ruler who gained control of the trade routes from Arabia. He greatly improved the system of justice throughout his kingdom, and he led his people in a return to the worship of God and obedience to the law of Moses. *1 Kings 22:41-45; 2 Chronicles 20:29–21:3, 12.*

JOASH, THE BOY KING

JEHU
(JAY-hoo)
The son of Jehoshaphat, he was king of Israel from about 841 to 814 B.C., when Elisha was a prophet in the land. Jehu led a blood revolt which was inspired by the prophet after being secretly anointed as king. His purpose was to rid the land of Baal worship and of the people who practiced it. Joram, king of Israel; Ahaziah, king of Judah; and Jezebel, the wife of Ahab, were assassinated. Finally Jehu summoned all the worshipers of Baal on the pretense of offering a great sacrifice in the temple which Ahab had built. Once these people were assembled, Jehu gave orders that they all be killed. *2 Kings 9:1–10:36; 2 Chronicles 22:8-9.*

JEPHTHAH
(JEF-thuh)

A Gileadite warrior who freed Israel from the constant raids by the Ammonites. His victories stopped invasions by the Ammonites until Saul became king. After his military victories he became a judge in Israel. Before defeating the Ammonites Jephthah vowed to offer as a sacrifice whatever came out of his house upon his return if God would give him success. His daughter and only child came dancing to meet him. When he sadly told her of his solemn promise, she insisted that he keep his word. *Judges 11:1–12:7; Hebrews 11:32.*

JEREMIAH
(jer-uh-MYE-uh)

One of the major OT prophets who lived in the last years before the Babylonians defeated Judah and destroyed Jerusalem. He lived from 626 to about 580 B.C. Jeremiah spoke to his own people throughout the reigns of five kings. There was a constant threat of disaster to the nation. He denounced the people of Judah for their neglect of the true service of God, for their injustices to one another, and for their worship of idols. He urged the people of Judah to repent and return to God. They would not listen, and the prophet was even punished for his efforts. As he had foretold, Jerusalem was taken by the Babylonians in 586, and the people were sent into exile. Jeremiah was permitted to remain in Judah. Later he was taken to Egypt against his will and died there. (See *Jeremiah, Book of.*)

JEREMIAH, BOOK OF

The book contains the prophecies of Jeremiah, usually set down in poetic form. It also contains history of those critical times which Jeremiah dictated to his secretary Baruch. It is possible that Baruch added to the book, material based on his personal knowledge of Jeremiah. *See the book itself.*

JERICHO
(JER-uh-koh)

A major city at the southern end of the Jordan Valley. It is the site of many ancient cities, the earliest of which dates back as far as 7000 B.C. At the time of the conquest of this strongly fortified city, Jericho stood in the path of the Hebrews as they entered Canaan under the leadership of Joshua. The OT tells how the armies of Israel marched around the city according to God's instruction, and the walls crumbled, and the city fell. Archeologists have always been interested in the city. It was excavated long before science was as developed as it is today. For this reason much valuable evidence was lost. However, many scientists think one city of Jericho may have been destroyed by earthquake and fire a century before the time of Joshua and then rebuilt. The NT Jericho, founded by Herod the Great, was a mile south of the old city. Zacchaeus, the famous tax collector, lived there. There are many stories in the Gospels that tell of Jesus' ministry in Jericho. *Joshua 2:1-14; 5:10–6:27; 1 Kings 16:34; 2 Kings 2:4-5, 15-18; Matthew 20:29; Mark 10:46; Luke 10:30; 18:35; 19:1-2; Hebrews 11:30.*

JEROBOAM
(jer-uh-BOH-uhm)

1. The first king of the northern kingdom Israel, who reigned from about 931 to 910 B.C. He was chosen by ten northern tribes when the kingdom was divided after the death of Solomon. He introduced pagan practices into the worship of God. Many later kings of Israel were described as following the ways of Jeroboam, "who made Israel to sin." *1 Kings 11:26-40; 12:20–14:20; 2 Kings 14:24; 2 Chronicles 9:29; 10:2-5, 12-15; 13:3-20.*

2. A later king of Israel (782–753 B.C.), son and successor of Joash. Under him the kingdom prospered, but the prophet Amos declared everything in the land was crooked. *2 Kings 14:23-29; Amos 1:1.*

JEREMIAH

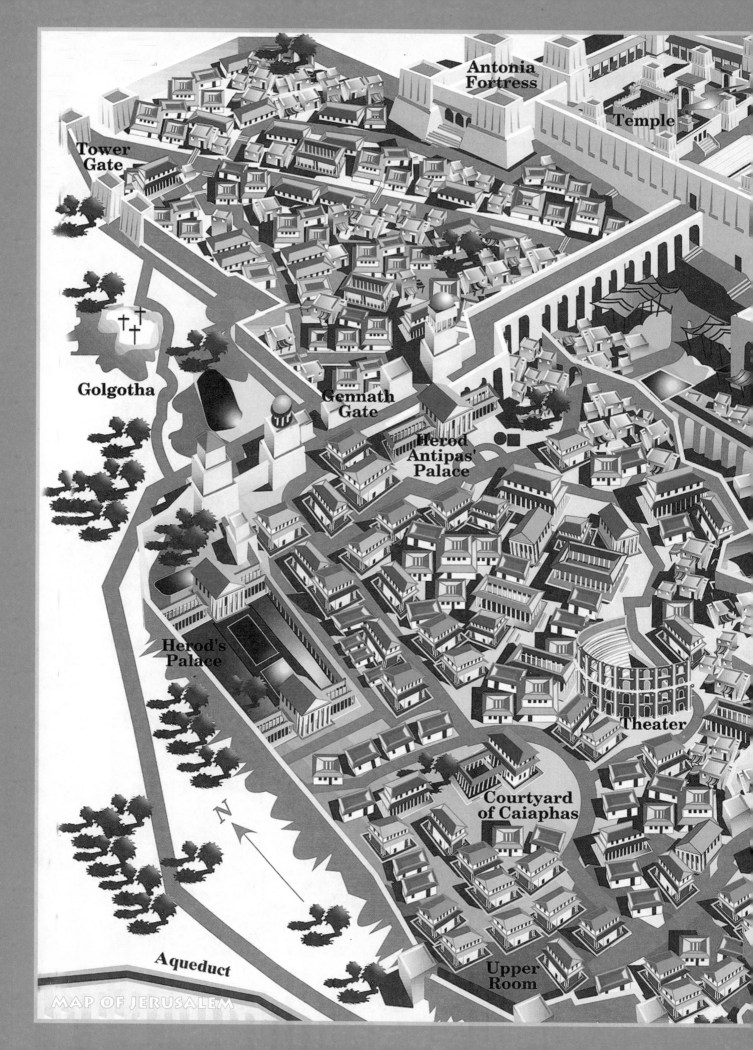

Antonia
Fortress

Temple

Tower
Gate

Golgotha

Gennath
Gate

Herod
Antipas'
Palace

Herod's
Palace

Theater

N

Courtyard
of Caiaphas

Aqueduct

Upper
Room

MAP OF JERUSALEM

JERUSALEM
(juh-ROO-suh-lem)

In the Bible, Jerusalem is referred to by several other names, such as Salem, Zion, Moriah, City of David, and Jebus. David captured Jerusalem from the Jebusites and made it his capital city. When he brought the ark to Jerusalem, the city became the religious center of the Hebrew people. David's son Solomon built the temple, and Jerusalem became a holy city. After Solomon's death when the kingdom was divided, Jerusalem was the capital of the southern kingdom, Judah. Many nations threatened Jerusalem. Finally it was conquered and burned by Nebuchadnezzar and part of its population carried off to Babylon. When the refugees returned from exile, they rebuilt the temple, and later the city and walls were restored. In NT times Jerusalem was under Roman rule, but the Jews were free to worship in the temple and to celebrate their feast days. Jesus spent his last days on earth in Jerusalem, and his trial and resurrection took place there. Jerusalem was very important in the early years of the Christian church. Today the city of Jerusalem is the capital of the state of Israel. It is sacred to Christians, Jews, and Muslims. *Joshua 15:8; 2 Samuel 5:6-10; 6:16-19; 1 Kings 3:1; 14:25-26; 2 Kings 12:17-18; 14:13; 2 Chronicles 3:1; 36:19; Ezra 1:5; 7:7-10; Nehemiah 2:17; Psalms 122:1-9; 137:5-7; Jeremiah 3:17; 39:1-3; Matthew 2:1; 16:21; Mark 11:11; Luke 2:22-25, 38, 41-45; 9:51; 13:33-35; Acts 1:8; 11:22; and many other references.*

JESSE
(JESS-ee)

The father of King David. He was of the tribe of Judah and lived in Bethlehem. *Ruth 4:17, 22; 1 Samuel 16:1-23; 17:17-19; 20:27; 1 Chronicles 2:12-13; 10:14; Isaiah 11:1, 10; Matthew 1:5-6; Luke 3:32; Acts 13:22.*

JESUS CHRIST
(JEE-zuhss kriste)

The central figure in the NT. Both God and human, Jesus is the one in whom the whole of OT history takes on a new and deeper meaning. Jesus was the personal name of the one whose title is "the Christ," from which the Christian religion gets its name. The name Jesus in the original Hebrew is a form of the name Joshua meaning "God saves." Jesus was born into an ordinary Jewish family from Nazareth—one which practiced deep devotion to God and which had ancestors in the line of David. After being baptized by John in the river Jordan Jesus began his ministry. His words and teaching had such power that he was called a prophet (see Matthew 21:11). As he preached his message that the kingdom of God was coming, in fact had already begun (Mark 1:15), he healed the sick of every sort and did other works that indicated the power of God was working through him. Those who believed his message and understood his mission, hailed him as the Son of David (see Matthew 21:15), the son of God (see John 1:49), and the Messiah (see John 1:41). Jesus proclaimed the personal nearness of God and spoke of him as the Father. He declared the mercy, the justice, and especially the love of God. Through his extraordinary life and mighty acts his disciples came to recognize him as the Christ, or Anointed One. However, it was only after his death and resurrection that they began to understand his role as the Lord and Savior of humankind. *Matthew 1:1, 21; 16:13-20; 26:71; Mark 1:1, 24; 10:47; 14:67; Luke 4:22; 18:37-38; John 1:17; 20:31; Acts 2:36; Romans 8:39; Galatians 3:26; 1 Timothy 1:1; and many other references.*

governance of Babylon or Persia. It also came to be used for any person who worshiped God and followed Judaism even if that person were not a Jew by birth. *2 Kings 25:25; Ezra 4:12; 5:5; Nehemiah 1:24; 4:1-2; Esther 3:6–9:31; Jeremiah 40:11-12; Daniel 3:8; Zechariah 8:23; Matthew 27:11; John 4:9; 11:33-36; Acts 2:10; 14:1; 21:39; Romans 2:28-29; Galatians 2:13; Colossians 3:11.*

JETHRO
(JETH-roh)

Priest of Midian and father-in-law of Moses. He is also called Hobab and Reuel. He advised Moses on giving counsel to the people in the wilderness. *Exodus 18:1-27.*

JEW
(joo)

There are three ways in which this word is used in the Bible. In the OT it was used from the time of the Exile to refer to the members of the southern kingdom of Judah who were in Babylon. Later it was used to refer to any of the people who were not Gentiles and who lived in the province of Judah under the

JESUS AND A CHILD

133

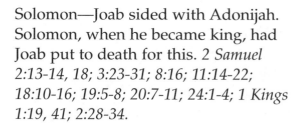

JEZEBEL
(JEZ-uh-bel)

A princess from Phoenicia who became the wife of King Ahab of Israel. Jezebel was a clever and strong-willed woman who influenced Ahab and the people of Israel to turn away from God and worship her god Baal. The prophet Elijah opposed the queen in her schemes. Jezebel succeeded in driving Elijah away, but not before he had won a victory over the prophets of Baal. *1 Kings 16:31-33; 18:4, 19; 19:1-2; 21:5-15; 2 Kings 9:22, 30-37.*

JEZREEL
(JEZ-ree-uhl)

An OT town located at the foot of Mt. Gilboa southwest of the Sea of Galilee. Here King Ahab had a royal residence. It was also the name of the entire valley that separated Galilee from Samaria. Jezreel is mentioned frequently in biblical history after the division of the kingdom. The prophet Hosea named his first child Jezreel, recalling the bloodshed in the city of Jezreel by which King Jehu came to power. *Joshua 17:16; Judges 6:33; 1 Samuel 29:1, 11; 2 Samuel 2:9; 4:4; 1 Kings 4:12; 18:45-46; 21:1; 2 Kings 8:29; Hosea 1:4-5.*

JOAB
(JOH-ab)

King David's nephew and commander of the army during many of David's important conquests. He was a fearless soldier and a loyal servant of the king in many private matters. In the dispute over who would be king after David's death—Adonijah or Solomon—Joab sided with Adonijah. Solomon, when he became king, had Joab put to death for this. *2 Samuel 2:13-14, 18; 3:23-31; 8:16; 11:14-22; 18:10-16; 19:5-8; 20:7-11; 24:1-4; 1 Kings 1:19, 41; 2:28-34.*

JOANNA
(joh-AN-uh)

Wife of the steward of Herod Antipas. She was healed by Jesus, and provided for the needs of Jesus and the Twelve out of her own money. She was one of the women who visited the tomb of Jesus after his resurrection. *Luke 8:3; 24:10.*

JOASH
(JOH-ash)

Sometimes written as Jehoash, it is the name of several people in the OT. The most important were two kings.

1. Joash, son of Ahaziah, who ruled the southern kingdom of Judah about 835 to 797 B.C. He came to the throne when he was seven years old with the priest Jehoiada acting as his teacher and regent until the boy king came of age. During his reign the temple was repaired. He is also called Jehoash. *2 Kings 1:2-3, 21; 12:1-21.*

2. Joash, son of Jehoahaz, was king of the northern kingdom of Israel from about 798 to 782 B.C. He recovered for Israel the territory lost to Aram in the reign of his father. He was a friend of the prophet Elisha. *2 Kings 13:10-13, 24-25; 14:8-16.*

JOB

to Job and gives him the key to the answer. (See *Job, Book of.*)

JOB, BOOK OF

The eighteenth book in the OT which tells the story of Job. The author and the date are uncertain, but it may have been written sometime between 600 and 450 B.C. *See the book itself.*

JOEL
(JOH-uhl)

A common name in the OT, but the most famous Joel was a prophet. Little is known about him, but he probably lived in Jerusalem at a time when there was a plague of grasshopper-like locusts which destroyed crops and trees until there was a serious food shortage. (See *Joel, Book of*).

JOB
(johb)

A righteous and godly man who is the hero of the OT poem in the book of Job. For no reason that he could understand Job suffered terrible troubles. All his possessions, his children, and finally his health were taken from him. Through all this his faith in God held steady (see James 5:11). He discussed his situation with his friends. They discussed the problem of why God allows good people to suffer, but they could not find the answer. At the end of the poem God himself speaks

JOEL, BOOK OF

The second of the twelve short books of prophecy that stand at the end of the OT. The prophet described a terrible locust plague which he understood to be a warning from God to the people of even worse disaster at the day of judgment. Joel urged the people to repent and predicted that they would be forgiven and the land restored. The book was probably written about 4000 B.C. *See the book itself.*

135

JOHN
(jon)

1. One of the twelve apostles and a member of the inner circle of men—Peter, James, and John—who were closest to Jesus. He was the son of Zebedee and brother of James. He was a fisherman and followed his trade on the Sea of Galilee. He may have been the one called the beloved disciple. John became an outstanding leader in the church at Jerusalem and was concerned with preaching the gospel to his fellow Jews. *Matthew 4:21-22; 10:2; 17:1-2; Mark 1:19-20; Luke 5:10; 22:8; Acts 1:13; 3:1-4, 11; Galatians 2:9.*
2. A prophet whose father was a priest. His mother Elizabeth was related to Mary, the mother of Jesus. He was called John the Baptist. John lived in Judea and began his ministry in the wilderness preaching repentance for the forgiveness of sins. Many came to hear him preach and to be baptized in the river Jordan, some of them thinking he was the Christ. Jesus came to be baptized by his cousin. John criticized King Herod for marrying his brother's wife. This made the woman so angry with the prophet that she had him beheaded (see *Herodias*). John the Baptist is often called the "forerunner" or the person who prepared the way for Jesus and the kingdom of God. *Matthew 3:1-15; 4:12; 11:2-19; 14:1-12; Mark 1:4-9; 6:14-29; Luke 7:18-27; John 1:6-8, 15-40; Acts 1:5; 13:24-25.*

JOHN, GOSPEL OF

The last of the four Gospels in the NT. It is different from the other three in that it does not tell a connected story of the life of Jesus but explains the importance of Jesus to all mankind. In small sermons John gives "signs" selected from Jesus' own acts that show Jesus to be the Christ, the Son of God. The book of John teaches that in Jesus people can better understand God. The book probably was written toward the end of the first century. It is not certain who the author was. *See the book itself.*

JOHN, FIRST, SECOND, AND THIRD

Three letters in the NT written to Christians in the early church encouraging them to be faithful and loyal in a time of trouble and danger. The writer warned them against false teachers who claimed Jesus was not the Christ. He emphasized that love and concern for others are important. The author of these letters does not identify himself by name. The letters were written toward the end of the first century. *See the books themselves.*

JOHN MARK

See *Mark, John.*

JONAH
(JOH-nuh)

The OT parable of a prophet who was commanded by God to go and preach to the people of Nineveh, a large and prosperous city. Jonah was unwilling to go to a non-Jewish city so he tried to run away by taking a ship. A storm so frightened the sailors that they threw Jonah overboard because they felt he was the cause of the storm. At

JOHN BAPTIZES JESUS

this point a great fish swallowed him and took him the rest of his journey. He went into the city and urged the people to turn from their sins. When they listened and did repent, God spared the city. Jonah was angry at this. However, God showed Jonah that these people who were not Jews also had a place in God's purpose (See *Jonah, Book of.*)

JONAH BOOK OF

The fifth of the twelve OT books known as the Minor Prophets. It is a story about a prophet rather than a book of prophetic sayings. It was written about 350 B.C. by an unknown writer who recognized that God's concern was not for Jews alone. It is a missionary book in which the chief character is a prophet called Jonah. *See the book itself.*

JONATHAN
(JON-uh-tuhn)

Eldest son of King Saul. He was a warrior who assisted his father in many military campaigns. He was a dear friend of David and proved his love even when King Saul turned against David. Jonathan died with his father and brothers in a battle with the Philistines at Gilboa. David was deeply grieved at the loss of Jonathan. This personal name was used frequently in OT times. *1 Samuel 13:2-3, 16; 14:1-45; 18:1-4; 19:1-7; 20:1-42; 23:16-18; 2 Samuel 1:4-5, 23-26, 21:12-14.*

JOPPA
(JOP-uh)

A city thirty-five miles from Jerusalem on the Mediterranean coast. It is now called Jaffa and is a part of Tel Aviv. In OT times it was a major seaport serving Jerusalem. In NT times there was an early Christian community there with which Peter was closely connected. *2 Chronicles 2:16; Ezra 3:7; Jonah 1:3; Acts 9:36-43; 10:5-6.*

JORAM
(JOHR-uhm)

Sometimes spell Jehoram.
1. King of the northern kingdom of Israel from 852 to 841 B.C. He was the brother and successor of Ahaziah and a son of Ahab. The prophet Elisha encouraged a revolt against the Omride family (the family of Ahab), and Jehu was secretly proclaimed king. When Jehu saw the wounded king returning from battle he murdered Joram. *2 Kings 1:17; 3:1; 8:28-29; 9:14-26.*
2. King of Judah from about 848 to 841 B.C. He was the son and successor of

Jehoshaphat. His wife was Athaliah, daughter of Ahab. During his reign he encouraged Baal worship and was remembered as a wicked king. *2 Kings 8:16-24; 2 Chronicles 21:16-17.*

JORDAN
(JOR-duhn)

The longest and most important river in Palestine. The name means "stream that descends rapidly." It rises 1,200 feet above sea level, flows south, and empties into the Dead Sea 1,200 feet below sea level. A straight line from its beginning to its end is about eighty miles, but its curves and twists make it a full two hundred miles long. It cannot be used for transportation, but there are many shallow places where it can be forded. In Bible times the Jordan was a great military barrier and armies fought for possession of the fords. Crossing the Jordan marked the Hebrews' entry into Canaan, and the stretch of river from the Sea of Galilee to the Dead Sea continued to play an important part in biblical history. *Genesis 13:10-11; 32:10; Numbers 13:29; Deuteronomy 3:8, 17, 23-27; Joshua 1:2; 3:1-17; 23:4; Judges 3:28; 7:24-25; Mark 1:5, 9; Luke 3:3.*

JOSEPH
(JOH-seph)

1. The son of Rachel and the favorite of his father Jacob. His older brothers were envious and plotted to kill him. However, they changed their plan a bit and sold him to a caravan of traders. Joseph became a slave in Egypt. But his intelligence and attractive personality made it possible for him to rise to power and into favor with the pharaoh. He managed the grain supply in such a way that there was

enough to feed the people during a great drought. Years later Joseph was reunited with his father and brothers, and his entire family came to live in Egypt. *Genesis 30:23-24; 37:2-35; 39:1–48:22; 50:1; Exodus 1:5-9; Joshua 16:1-4.*

2. The carpenter who was the husband of the mother of Jesus. He is mentioned only a few times in the NT. Matthew and Luke mention him in the birth and childhood stories of Jesus. Mark does not refer to him at all, and the Gospel of John twice refers to Jesus as the "son of Joseph." It is probable that Joseph died before Jesus' ministry began. Mary seems to have been a widow at the time of the Crucifixion (see John 19:25-27). *Matthew 1:16, 19-25; 2:13-15, 19-23; 13:55; Luke 2:4-7, 16; 3:23; John 1:45; 6:42.*

3. Joseph of Arimathea was a wealthy member of the Jewish Sanhedrin who probably became a follower of Jesus. He begged the body of Jesus from the Roman governor and buried it in a newly hewn tomb on his own property. *Matthew 27:57-60; Mark 15:43-46; Luke 23:50-53; John 19:38-41.*

JOSEPH

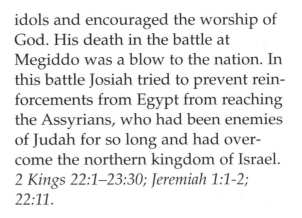

JOSHUA
(JOSH-oo-uh)

The son of Nun and a major figure in the OT book of Joshua. He was Moses' assistant in the journey from Egypt to Canaan. Before Moses died, he appointed Joshua his successor. Joshua had great military skill and was a forceful leader. He brought the tribes together and led them in conquering the land of Canaan. Before his death he challenged the people to be faithful in their worship and service of God and not to accept the gods of the Canaanites. (See *Joshua, Book of.*) *Exodus 24:13; Numbers 14:6-8, 38; 27:18-23; 34:17; Deuteronomy 1:38; 3:28; 31:7-8, 14, 23; 34:9; Judges 2:8; 1 Chronicles 7:27; Acts 7:45.*

JOSHUA, BOOK OF

The sixth book in the OT. It describes the invasion of Canaan after the exodus of the Israelites from Egypt and their wanderings in the wilderness. It tells of the division and allotment of the land of Canaan among the tribes of Israel. The central figure is Joshua, who was the leader at this time. The book probably was written by several authors drawing from various sources. *See the book itself.*

JOSIAH
(joh-ZYE-uh)

King of Judah from about 641 to 609 B.C. He was the son and successor of Amon. Josiah was one of Judah's able and faithful kings. The discovery of the book of the law in the temple led him to make many major reforms in the life of the nation. He removed the idols and encouraged the worship of God. His death in the battle at Megiddo was a blow to the nation. In this battle Josiah tried to prevent reinforcements from Egypt from reaching the Assyrians, who had been enemies of Judah for so long and had overcome the northern kingdom of Israel. *2 Kings 22:1–23:30; Jeremiah 1:1-2; 22:11.*

JOTHAM
(JOTH-uhm)

1. One of Gideon's sons who told the story of the fable of the trees. *Judges 9:7-15.*
2. A king of Judah from about 740 to 732 B.C. He was the son and successor of Uzziah (Azariah). During his reign there was great building activity in Jerusalem and all of Judah. It was a time of prosperity. *2 Kings 15:32-36; 2 Chronicles 27:1-9.*

JUBILEE, YEAR OF
(JOO-buh-lee)

In OT times every fiftieth year was set by law as the time when all slaves of the preceding forty-nine years (seven, seven-year periods) were to be released and all property, sold during that time, returned to its original owners. This year was also called the "year of liberty." The biblical records seem to show that this legislation never became effective. The probable use of the term "jubilee year" was to name a fifty-year period of time, like the present half-a-century. *Leviticus 25:8-14; Numbers 36:4.*

140

JUDAH
(JOO-duh)

The fourth son of Jacob and leader of the tribe descended from him which took his name. In the OT, King David was the most famous descendant of the tribe. The NT genealogies of Jesus Christ list Judah as an ancestor. The territory of Judah was a narrow mountain ridge about twenty miles long between Jerusalem and Hebron.

Judah and several other tribes gradually occupied the whole of the southern country of Palestine. There were none of the strong Canaanite cities to be dealt with, and the land was cleared of forest to make it suitable for farming. The tribe of Judah gradually expanded to the south and mingled with the other Judean hill clans. The tribes and territory of Judah became the southern kingdom of

Judah (see *Israel*) after the death of King Solomon. *Genesis 29:35; Judges 1:1-19; 2 Samuel 2:4; 1 Kings 12:17; 14:21; 2 Kings 18:1; 25:21-22; Psalm 78:68-70; Isaiah 40:9; Lamentations 1:3; Matthew 1:2-3; Luke 3:33; Revelation 5:5; and many other references.*

JOSHUA CONQUERS THE CITY OF JERICHO

141

JUDAISM

(JOO-dee-iz-uhm)

The belief and total way of life of the Jewish community. This community was unlike most in that it was bound together by its sense of having been chosen by God and bound to God by the covenant, their agreement to serve God. In Jesus' day the beliefs and practices differed in various Jewish sects, such as the Pharisees and Sadducees, but all Jews believed in the one God of Israel and acknowledged the Law. *Acts 13:43; Galatians 1:13-14.*

JUDAS

(JOO-duhss)

1. Judas Iscariot, one of the twelve apostles and the betrayer of Jesus. There are many puzzling questions about this man: Why was he attracted to Jesus? Why did Jesus include him in the Twelve? Why did Judas turn against Jesus? For a sum of money he agreed to help the religious authorities in Jerusalem take Jesus in a quiet place where they would not arouse the people. Later Judas was sorry for his deed and killed himself. *Matthew 10:2-4; 26:14-16; 27:3-5; Mark 4:10-11; Luke 22:3-6; John 12:4-6; 13:2, 21-30; 18:2-5; Acts 1:16-26.*

2. Another apostle was called Judas and is referred to as a son of James. He is sometimes called Thaddaeus. Tradition tells that this apostle went to preach the gospel with Bartholomew in Armenia. *Mark 3:18; Luke 6:13-16; John 14:22; Acts 1:13.*

3. A relative of Jesus was also called Judas. At the beginning of Jesus' ministry Judas doubted him and was not interested. This was also true of James, another "brother." After the Resurrection they did believe and become leaders in the early church. *Matthew 13:55; Mark 6:3; Jude 1:1.*

JUDE, LETTER OF

(jood)

A short letter in the NT written around the beginning of the second century. The writer appealed to all the churches to keep their faith strong and warned them against false teachings. It is not certain who was the author. *See the book itself.*

JUDEA

(joo-DEE-uh)

In NT times a division of the Roman province of Syria. It is a variation of the name Judah of OT times. During Judea's long history political changes at times enlarged the area, but Judea proper was a small area about forty-five miles square around Jerusalem, usually ruled by a tetrarch, or governor. In Judea the Herods rose to power with the support of Rome and were ruling when the Christian era began. Judea was important in the life of the Jewish people, chiefly because the holy city Jerusalem was located there. *Matthew 2:1; Mark 1:5; 10:1; Luke 3:1; John 3:22; Acts 8:1; 9:31; Galatians 1:22.*

JUDGE

An official with authority to settle disputes in a court of law; also the act of deciding disputes. In the OT between the time of Joshua and David the judges were military leaders who delivered the Israelites from their

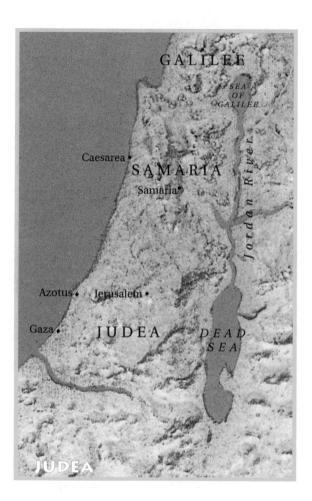

JUDEA

enemies. After the establishment of the kingdom the king often acted as judge or appointed others to fill this office. "Judge" was also used as a title for God, who is the Judge of all the earth, and for Jesus, who set a new standard of judgment. *Genesis 18:25; 19:9; Exodus 2:14; 18:13-26; Leviticus 19:15; Deuteronomy 16:18; 17:8-12; 1 Samuel 7:15; 2 Samuel 15:1-6; 1 Chronicles 23:4; 2 Chronicles 19:5-7; Psalm 94:2; Isaiah 2:4; 33:22; Luke 6:37; John 7:24; 8:16; Acts 7:27; 10:42; 2 Timothy 4:1.*

JUDGES, BOOK OF

The seventh book in the OT. It records the history of the Israelites from the time of their entrance into Canaan to the beginning of the kingdom. The book emphasizes that the spirit of God was moving through the history of time. It tells the stories of the chief Israelite leaders who were called judges and contains stories, songs, poems, and some fragments of very ancient literature. *See the book itself.*

JUDGMENT SEAT

See *Tribunal.*

JULIUS
(JOOL-uhss)

A Roman centurion, or officer, assigned to take Paul from Caesarea to Rome. He was kind to Paul and permitted him to go ashore at Sidon to visit friends. *Acts 27:1, 3, 9-11, 42-44; 28:16.*

JUSTICE

See *Law, Righteousness.*

JUSTIFY
(JUHS-teh-figh)

In biblical use a term for the action of God which forgives and restores men to goodness and righteousness. Several ideas are combined in this thought: (1) God is a holy and righteous God. (2) He demands holiness and righteousness of his people. (3) Men are not holy, they are sinners. (4) This sinfulness deserves punishment. The NT solution for this problem was God's offer of forgiveness through Jesus Christ. When men respond to this offer they are justified. *Job 32:2; Psalm 51:4; Isaiah 43:9; Luke 10:29; Romans 3:20-26; 8:33; Galatians 2:15-21.*

KADESH, KADESH-BARNEA
(KAY-desh-BAR-nee-uh)
An oasis in the Wilderness of Zin south of Canaan. Here the Israelites encamped for a lengthy time during their travels from Egypt to Canaan. It was from here that the Israelites sent men to spy out the land of Canaan. *Genesis 14:7; 16:14; Numbers 13:25-26; 20:14-16; 32:8; Deuteronomy 1:19; 2:14; Joshua 10:41; Psalm 29:8.*

KADMONITES
(KAD-muhn-ites)
Meaning "easterners." The Kadmonites were a nomadic tribe living in the desert between Canaan, Syria, and the river Euphrates. Their lands were included in those promised by God to Abraham and his descendants. *Genesis 15:18-19.*

KIDRON, BROOK
(KID-rehn)
A valley east of Jerusalem dividing the eastern parts of the city from the Mount of Olives. After heavy rainfalls a brook runs down the valley and waters the orchards and gardens near Jerusalem. Jesus crossed this valley on his way to Gethsemane. Part of the valley was used as a burial ground for the poor. *2 Samuel 15:23; 2 Kings 23:6, 12; 2 Chronicles 15:16; 29:16; 30:14; John 18:1.*

KING, KINGSHIP
A male ruler who had power over a city or a nation. He had the right to hand his royal power on to his descendants. A kingship refers to the office and dignity of a king, his power and authority, and the territory governed by him. In Israel the king was also the military leader who led the army into battle and the judge who

settled disputes and corrected injustices. The king also had authority over the religious life of the people. The Israelites recognized the supreme kingship of God and looked on all earthly kings as his anointed representatives. By NT times "king" had become an honorary title for the governor appointed, as the Herods were, by Rome to rule a province. All four Gospels report that Pilate and others called Jesus King of the Jews when questioning him or when mocking him during the trial and crucifixion. *Joshua 12:9-24; 1 Samuel 8:4-22; 2 Samuel 5:1-3; 15:2; Psalms 10:16; 24:7-10; Matthew 27:11, 27, 37, 42; Mark 15:2, 9, 12, 18, 26; Luke 23:3, 37-38; John 19:14-15, 19-22; 1 Timothy 1:17; 6:14-16; Revelation 17:14; and many other references.*

KINGDOM OF GOD, OF HEAVEN

The rule or reign of God. This is one of the most important ideas in the Bible. It deals with a kingdom which is not only in the world that we know, but which includes all places and all times. It is a kingdom designed to carry out the purposes of God. There are three parts to the idea of the kingdom: First, the ruler is and always has been God. Second, the establishment of the kingdom on the earth becomes a reality whenever people pledge their allegiance to God and try to keep God's law. Third, a fulfillment, or completing of, God's purpose is expected and hoped for by God's people. The idea of the kingdom of God was important to the Hebrews of the OT, and when Jesus came the NT

records that he began his ministry by announcing that the "kingdom of God is at hand." He taught that his life, work, and death were necessary for the coming of the kingdom. Jesus also spoke of a future completion. Therefore, the kingdom has come in the person and the acts of Jesus. Those individuals who believe that Jesus is lord become part of the community of the kingdom here and now. They may look forward to a place in the fulfilled kingdom of the future. *Matthew 4:17; 5:3, 10, 19-20; 6:10; 7:21; 10:7; 13:24-52; 18:1-4; Mark 1:14-15; 4:1-33; 12:28-34; Luke 9:2, 61-62; 10:9; 19:11-27; John 3:3, 5; Acts 14:21-22; Romans 14:17; Ephesians 5:5.*

KINGS, FIRST AND SECOND

The eleventh and twelfth books in the OT. They give the history of the Hebrews from the beginning of Solomon's reign, through the division of the kingdom into two separate states, through the fall of Samaria to the Assyrians, through the fall of Samaria to the Assyrians, through the fall of Jerusalem and the exile into Babylon. The materials in the books of Kings were collected from many sources such as old histories and court records. The writers, or authors, of the books show how the kings behaved toward God and tell of those who failed in their loyalty to God. *See the books themselves.*

TABLE OF OLD TESTAMENT KINGS

The United Kingdom

Saul	1020–1000 B.C.
David	1000–965 B.C.
Solomon	965–931 B.C.

The Divided Kingdom

JUDAH

Rehoboam	931–913 B.C.
Abijam	913–911
Asa	911–870
Jehoshaphat	870–848
Jehoram	848–841
Jehoahaz (Ahaziah)	841
Athaliah	841–835
Joash (Jehoash)	835–797
Amaziah	797–792
Uzziah (Azariah)	792–740
Jotham	740–732
Ahaz	732–716
Hezekiah	716–687
Manasseh	687–643
Amon	643–641
Josiah	641–609
Jehoahaz	609
Jehoiakim	609–598
Jehoiachim	598–597
Zedekiah	597–586

(Fall of Jerusalem)

ISRAEL

Jeroboam	931–910 B.C.
Nadab	910–909
Baasha	909–886
Elah	886–885
Zimri	885
Omri	885–874
Ahab	874–853
Ahaziah	853–852
Joram (Jehoram)	852–841
Jehu	841–814
Jehoahaz	814–798
Joash (Jehoash)	798–782
Jeroboam II	782–753
Zechariah	753–752
Shallum	752
Menahem	752–742
Pekahiah	742–740
Pekah	740–732
Hoshea	732–722

(Fall of Samaria)

KING'S HIGHWAY

In Bible times a well-known road that ran from Damascus to the Gulf of Aqabah along the length of eastern Palestine. It passed through the territories of Bashan, Gilead, Ammon, Moab, and Edom and connected with other roads that led to Egypt. Fortresses lined the road. The Israelites on their way from Egypt to Canaan were prevented by the Edomites from using the highway through Edomite territory, and they had to go around it. There is a modern road which closely follows the course of the old road. *Numbers 20:17-21; 21:22.*

KISHON

(KISH-on)

A river draining the western part of the Valley of Jezreel. It winds its way for twenty-three miles to the Mediterranean Sea. During the rainy months of winter the river bed is muddy, but in summer it is usually dry. It is chiefly remembered as the scene of the defeat of Sisera by Barak and Deborah, recorded in the OT. *Judges 4:7, 13; 5:19-21; 1 Kings 18:40; Psalm 83:9.*

KITTIM

(KIT-im)

OT name for the island of Cyprus. It was known to the Israelites as a land across the sea, and they associated Kittim with ships. People of Tyre and Sidon fled to Kittim to escape from the Assyrians. It was captured by the Assyrians under Sargon. Pine for the decks of Phoenician ships came from Cyprus. *Numbers 24:24; Daniel 11:30.*

KNEAD

(need)

To pound or press dough with the hands until it forms a well-mixed mass. Flour and water were mixed along with a small piece of leavened dough left from the previous day in shallow containers made of wood, bronze, or pottery and called a kneading bowl or kneading trough. *Genesis 18:6; Exodus 8:3; 12:34; Deuteronomy 28:5, 17; 1 Samuel 28:24; 2 Samuel 13:8; Jeremiah 7:18; Hosea 7:4.*

KNEADING BREAD

KOHATH

(KOH-hath)

A son of Levi and the grandfather of
Aaron, Moses, and Miriam. *Exodus
6:16-20; Numbers 3:17-19; 4:1-15; 7:9.*

KOHATHITE

(KOH-hath-ites)

The Kohathites were one of three
important Levitical families who were
responsible for the care and transportation of the tabernacle during the
journey through the wilderness.
*Numbers 3:27-31; 4:34-37; 10:21; 26:57;
Joshua 21:4-5, 9-26; 1 Chronicles 9:32; 2
Chronicles 20:19.*

KORAH

(KOR-uh)

1. A son and a grandson of Esau.
Genesis 36:5, 14, 16, 18.
2. An Israelite who quarreled with
Moses because he felt Aaron and his
family should not be the only ones
who could be priests. Korah declared
that all the families were holy and
could be religious leaders. *Numbers
16:1-50.*

KORAHITES

(KOR-uh-hites)

In 1 Chronicles the Korahites are
named with the Kohathites as gate-
keepers and helpers in the temple
service. The "Sons of Korah" appear
in the headings of several psalms
(Psalms 42; 44–49; 84–85; 87–88), indicating that there was a guild or group
of temple singers called Sons of
Korah. *1 Chronicles 9:19, 26:1, 19; 2
Chronicles 20:19.*

LABAN
(LAY-buhn)

A relative of Abraham who lived in the area of Paddan-aram in northern Mesopotamia. He was the brother of Issac's wife Rebekah and the father of Leah and Rachel, who became the wives of Isaac's son Jacob. *Genesis 25:20; 28:5; 29:1-30; 31:1-55.*

LACHISH
(LAY-kish)

An ancient Canaanite city between Jerusalem and Gaza, captured and destroyed by the Israelites when Joshua led their invasion of the hill country. During Solomon's reign it was rebuilt, and it later became a city of the southern kingdom Judah. Great fortifications were added. About 700 B.C. Lachish was captured and burned by the Assyrians. Wall carvings found in the ruins of Sennacherib's palace at Nineveh show the siege of Lachish. The city was rebuilt and stood until captured by Nebuchadnezzar in 588–586 B.C. Archaeologists have uncovered in the ruins of Lachish evidence of great fires and battles. They have also found bits of pottery with writing which appear to have been the letters of a military man, written just before Nebuchadnezzar's destruction of Jerusalem. *Joshua 10:3-5, 31-35; 12:11; 2 Kings 18:14-17; 19:8; 2 Chronicles 11:5-12; 25:25-28; 32:9-10; Nehemiah 11:30; Isaiah 36:1-2; 37:8; Jeremiah 34:6-7; Micah 1:13.*

LAMB

A young sheep. In OT times the lamb was used for food and in sacrifices in the temple. It was especially important at the Passover. For the Israelites, flocks of sheep and herds of goats were of great importance. Sheep were a source of meat, milk, cheese, wool, and hides. So the lamb offered as sacrifice was an object of great value. Unlike most animals, sheep quietly submit to such things as being sheared or clipped, and even to being sacrificed. It isn't surprising that for the Israelites the lamb symbolized innocence and gentleness. In the NT the term is used as a figure of speech in referring to Jesus. *Exodus 12:3-14; 29:38-42; 1 Samuel 7:9; 2 Chronicles 35:13; Isaiah 65:25; Luke 22:7; John 1:29, 35-36; Acts 8:32; 1 Corinthians 5:7.*

LAMENTATION

(lam-en-TAY-shuhn)
See *Mourning.*

LAMENTATIONS, BOOK OF

An OT book of five poems mourning the destruction of Jerusalem. The poems are sad, yet there is confession of sin and hope for the future in chapter 3. All the cruelty of the invading army of the Babylonians in 586 B.C., the sickness and hunger, the helplessness of the Jewish leaders, and the destruction of the temple are described. Yet the writer of chapter 3 had confidence in God and hope for the future (see Lamentations 3:21-27). Called the "Lamentations of Jeremiah," it was once thought that the prophet had written these pieces, but probably they were written by several authors. *See the book itself.*

LAMP

In early Bible times a pottery saucer filled with olive oil, having a wick of twisted threads resting on the edge. Later the rim of the saucer was pinched in several places to hold the wick. Still later covered lamps with spouts for holding the wick became popular. Usually a lamp was kept burning in a house day and night. The word was also used in a figure of speech to represent the law, to symbolize life as opposed to death, or to symbolize the change from the darkness of evil into the light of goodness and truth. *Exodus 27:20; 1 Samuel 3:3; 2 Samuel 21:17; 22:29; 2 Chronicles 21:7; Psalm 119:105; Proverbs 31:18; Matthew 5:15; Mark 4:21; Luke 8:16-17; John 5:35; Revelation 21:23; 22:5.*

LAMPSTAND

A device for raising a lamp high so that its light will cover a large area. Lampstands were used in the tabernacle, the temple, and palaces. Originally the stand probably held a pottery lamp with seven spouts. This was developed into a seven-branched lamp which became and still is one of the best-known symbols of Judaism. *Exodus 25:31-40; 26:35; 37:17-24; 1 Kings 7:49; 1 Chronicles 28:15; Zechariah 4:2-14; Hebrews 9:2; Revelation 1:12-20; 2:5.*

LAMP

they had contact. In the story of Joseph in Egypt, Egyptians words are quoted (see Genesis 41:43, 45). Babylonian and Assyrian words and names found their way into the Bible (see 2 Kings 18:17; Daniel 1:7) as did Persian words (see Daniel 3:2-3). Whole chapters in Daniel and Ezra were written in Aramaic. Jesus spoke in Aramaic, and the NT contains many Aramaic expressions (see Matthew 27:46; Mark 5:41). The Gospels state that the inscriptions aove the cross were in Latin, Greek, and Hebrew (see John 19:20). The names of many places found in the Bible have come from a variety of languages, and there are some whose meaning and origin are unknown. *Nehemiah 13:23-24; Esther 3:12.*

LANDMARK

A mark showing the boundaries of an area of land. In Bible times stones were piled to mark the boundaries between the fields of one man and those of his neighbors. They also marked districts and nations. It was a serious offense to remove the landmarks. *Deuteronomy 19:14; 27:17; Job 24:2; Proverbs 22:28; 23:10; Hosea 5:10.*

LANGUAGES OF THE BIBLE

The OT in its final form was in Hebrew, and the NT in Greek. However, biblical writers sometimes used names, words, and phrases, from languages of other nations with which

LAODICEA
(lAY-oh-di-SEE-uh)

A city in southwestern Asia Minor. In NT times it was one of the main cities of Phrygia (now part of Turkey), located in the Lycus River Valley. Laodicea was a prosperous city, famous for its black sheep whose wool was woven into especially fine garments and carpets. In NT times the population included Greek-speaking Syrians, Romans, and also many wealthy Jews. *Colossians 2:1; 4:13-16; Revelation 1:11; 3:14-17.*

LAST SUPPER, THE

The final meal which Jesus ate with his disciples on the evening before his death. Jesus spoke of his coming death and said it would be used by God to establish his kingdom. Christians recall the Last Supper in the sacrament, or sacred observance, called the Communion service or Eucharist. (See *Lord's Supper.*) The Last Supper is described in: *Matthew 26:17-30; Mark 14:12-26; Luke 22:7-30; 1 Corinthians 11:23-26.*

LATIN

The language spoken by Romans in Bible times. In Italy in NT times every educated Roman spoke Greek as well as Latin, for Greek was the international language. In the Judean and Galilean provinces only those who were officers of the law, the government, and the army spoke Latin. *John 19:20.*

LAVER
(LAY-vur)

A large metal basin or bowl for water in the tabernacle or temple. It was used by the priests for washing before they offered a sacrifice. *Exodus 30:17-19; 1 Kings 7:38.*

LAW

Rules or ordinances for living together in a community. The OT law was based on a covenant, or agreement, between God and the Hebrew people. The basis for Hebrew law was the Ten Commandments, but the first five books of the OT, called the Torah, con-

tained most of the Hebrew laws and ordinances. The OT prophets constantly challenged the people to keep the laws in obedience to God. Jesus observed the customs and laws of his people but criticized the way many religious leaders insisted upon exact performance of ceremonial laws and forgot that the most important law in all relationships is the law of love. *Exodus 13:9, 21:1, and other verses; Leviticus 7:37; Deuteronomy 1:16-18; 4:8; 5:1-20; 6:1-9; Joshua 1:7; 24:25-26; Ezra 7:10, 14; Isaiah 5:24; Jeremiah 32:23; Daniel 6:5; Matthew 5:17; 22:34-40; John 7:19; Acts 13:15; Romans 2:17-23; Galatians 3:21-26.*

LAWYER

In NT times one who knew and interpreted the law, especially the law of Moses. The lawyers were among those who opposed Jesus for healing on the sabbath. In the NT a lawyer was also called a scribe. *Matthew 22:35; Luke 7:30; 10:25; 11:45-52; 14:3-5.*

LAZARUS
(LAZ-ur-uhss)

1. The name of a beggar in Jesus' parable about a beggar and a rich man. His name means "God's help of a needy beggar." *Luke 16:19-31.*
2. A friend of Jesus whom Jesus raised from the dead. He lived in Bethany with his sisters Mary and Martha. *John 11:1-44.*

THE LAST SUPPER

LEAH
(LEE-uh)
The older daughter of Laban and Jacob's first wife. She was not as high in Jacob's favor as her younger and more beautiful sister Rachel. In fact, Jacob was tricked into marrying her. She was the mother of six sons. *Genesis 29:15-35; 30:17-21; 49:31.*

LEATHER
Animal skins tanned and prepared for use as garments, girdles, belts, footwear, coverings for tents, skin bottles for water or wine (see 1 Samuel 1:24; Job 38:37), and writing materials. Some scrolls were made of strips of leather sewn together. *Exodus 26:14; 2 Kings 1:8; Ezekiel 16:10; Matthew 3:4; Mark 1:6.*

LEAVEN
(LEV-en)
Any substance such as yeast that was added to bread dough to make it rise. In biblical times leavening was done with a portion of active dough kept from a previous day's baking. During the Passover festival each year the Hebrews did not eat bread that had been made with leaven. They used unleavened bread as a reminder of the hardships their ancestors suffered during the exodus from Egypt. Only unleavened bread could be used in any sacrifices to God. In the NT "leaven" is often used as a figure of speech to show how the actions of a person, whether good or bad, can have a wide influence, affecting a group of people as yeast affects dough. *Exodus 12:19-20, 34, 39; 34:25; Leviticus 2:11; 27:13;*

Deuteronomy 16:3-4; Matthew 13:33; 16:6, 11-12; Mark 8:15; Luke 12:1; 13:21; 1 Corinthians 5:6-8; Galatians 5:9.

LEBANON
(LEB-uh-non)
The name of a country and of a mountain range that follows the eastern coastline of the Mediterranean Sea. In OT times it formed the northwestern boundary of the lands of the Hebrews and was famous for its great forests of cedars and cypresses. The snow-capped mountain peaks probably gave the mountains the name Lebanon, which means "white." *Deuteronomy 1:7; 3:25; 11:24; Judges 3:3; 1 Kings 5:6, 8-10, 14; 7:2; 2 Kings 19:23; Ezra 3:7; Psalms 37:35; 92:12; Isaiah 40:16; Jeremiah 18:14; Hosea 14:6-7.*

LEES
(leez)
The dregs of wine which were allowed to settle at the bottom of a wineskin until the wine was strong and well flavored. In the Bible the word was used in a figure of speech to describe people who had never been unsettled by calamity. *Isaiah 25:6; Jeremiah 48:11; Zephaniah 1:12.*

LEGION
(LEE-juhn)
The main unit of the Roman army. In NT times a legion usually consisted of about six thousand men divided into ten cohorts or regiments. The legions were made up of the best and most-trusted Roman soldiers. In the NT the

word is used to refer to a large number or group. *Matthew 26:53; Mark 5:9, 15; Luke 8:30.*

LENTILS
(LEN-tehlz)

The fruit of a plant of the pea family. *Genesis 25:34; 2 Samuel 17:27-29; Ezekiel 4:9.*

LEOPARD
(LEP-ehrd)

A spotted animal of the cat family. The cheetah, which is a variety of leopard, was known in the biblical world. It is noted for its speed and is sometimes trained for hunting. In the Bible "leopard" is often used as a figure of speech. Early Christians likened the Roman Empire to a beast such as a leopard, ready to spring upon them and destroy them. *Isaiah 11:6; Jeremiah 13:23; Hosea 13:7; Habakkuk 1:8; Revelation 13:2.*

LEPROSY
(LEP-ruh-see)

A serious skin disease. In Bible times persons who had leprosy were forced to live apart from others.

They were considered religiously unclean. The term "leprosy" in Bible times was probably used for many types of skin diseases. The priest had to observe the skin disease and determine whether or not it was leprosy. Today leprosy is often called Hansen's disease, and some forms are curable. *Leviticus 13:1–14:54; Numbers 5:2; 2 Kings 5:1-27; 2 Chronicles 26:19-21; Matthew 8:2-4; 10:8; Mark 1:40-44; Luke 5:12-15; 17:11-19.*

CEDARS OF LEBANON

LETTER

A written message sent to a person or persons at a distance. The earliest letters were written on clay tablets or pieces of pottery. Later, writing was done on sheets of papyrus which were folded or rolled, then sealed and carried to their destination by runners. Many of the books in the NT were written in the forms of letters. Paul is the most famous NT author of this type of book. *1 Kings 21:8-12; 2 Chronicles 30:6; Ezra 4:7-24; Acts 15:22-31; Romans 16:22; Colossians 4:16.*

LEVI

(LEE-vye)

1. In the OT one of the twelve sons of Jacob whose descendants were called "sons of Levi," "tribe of Levi," or "Levites." *Genesis 29:34; 35:23; 49:5; Exodus 1:2; 6:16; 32:25-29; Deuteronomy 33:8-11; Joshua 13:14; 1 Chronicles 2:1.*
2. In the NT the name of a tax collector in Capernaum who became a follower of Jesus. He was sometimes called Matthew, but it is not certain that he was the same Matthew listed as one of the twelve apostles. *Mark 2:14; Luke 5:27-32.*

LEVIATHAN

(li-VYE-uh-thuhn)

In the OT the name of a dragon, a symbol of disorder and evil, subdued by God at the time of creation. The name is also used to refer to any sea monster. *Job 41:1; Psalms 74:14; 104:26; Isaiah 27:1.*

LEVITES

See *Priests and Levites.*

LEVITICAL CITIES

(le-VIT-i-kuhl)

Forty-eight cities in Canaan which were to be set apart as the dwelling places of the tribe of Levi, who were priests. *Leviticus 25:32-34; Numbers 18:21-30; 35:1-34; Deuteronomy 14:28-29; Joshua 20:1–21:42.*

LEVITICUS

(li-VIT-i-kuhss)

The third book of the Bible. It deals mainly with the duties of the priests and contains laws and regulations about worship, sacrifices, food, dress, and the conduct of everyday living. Jesus used Leviticus 19:18 as part of his summary of the law. Leviticus probably was compiled after the Exile. *See the book itself.*

LIBERTY

Freedom from bondage, slavery, or the control of another. In the OT it almost always refers to those who are free from slavery or forced labor. The NT uses "liberty" to mean freedom from the slavery of sin. This liberty is gained through Jesus Christ and makes one able to lead a new life ruled by God's love. *Isaiah 61:1; Luke 4:16-21; Romans 8:21.*

LILY

A general term for a variety of springtime flowers that grew in Bible lands. Hebrew poets often referred to lilies in figures of speech. Jesus was probably thinking of the crimson and purple blossoms of the wild anemone, or wind flower, when he spoke of the lilies of the field. The bowl-shaped decorations on the tops of the pillars at the entrance to Solomon's temple resembled open flowers and were called lily-work. *1 Kings 7:19, 22; Song of Solomon 2:1-2; Hosea 14:5; Matthew 6:28-29; Luke 12:27.*

LION

A large, meat-eating, honey-colored, shaggy animal. The lion of Bible times was the small Persian lion, about five feet long. Lions were common in Bible times, and some survived in Bible lands until the end of the nineteenth century. Lion hunting was the sport of Assyrian kings. It is reported that David and Samson each killed a lion. Shepherds kept a sharp watch for lions, for they could quickly destroy a flock of sheep. The lion was mentioned in Hebrew poetry as a symbol of strength and cruelty. Carved lion figures decorated Solomon's temple. The lion may have been the symbol of Hebrew royalty. *Judges 14:5-6, 18; 1 Samuel 17:34-37; Psalms 10:9; 104:21; Proverbs 28:1; 30:29-30; Isaiah 11:7; Jeremiah 51:38; Amos 3:4, 8; Revelation 5:5.*

LILY-WORK

LOCUST

A flying grasshopper-like insect capable of causing great destruction to vegetation. The locust may be eaten raw or roasted, or may be dried and ground into powder and mixed with honey and dates. This was a common food in the Near East in Bible times and is still eaten today. *Exodus 10:13-15; Leviticus 11:21-22; Deuteronomy 28:38; Judges 6:5; 7:12; 1 Kings 8:37; Job 39:20; Jeremiah 46:23; Joel 1:1–2:27 (the prophet describes a locust plague); Nahum 3:15.*

LOG

The OT liquid measure equal to about a pint in modern terms. Also a length of tree trunk. *Leviticus 14:10, 12, 15, 21, 24; 2 Kings 6:5; Matthew 7:3-5.*

LORD

A title for anyone who commands respect or has authority over others. The OT uses "Lord" as a title of honor and majesty for God. The NT uses the word as a title for God and also for Jesus. Early Christians used the expression "Jesus is Lord" to indicate that God had sent Jesus as the Christ. *Deuteronomy 14:1-2; Joshua 1:9; 13:33; 1 Samuel 2:1-10; Isaiah 42:5-8; Jeremiah 16:19-20; Amos 4:13; Matthew 1:20; Luke 2:22-23; 7:19; John 13:13-14; Acts 10:36; 1 Corinthians 1:3; and many other references.*

LORD'S PRAYER

The title given to the prayer Jesus taught his disciples. *Matthew 6:9-13; Luke 11:2-4.*

LOT CHOOSES LAND

LORD'S SUPPER

The title given by Paul to the holy meals of the church. These were a continuation of the fellowship of Jesus with his disciples begun at the Last Supper (see Last Supper). The celebration of the Lord's Supper or Holy Communion in Christian churches today are a continuing memorial to Jesus Christ. *1 Corinthians 11:17-26.*

LOT

A nephew of Abraham who first settled in Canaan with his uncle. As his flocks grew, he quarreled with Abraham over the grazing. Abraham offered Lot his choice of land and the younger man chose the rich, well-watered Jordan Valley. He escaped from the judgment that fell upon Sodom and Gomorrah, but his wife perished. *Genesis 11:27–13:13; 19:1-38.*

LOTS

Small stones or cubes used to make choices, like the modern day throwing of dice. In the OT there are instances of casting lots to determine the will of God, to determine which priest would serve at a certain time, and to divide land and property. In the NT, Judas' replacement was determined by the use of lots. The soldiers at the cross used lots to divide Jesus' clothing among themselves. *Leviticus 16:8; Joshua 7:14, 14; 1 Corinthians 24:3-19; Matthew 27:35.*

CASTING LOTS

LOVE

The deep, personal attachment that includes loyalty, goodwill, devotion, knowledge, and responsibility. In the OT love is looked upon as God's activity in redeeming humanity and is seen most clearly in God's steadfast care for the Hebrews. People are the object of God's love, while humanity's love for God is the response we make to God's love. The love of person for person is based on God's love and requires love and justice in all relationships. In the NT Jesus showed clearly the meaning of God's love by his concern and care for others and by his life and his death. *Leviticus 19:18; Deuteronomy 6:5; 7:7; Psalms 17:17; 136:1-26; Matthew 22:37-39; Mark 12:30-31; Luke 6:27-36; John 14:23; 15:9-13, 17; Romans 5:8; 12:9-10; 13:8-10; 1 Corinthians 13:1-13; 2 Corinthians 5:14; Galatians 5:13-14; Ephesians 6:24; Hebrews 13:1; 1 John 3:1–4:21.*

LUKE, EVANGELIST

A Gentile Christian, probably the author of the Gospel of Luke and the book of Acts. Luke was a physician and a close friend and traveling companion of Paul. Luke's native country is uncertain. (See *Luke, Book of.*) *Colossians 4:14; 2 Timothy 4:11; Philemon 1:24.*

LUKE, GOSPEL OF

The third book of the NT, probably written by Luke, the beloved physician and companion of Paul. The book tells of the life, ministry, death, and resurrection of Jesus Christ. The author used information from reports and stories he had heard about Jesus and also from such written accounts as are found in the Gospel of Mark. He was writing to tell Gentile Christians that what they had been taught about Christ was true. He may have had in mind also recommending Christianity to members of the Roman court circle. The Gospel of Luke, probably written about A.D. 70–80, and the book of Acts make a two-volume account of the life of Jesus and the beginnings of the early church. *See the book itself.*

LUTE

(loot)
See *Musical Instruments.*

LYCAONIA

(LIK-ay-OH-nee-uh)
A region in south central Asia Minor, bounded on the north by Galatia. Paul traveled and preached in the cities of Lycaonia, including Lystra, and made many disciples. *Acts 14:3-7.*

LYDIA

(LID-ee-uh)
A woman from Thyatira in Asia Minor who sold purple-dyed cloth in Philippi. She heard Paul preach, and she and her family were baptized. Paul and his companions stayed in Lydia's house, and thus he did not have to earn his living while he was in Philippi. The church at Philippi supported Paul as he allowed no other church to do. Lydia's help may have been the chief reason Paul allowed the church to do this. *Acts 16:11-15, 40.*

LYRE

(LYE-ur)
See *Musical Instruments.*

LYSTRA

(LYE-struh)
A city in the highlands of the region of Lycaonia in southern Asia Minor. Paul and Barnabas preached in Lystra and made disciples there. *Acts 14:5-8, 21; 16:1-2; 2 Timothy 3:10-11.*

MACEDONIA

(may-suh-DOh-nee-uh)

The region north of Achaia in what is now the northern part of Greece. In NT times Macedonia was a Roman province. Its mountains and plains stretched from the Adriatic Sea to the Aegean Sea, with its most important cities situated on the Aegean coast. Macedonia was the first European territory in which the gospel was preached. Paul preached in many of the cities, among them Philippi and Thessalonica. Paul later wrote letters to the churches which he had started in these two cities. *Acts 16:9-12; 18:5; 19:21-22; 27:2; 1 Corinthians 16:5; 2 Corinthians 8:1; Philippians 4:15; 1 Thessalonians 1:7-8.*

MACHIR

(MAY-kur)

1. Son of Manasseh and grandson of Joseph. The name of a tribe that settled west of the Jordan. The Machirites probably helped to conquer part of Canaan. *Genesis 50:23; Numbers 26:29; 32:39-40; Deuteronomy 3:15; Joshua 13:29-31; 17:1, 3; Judges 5:14; 1 Chronicles 7:14, 16.*
2. A follower of King Saul who gave shelter to Mephibosheth, the lame son of Jonathan, until David took the prince to his court. Machir was so moved by the king's kindness that he became a loyal supporter of King David. *2 Samuel 9:3-5; 17:27-29.*

MACHPELAH

(mok-PEL-uh)

A field near Hebron where Abraham bought a cave to use as a family burying place. Sarah, Abraham, Isaac, Rebekah, Leah, and Jacob are buried there. *Genesis 23:19; 25:9; 49:29-32; 50:13.*

MAGADAN, MAGDALA, DALMANUTHA

(MAG-uh-dan, MAG-duh-la, dal-men-NOO-thuh)

A city on the western shore of the Sea of Galilee. In NT times the Greek name for Magadan, or Magdala; was probably Tarichea. It was the center of a prosperous fishing industry and was the home of Mary Magdalene, one of the followers of Jesus. Today it is called Mejdel. *Matthew 15:39; Mark 8:10.*

MAGDALENE

(MAG-duh-leen)

Meaning "from Magadan" or "Magdala." It is used in the Gospels to identify one of Jesus' followers, Mary Magdalene, a Galilean woman. (see *Magadan.*) *Matthew 27:55-56, 61; 28:1; Mark 15:40, 47; 16:1; Luke 8:2; 24:10; John 19:25; 20:1, 18.*

MAGIC, MAGICIAN

(MAJ-ik, muh-JI-shun)

In ancient times power which was believed to be supernatural. This power could be set into action, it was believed, by use of certain acts and words. Various kinds of magic and sorcery were practiced among ancient peoples. The laws of the Israelites forbade the practice of magic. The prophets condemned its use. Still, some Hebrews were influenced by the Egyptian and Babylonian sorcery and did engage in magic practices. In the NT, Paul called magicians the enemies of all righteousness. Other terms used for a magician are "diviner," "soothsayer," "sorcerer," "medium," and "necromancer." *Genesis 41:8; Deuteronomy 18:10-14; 1 Samuel 28:3, 7; 2 Chronicles 33:6; Isaiah 3:2-3; Jeremiah 27:9; Ezekiel 13:18-20; Acts 8:9-24; 13:6-8; 19:19.*

MAGISTRATE

(MAJ-i-strate)

In the NT the term was used for a judge or governing official in the Roman provinces. *Luke 12:58-59; Acts 16:20, 22, 35-36, 38.*

MALACHI

(MAL-uh-kye)

The last of the short books that make up the collection of the Twelve Prophets; the last book of the OT. It tells of the religious and social conditions after the Jews' return from exile, when the land was under Persian rule. The writer's chief concern was for the Jews to be faithful to their covenant with God. He urged them to practice proper worship in the temple. He warned against the danger of foreign religious practices which were introduced when Jews married non-Jews. The author probably wrote the book about 450 B.C. *See the book itself.*

MALLOW

(MAL-oh)

Probably a shrub that grows in the salt marshes in Palestine. It is often called the salt plant. The leaves are thick and fleshy and can be eaten in times of food shortages. *Job 24:24; 30:3-4.*

MALTA
(MAWL-tuh)

An island south of Sicily. In NT times Malta belonged to Rome. Paul was shipwrecked in a bay off the coast of Malta on his way to prison in Rome. Although Paul stayed for three months on the island, it is uncertain whether he organized a Christian group. But early art found on Malta shows Christian influence. Jewish and Christian catacombs have been found on the island. *Acts 28:1.*

MAMMON
(MAM-uhn)

A word meaning "wealth," "money," "property," or "profit." Jesus used the term to describe the love of material things which makes a person forget God and to use energy to earn money instead of serving God. *Matthew 6:24; Luke 16:9, 11, 13.*

MAMRE
(MAM-ree)

A place near ancient Hebron in Canaan in the general area in which Abraham lived. It is often associated with the oak trees near which Abraham built an altar. The burial place of Abraham's family was located nearby. *Genesis 13:18; 14:13, 24; 18:1; 23:17-19; 35:27.*

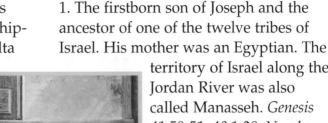

MARY MAGDALENE

MANASSEH
(muh-NASS-uh)

1. The firstborn son of Joseph and the ancestor of one of the twelve tribes of Israel. His mother was an Egyptian. The territory of Israel along the Jordan River was also called Manasseh. *Genesis 41:50-51; 48:1-20; Numbers 1:34-35; Joshua 4:12; 17:5-12; Judges 1:27; 2 Chronicles 30:10-11; Psalm 60:7; Isaiah 9:21.*

2. The name of a king of Judah who reigned about 687–643 B.C. He was the son and successor of Hezekiah. King Manasseh attempted to restore the places of pagan worship that his father had destroyed. *2 Kings 21:1-18; 23:26; 24:3-4; 2 Chronicles 33:10-12.*

MANDRAKE

A stemless herb with large leaves shooting out from the roots to form a flat circle on the earth. Creamy-yellow blossoms veined with purple come out on single stems. The small, bright yellow, pulpy fruit is sometimes eaten, although it is slightly poisonous. The root of the plant is dark brown and is shaped so much like a person that many superstitious ideas about its magic powers were held in early Bible times. *Genesis 30:14; Song of Solomon 7:13.*

163

MANGER

In Bible times a trough or box made of stones or hollowed out of rock and used for feeding cattle. Sometimes it was located on the lower level of a Palestinian house where the poorer people kept their animals in bad weather or in a natural cave near the house. The first bed of the baby Jesus was a manger. *Luke 2:7, 12, 16; 13:15.*

MANNA
(MAN-uh)

Meaning "What is it?" The substance that the Israelites gathered and ate for part of their food during the long journey through the wilderness. After the hungry people began to murmur for bread, God told Moses God would rain bread from heaven. From this time on the people found manna on the ground each morning. Some scholars believe this may have been a natural substance secreted from certain insects; if so this sticky, sweet honeydew is still gathered and dried into wafers of sticky solids. Today Arabs eat it as a relish on bread. Other scholars, however, believe that manna appeared when the Israelites cried out for food and disappeared when the people entered Canaan and had access to normal food. In any case, manna appeared as a direct action of God, sent to ease the suffering of God's wandering people. *Exodus 16:3-5, 13-17; Numbers 11:6-9; Deuteronomy 8:3, 16; Nehemiah 9:20; Psalm 78:23-24.*

MANTLE
(MAN-tl)

A loose, sleeveless coat. A rough mantle made of hair was worn by the prophets as a sign of their office. Priests, kings, and other people in authority wore rich mantles suitable to their position. The word is used as a figure of speech in which praise, prosperity, or beauty is spoken of as a covering wrap, or adornment. *Exodus 12:34; Joshua 7:21, 24; 1 Kings 19:13, 19; 2 Kings 2:8, 13-14; Ezra 9:5; Isaiah 3:22; 59:17; 61:3; Zechariah 13:4; Mark 14:63; Luke 22:36.*

MARK, JOHN
(mark, jon)

A member of the church in Jerusalem, who may have been the author of the Gospel of Mark. The home of his mother Mary was a gathering place for Christians. He was a close friend of Peter and became a companion of some of the early Christian missionaries. He traveled with Paul and Barnabas on their first missionary journey. (See *Mark, Book of.*) *Acts 12:12, 25; 15:37-39; Colossians 4:10; 2 Timothy 4:11; Philemon 1:23-24.*

MARK, GOSPEL OF

The second book in the NT. Most scholars believe it to be the first Gospel written down. This Gospel may have been written in Rome by John Mark between A.D. 65 and 70. It was based on information Mark gathered from Peter and perhaps from some other eyewitnesses to the events in the life of Jesus. It is the story of Jesus' life, teachings, death, and resurrection; written to strengthen the church in Rome during persecution and for use in the church's mission to non-Christians. The writers of Matthew and Luke made use of the material in Mark. *See the book itself.*

MARTHA
(MAR-thuh)

Sister of Mary and Lazarus of Bethany and friend of Jesus. Martha was a homemaker and provided for Jesus' needs whenever he visited their home. It was to Martha that Jesus declared "I am the resurrection and the life." Her reply was, "I believe that you are the Christ, the Son of God." *Luke 10:38-42; John 11:1-6, 17-30; 12:1-2.*

MARY
(MAIR-ee)

1. The mother of Jesus. Very little is said about Mary in the Gospels after the stories of Jesus' birth and childhood. The NT tells us that during Jesus' ministry Mary lived in Nazareth with his brothers and sisters, that she was present at the Crucifixion, and afterwards with his brothers and disciples took part in a prayer meeting. *Matthew 1:18-25; 2:10-15, 21; Mark 3:31-35; 6:3; Luke 1:26-56; 2:1-19; John 2:1-12; 19:25-27; Acts 1:14.*
2. Mary Magdalene, a friend of Jesus who was present at the Crucifixion and went to the tomb. (See *Magdalene.*) *Mark 16:9; Luke 8:1-2; John 20:1-2, 11-18.*
3. Mary of Bethany, the sister of Lazarus and Martha. This Mary felt a deep devotion to Jesus. The gospel stories show that she was a thoughtful person who spent much time considering the words of Jesus and their meaning. *Luke 10:38-42; John 11:1–12:8.*
4. There are several other Marys mentioned in the Gospels who were relatives of the disciples and so associated in the ministry of Jesus. *Matthew 27:55, 61; 28:1; Mark 15:40, 47; 16:1; Luke 24:9-11; John 19:25.*

MASTER
(MAS-tuhr)

Meaning "manager" or "chief"; a person with authority over others. Used in the NT as a title for Jesus Christ. *Genesis 24:27; Judges 19:11-12; 2 Kings 6:23; Isaiah 37:4; Malachi 1:6; Matthew 24:45-51; 26:25; Mark 9:5; Luke 8:24; 9:49; Ephesians 6:9.*

MATTHEW
(MATH-u)

One of the twelve apostles of Jesus. A collector of taxes on the goods carried over the Damascus Road, and perhaps on the fishing industry and other industries in Capernaum. It is possible that Matthew and Levi are the same person. (See *Matthew, Book of.*) *Matthew 9:9; 10:3; Luke 6:15; Acts 1:13.*

MATTHEW, GOSPEL OF

First in the arrangement of books in the NT, this book probably was written sometime close to A.D. 100. Matthew based his writing on the material in Mark's Gospel and on a collection of Jesus' sayings which had been made at that time. Written especially for the Jewish Christians of the time, the book used many quotations from the OT to show how Jesus was the fulfillment of old prophecies, and had given the old laws new meaning. *See the book itself.*

MATTHIAS
(muh-THYE-uhss)

The apostle chosen by casting lots to fill the place left vacant by Judas

Iscariot. He is credited with helping to bring the gospel to Armenia, which is part of Russia today. *Acts 1:23-26.*

MEAL

A coarse type of flour ground from whole kernels of wheat or barley. Fine flour was prepared from the inner kernels only. In early Bible history meal was more commonly used than flour. Meal was ground by the women before dawn and only enough was ground for a day's use. *Genesis 18:6; Numbers 5:15; 1 Kings 17:12; 1 Chronicles 12:40; Nehemiah 10:37; Hosea 8:7; Luke 13:21.*

MEDIA
(MEE-dee-uh)

In OT times a province in the Persian Empire in what is now northwestern Iran. The Israelites were exiled to the "cities of the Medes" by the Assyrian king who conquered Samaria in 722 B.C. According to the report in Daniel, the laws of the Medes and Persians could not be changed. Today the phrase "of the Medes and Persians" is used to indicate any law that is firm. *2 Kings 17:6; 18:11; Ezra 6:2-4; Esther 1:3, 14, 18-19; Daniel 5:28; 6:8, 12, 15; 8:20.*

MARY OF BETHANY

MEEKNESS

In OT usage, complete dependence upon God rather than on oneself. The opposite of pride. In the NT the word is used by Jesus in the Beatitudes to indicate one attitude needed to be blessed, and by Paul in the Epistles to show that meekness is becoming to a Christian. In general usage, it is the quality of a person with a gentle and quiet spirit of thoughtful courtesy in dealing with others. *Numbers 12:3; Psalms 10:17; 37:11; Matthew 5:5; 2 Corinthians 10:1; Ephesians 4:2; James 1:21; 3:13.*

MEGIDDO
(meh-GID-oh)

An important Canaanite and later Israelite city in north central Palestine overlooking the Valley of Jezreel. It controlled an important mountain pass. King Solomon made Megiddo into a royal chariot city, and archaeologists have uncovered the remains of his fine stables. *Joshua 12:21; 17:11; Judges 1:27; 5:19; 1 Kings 9:15; 2 Kings 23:29-30; 2 Chronicles 35:20-22.*

MELCHIZEDEK
(mel-KIZ-uh-dek)

In early OT times, a Canaanite king and priest who prepared a meal for Abraham and blessed him. Since Melchizedek had both royal and priestly authority in the city of Salem (Jerusalem) before the Israelites came, David claimed to be his successor. Melchizedek became the symbol of an ideal priest-king. *Genesis 14:18-20; Psalm 110:4; Hebrews 5:6, 8-10; 6:20; 7:1-4, 10-11, 15-17.*

MENAHEM
(MEN-uh-hem)

King of Israel about 752–742 B.C. He gained the throne by murdering Shallum. He was obliged to pay tribute to Tiglath-pileser III of Assyria. *2 Kings 15:13-22.*

MEPHIBOSHETH
(me-FIB-oh-SHETH)

Jonathan's lame son and a grandson of King Saul. King David showed great kindness to Mephibosheth and took him into his own household in memory of his friendship with Jonathan. (See *Machir.*) *2 Samuel 4:4; 9:1-13; 16:1-4; 19:24-30; 21:7-8.*

MERCY, MERCIFUL
(MUR-see)

In the OT the continued steadfast love of God by which he keeps his covenant relationship with his people Israel; the quality of having mercy. Human mercy is the quality of kindness and consideration for the needs of others that God requires of God's people. This understanding of mercy is also found in the NT, especially in the Beatitudes where Jesus' words seem to mean that to expect mercy for himself a person must show mercy to others. *Exodus 34:6; 2 Samuel 24:14; Psalms 23:6; 51:1; 103:4; 145:8; Jeremiah 6:23; Lamentations 2:21; Matthew 5:7; 9:13; 15:22; Luke 10:36-37; 2 Corinthians 1:3; and other references.*

MERCY SEAT

A slab of especially refined gold with a cherub at each end on top of the ark of the covenant. It was reverenced as God's throne, the symbol of God's presence in the temple. The mercy seat was sprinkled with blood on the Day of Atonement. *Exodus 25:17-22; 26:34; 37:6-9; Leviticus 16:2-5; Numbers 7:89; 1 Chronicles 28:11; Hebrews 9:5.*

MEROM, WATERS OF
(MEE-rom)

A body of water near the Jordan and not far from the Sea of Galilee. Where the Israelites led by Joshua defeated a large army of Canaanites. *Joshua 11:1-9.*

MESHACH

See *Shadrach, Meshach, Abednego.*

MESOPOTAMIA
(mess-uh-poh-TAY-mee-uh)

In OT times the land between the Tigris and Euphrates rivers. The borders of Mesopotamia changed many times in its long history. It now lies partly in Syria and partly in Iraq. Much of the culture of the Hebrews came from this region. Abraham came from Haran, an area in northern Mesopotamia known as Paddan-aram, and the Hebrews had connections with this area throughout their history. *Genesis 24:10; Deuteronomy 23:4; Judges 3:8, 10; 1 Chronicles 19:6; Acts 2:9; 7:2.*

KING DAVID CARES FOR MEPHIBOSHETH

MESSIAH
(muh-SYE-uh)
Meaning "anointed one." The word does not appear in the OT. However, the Hebrews throughout their history had looked forward to the coming of an ideal king whom they believed God would send to restore a kingdom to Israel. The title of Messiah was given to Jesus by some who recognized him as the long-awaited king. (See *Holy One*.) *John 1:41; 4:25.*

MICAH
(MYE-kuh)
A prophet of the southern kingdom of Judah during the reigns of Jotham, Ahaz, and Hezekiah. Micah must have had a long life in the years between 740 and 687 B.C. At this time Isaiah was preaching in Jerusalem. Micah was from a small village of the Shephelah, low foothills of southwestern Palestine, and he loved the country people and their ways better than the corrupt city dwellers of his day. (See *Micah, Book of*.)

MICAH, BOOK OF
A prophetic book in the OT containing prophecies and warnings of the prophet Micah. There are also a few of what appear to be writings of a later prophet. Having watched the northern kingdom of Israel and its capital Samaria fall to the Assyrians in 722 B.C., Micah warned the people of Judah to return to the law of God and to pure worship of God so that a similar disaster would not befall them. *See the book itself.*

MICAIAH
(mye-KYE-uh)
A prophet in the ninth century B.C. during the reign of King Ahab of Israel. He was put in prison for speaking the truth to the king in contrast to four hundred false prophets who gave the king favorable answers to his questions concerning a military undertaking at Ramoth-gilead. Ahab was killed there. *1 Kings 22:8-28; 2 Chronicles 18:7-27.*

MICHAEL
(MYE-kuhl)
A name used to refer to a heavenly being who was the protector of Israel. The Revelation describes Michael as fighting Satan and the rebel angels during the war in heaven. *Daniel 12:1; Jude 1:9; Revelation 12:7-8.*

MICHAL
(MYE-keul)
Daughter of Saul and wife of David. Michal had no children. *1 Samuel 14:49; 18:20-27; 19:11-17; 25:44 2 Samuel 3:13-16; 6:16-23.*

MICHMASH
(MIK-mash)
A city in the mountains about seven miles northeast of Jerusalem. The rugged mountain area made a kind of natural fortress for this city. The Philistines made their camp in this place and fought with the armies of Israel led by Saul and Jonathan. Later, Nehemiah mentions the men of Michmash (Michmas) as people returned from exile. *1 Samuel*

MIDIANITES

13:2, 5, 11, 16-18, 23; 14:5, 31; Ezra 2:27; Nehemiah 7:31; 11:31-35; Isaiah 10:28.

MIDIAN
(MID-ee-uhn)
Son of Keturah, Abraham's third wife. He was the ancestor of the wandering tribes of Midianites. The "land of Midian" lay in northwestern Arabia on the eastern shore of the Gulf of Aqabah. *Genesis 25:2, 4; Exodus 2:15-16; 3:1; Judges 6:1-14; 7:1-25; 1 Kings 11:18; Psalm 83:9; Isaiah 9:4; 10:26; 60:6; Habakkuk 3:7.*

MIDIANITES
(MID-ee-uhn-ites)
Riding swift camels, these fierce nomads frequently made raids upon the Israelites in Canaan after the exodus from Egypt. As far as is known, the Midianites were among the first people to make effective use of the camel, thus increasing their swift striking power. *Genesis 37:28; Judges 6:1-16; 7:1-25.*

MIDWIFE
A woman skilled in helping during childbirth. Both Rachel and Tamar were attended by midwives. The best-known midwives in the Bible are the two who refused to carry out the command of Pharaoh to kill all male children born to the Israelites. *Genesis 35:17, 18; 38:28; Exodus 1:15-21.*

MIKTAM
(MIK-tam)
The heading of Psalms 16 and 56–60. The meaning is uncertain, but it may mean "to atone" (restore friendly relations with God) or "to cover the sin." Thus these would be psalms of atonement, that is, songs of praise and thanksgiving that someone who has been separated from God by sin has been restored to God. *Psalm 16; 56; 60.*

MILETUS
(mye-LEE-tuhs)
An ancient Greek city on the west coast of Asia Minor. In the days when Paul visited Miletus the port was still active and prominent. Its location made it a natural stopping place for Paul on his way to Jerusalem from Europe. It was close enough to Ephesus so that the church elders from that city were able to visit him at Miletus. The city has been excavated by archaeologists. *Acts 20:15, 17; 2 Timothy 4:20.*

MILL, MILLSTONES

A machine made from two hard rough stones used for grinding grain into meal or flour; the stones themselves. One type of mill consisted of a rectangle stone, slightly hollowed out, upon which a smaller stone, flat on one side, was placed. Grinding was done by pushing the upper, smaller stone back and forth on the larger stone where the grain had been placed. Another type of mill consisted of two round stones fitted together snugly. The top stone often had a hole in the center, through which grain was poured, and a handle for turning the top stone. Both types of mills were used in the home and were usually worked by women. There were also large community mills in which a heavy stone shaped like a wheel was placed on a large, round, lower stone and rolled around by an animal. The upper stone of a mill, called a millstone, was sometimes used as a weapon. *Deuteronomy 24:6; Judges 9:53; Job 41:24; Isaiah 47:2; Jeremiah 25:10; Matthew 18:6; 24:41; Mark 9:42; Luke 17:2; Revelation 18:21-22.*

MILLET

(MIL-et)

The smallest of grass seeds cultivated for food. It makes poor quality bread and is usually mixed with other grains. *Ezekiel 4:9.*

MILLO

(MIL-oh)

A part of the fortifying structure around the city of David. It was probably built on a platform of packed earth. This defense of Jerusalem was started by David but credited to Solomon. *2 Samuel 5:9; 1 Kings 9:14-15, 24; 11:27; 1 Chronicles 11:8; 2 Chronicles 32:5.*

MINISTER

(MIN-i-stur)

As a noun it means "one who serves." In the OT it was used most often as a verb meaning "to serve," especially to serve God in worship and in carrying out sacrifices. In the NT Jesus showed by his own life the importance of humble service. He said, "I am among you as one who serves." Paul referred to himself as a minister or servant of the gospel. *Exodus 28:43; Numbers 11:28; Ezra 8:15, 17; Isaiah 61:6; Jeremiah 33:21; Joel 1:9; Acts 8:27; Ephesians 3:7; 6:21; Colossians 1:7, 23, 25; 1 Timothy 4:6.*

MINT

A sweet-smelling herb used in medicine and for seasoning food. The Pharisees required that mint and other herbs be included by the Jews in their tithe (tenth). Mint was probably included in the bitter herbs eaten with the Paschal lamb (see Exodus 12:8). *Matthew 23:23; Luke 11:42.*

MIRACLE

(MIHR-uh-kuhl)

In a broad definition any event in which one sees the supernatural power of God at work. Other words used to mean miracle in the Bible are "signs," "wonders," "mighty acts" (see John 2:11; 6:14). *Exodus 4:21; 7:9; 15:11; Psalm 105:5; Acts 8:13; 19:11; 1 Corinthians 12:10; Galatians 3:5.*

MIRIAM

MIZPAH, MISPEH

(MIZ-pah)

Meaning "watchtower" or "lookout point." When Jacob and his uncle Laban settled an argument, they erected a pillar called Mizpah (watch post) in memory of Jacob's words, "The Lord watch between you and me, when we are absent one from the other." This has come to be called the Mizpah benediction and is often used in churches today (Genesis 31:49). It was the name of several towns and cities in OT times, the most important of which was on the border between the southern kingdom of Judah and the northern kingdom of Israel. Here archaeologists have discovered what are probably the ruins of the fortifications built by King Asa. This city was a boundary fortress between Judah and Israel. After the fall of Jerusalem to the Babylonian province with Mizpah as its capital. Mizpah seems to have become a center of worship also, thus taking the place of Jerusalem as both a political and religious center. *Joshua 11:3, 8; Judges 10:17; 11:11, 29; 1 Samuel 7:5-16; 2 Kings 25:23, 25; 2 Chronicles 16:6; Nehemiah 3:7, 15, 19; Jeremiah 40:6; 41:3.*

MIRIAM

(MIHr-ee-uhm)

Sister of Moses and Aaron. She is mentioned in several stories with Moses and Aaron. Though she is not named, we are told that the sister of the infant Moses kept watch over the baby in the basket and after his discovery ran to get their own mother for his nurse (see Exodus 2:4, 7-8). Her song of victory when the Israelites crossed the Red Sea is one of the earliest fragments of Hebrew poetry. *Exodus 15:20-21; Numbers 12:1-15; 20:1; Micah 6:4.*

MOAB
(MOH-ab)

A high rolling plateau east of the Dead Sea about three thousand feet above sea level. The Moabites were considered to be descended from Abraham's nephew Lot and so related to the Israelites. They were among those tribes who opposed the Israelites on their way from Egypt to Canaan. From the time of the Exodus until the fall of Jerusalem, Moab was often in conflict with Israel. At one time under King David the Moabites were forced to pay tribute to Israel. A Moabite stone found in 1868 and now in the Louvre in France bears an inscription to King Mesha of Moab, who won a victory over Israel. *Numbers 21:11, 26; 22:1; Deuteronomy 2:8-37; 29:1; 34:1-8; Judges 3:12-14; 2 Kings 1:1; 1 Chronicles 18:2; Isaiah 15:1–16:14; Jeremiah 48:1-47; Amos 2:1-3.*

MOLECH, MOLOCH
(MOH-lek)

A god of the Canaanites to whom children were sacrificed by forcing them to walk through fire. Although it was forbidden by their law, some Israelites also sacrificed their children. Most of these sacrifices took place in the Valley of Hinnom, southwest of Jerusalem. In King Josiah's reign the place of sacrifice was destroyed. *Leviticus 18:21; 20:2-5; 1 Kings 11:7; 2 Kings 23:10; Jeremiah 32:35.*

MOLTEN IMAGE

A representation of a god made from melted metal. Among ancient peoples it was the practice to make an image of a god for use in worship. Molten images were made by pouring melted gold, silver, iron, or bronze over a prepared form of wood or clay or into a mold. This practice was forbidden to the Hebrews. *Exodus 34:17; Leviticus 19:4; Deuteronomy 27:15; Nahum 1:14; and other references.*

MONEY

Something which is generally accepted as a means of payment for goods. In early Bible times cattle, oil, corn, wine, and wheat were used as payment in barter or exchange for other goods. Later, pieces of copper, silver, and gold molded into various shapes came into use. To make certain full value was being received, the metal was always weighed before it was accepted as payment. When coins came into use, they were stamped with the weight of the coin which also became the name of the coin. For example, "shekel" could refer to a coin or to its weight. Many coins of different nations were in use in NT times, circulating throughout the world. *Genesis 33:19; Exodus 30:13-16; Leviticus 25:37; Numbers 3:48-51; Joshua 24:32; Judges 17:2-4; 2 Kings 5:26; 12:4-16; Jeremiah 32:9-10; Matthew 22:19; 25:18; Luke 9:3; 19:23; John 12:5-6; Acts 4:37; 8:18.*

MONEY-CHANGER

The term used in ancient times for a man who carried on many of the duties of a modern banker. One of his important services was exchanging coins of one country or province for those of another. In NT times a money-changer was a person who exchanged foreign coins for the half-shekel silver coins minted in Tyre that were used to pay the annual temple tax. Roman and other foreign coins were not acceptable to the Jews because they usually had stamped on them representations of pagan gods. The money-changers received a small fee for their services, but sometimes their charges were excessive. At Passover time money-changers set up their tables in the temple courts. On one of his visits to the temple Jesus drove out the money-changers. *Matthew 21:12; Mark 11:15; John 2:13-15; 17:24.*

MORDECAI
(MOR-duh-kye)
The Jewish hero of the book of Esther. The story tells how he and his cousin, Esther, queen of the Persian king

Ahasuerus, uncovered a plot to kill Mordecai and all other Jews in the Persian Empire. *Esther 2:5–10:3.*

MORESHETH
(MOR-uh-sheth)
Home of the prophet Micah in the foothills of southwestern Judah. It is now Tell ej-Judeideh. *Jeremiah 26:18; Micah 1:1.*

MORIAH
(mor-EYE-uh)
A rocky hilltop north of Jerusalem where Solomon built the temple. It was said to be the place where Abraham made ready to sacrifice his son Isaac. *Genesis 22:2; 2 Chronicles 3:1.*

JESUS AND THE MONEY-CHANGERS

MORTAR

A building material, usually clay mixed with straw and used while damp and soft to bind bricks or stones together. Also, a bowl in which grain, herbs, spices, and dyes were powdered and crushed with a club-shaped implement called a pestle. *Genesis 11:3; Exodus 1:14; Numbers 11:8; Proverbs 27:22; Isaiah 41:25; Nahum 3:14.*

MOSES

(MOH-zuhss)

Leader of the Hebrew tribes in their escape from Egypt and on their journey to Canaan. In the OT, Moses is considered the most significant figure in the history of Israel. He was prophet, priest, judge, and lawgiver. He was the interpreter of God's laws by which the people were expected to live in their special covenant relation. The Exodus under Moses' leadership was the beginning of Israel as a people. His life story is told in the first part of the OT known as the Pentateuch. It tells of his birth, when he narrowly escaped death by being hidden in a basket-like boat. It describes his struggles with the pharaoh in Egypt and with the Israelites in the wilderness. Moses died on Mt. Nebo just as he had brought the Hebrews to the border of the Promised Land of Canaan. *See the book of Exodus, Leviticus, Numbers and Deuteronomy. Psalm 103:7; Matthew 17:3-4; Luke 16:29-31; John 1:17; Acts 7:20-44; Hebrews 11:23-24.*

MOST HOLY PLACE

The innermost room of the tabernacle and temple in which the ark of the covenant was placed. The place where the priests of Aaron ate the offerings not burned was also called a most holy place. (See *Sacrifices and Offerings.*) *Exodus 26:33-34; 2 Chronicles 3:8, 10; 5:7; Ezekiel 41:4.*

MOUND, SIEGE

In OT times a temporary ramplike structure built outside the wall of a city in order to lay siege to it. From the siege mound arrows and stones could be hurled over the wall into a city by a siege engine, and the wall could be climbed. *2 Samuel 20:15; Isaiah 37:33; Jeremiah 6:6; 32:24; Ezekiel 17:17; 21:22.*

MOURNING

An expression of grief. Funeral customs in Bible times included tearing one's clothing, sitting in ashes, fasting, wailing, and singing songs of lamentation. Sometimes there were paid professional mourners who sang songs of lament accompanied by musical instruments. *Genesis 37:34; 50:10-11; 1 Samuel 25:1; 2 Samuel 1:11-12; 3:31; 11:27; 1 Kings 14:13; 2 Chronicles 35:24; Jeremiah 4:28; Lamentations 1:4; Amos 5:16; 8:10; Zechariah 12:11-14; Matthew 11:17.*

MOSES AND THE PRINCESS

MUSICAL INSTRUMENTS

The Bible refers to musical instruments mainly as part of temple worship, but they were also used along with songs and chants at weddings, banquets, and funerals. There was a wide variety of instruments: stringed instruments such as the harp (small enough to be held in the hand) and the lute (gut strings on a wooden frame); wind instruments such as the flute (made of reed pipes), horns (made of an animal horn), and trumpets (of metal); noisemakers such as bells, tambourines, or timbrels (usually played by women for dancing), cymbals, castanets, and gongs. The shophar, or ram's horn, is still used in synagogues today. *Exodus 39:25-26; 1 Samuel 10:5; 1 Chronicles 16:42; 25:1; 2 Chronicles 5:11-13; 29:25-30; Ezra 3:10-11; Nehemiah 12:27; Psalm 150:3-5; Daniel 3:7, 10; Matthew 9:23; 1 Corinthians 13:1; Revelation 14:2-3.*

MYRRH
(mur)

A fragrant gumlike substance derived from various shrubs and trees found mostly in southern Arabia. In the OT an important ingredient in the sacred anointing oil and in perfumes. Myrrh mixed with wine was given to relieve pain. *Genesis 37:25; Exodus 30:22-25; 2 Chronicles 9:24; Psalm 45:8; Proverbs 7:17; Song of Solomon 1:13; 3:6; 4:6, 14; Matthew 2:11; Mark 15:23; John 19:39.*

MYRTLE
(MERT-uhl)

A leafy shrub used with other shrubs for covering the festival booths in which the Hebrews lived during Feast of Booths. *Nehemiah 8:15; Isaiah 41:19; 55:13; Zechariah 1:7-11.*

MYSTERY

A hidden religious truth. In the NT the word refers to the plan and purpose of God hidden from all except those who see it revealed in the life and ministry of Jesus. *Daniel 2:18-19, 27-28; 1 Corinthians 15:51; Ephesians 1:9-10; 3:3-4, 9-10; 6:19; Colossians 1:26-27; 1 Timothy 3:9, 16; Revelation 10:7.*

MYTH
(mith)

A story told to explain an event or happening which is not understood or a custom or practice the beginning of which has been forgotten. (See *Allegory, Parable.*) *1 Timothy 1:4; 4:7; Titus 1:14; 2 Peter 1:16.*

SHOPHAR

NAAMAN
(NAY-uh-muhn)
Commander of the Syrian army who was cured of his leprosy by Elisha, a Hebrew prophet. *2 Kings 5:1-17.*

NABOTH
(NAY-both)
Owner of a vineyard in Jezreel close to King Ahab's country palace. The king wanted the vineyard and offered to buy it, but Naboth did not wish to sell his land. Hebrew law forbade the king to take away land belonging to the people. Jezebel, Ahab's wife, had a deceitful plan to get the land, and Naboth lost his vineyard and his life. *1 Kings 21:1-29; 2 Kings 9:21-26.*

NADAB
(NAY-dab)
King of Israel about 910–909 B.C., son and successor of Jeroboam I. He was murdered by Baasha, who then succeeded him on the throne. Also the name of several other men mentioned in the OT. *1 Kings 15:25-27.*

NAHASH
(NAY-hash)
Ruler of the Ammonites who was defeated by Saul. This military victory led to Israel's acceptance of Saul as king. *1 Samuel 11:1-2; 2 Samuel 10:2.*

NAHOR
(NAY-hor)
1. In the OT genealogies the name of the grandfather of Abraham and also of Abraham's brother. *Genesis 11:22-26;*

22:20; *Joshua 24:2.*

2. The name of a city near Haran in Mesopotamia. *Genesis 24:10.*

NAHUM

(NAY-huhm)

A prophet in the southern kingdom Judah in the seventh century B.C. At this time the Babylonian Empire was growing strong. The armies of the Babylonians attacked and defeated the Assyrian capital of Nineveh. Nahum saw the fall of the Assyrian enemy as a great blessing from God to Israel. (See *Nahum, Book of.*)

NAHUM, BOOK OF

A short prophetic book in the OT containing the prophecies of Nahum. Nahum's writing is different from other OT prophets in that he emphasizes the downfall of an enemy rather than the corruption of the Hebrew nation. *See the book itself.*

NAME

The title by which a person is known. For the Hebrews a person's name was an expression of his character or personality. In the Bible when a name was changed, as from Jacob to Israel or Saul to Paul, it meant a change in character or, as in Abram to Abraham, a change in relationship with God. Many names were given that recalled some particular event or a circumstance attending a person's birth or that expressed gratitude for his birth. Many of the place names in Palestine were established before the Israelites conquered the land and so do not necessarily show Israel's beliefs and practices. Many of these names indicate social or religious customs, the size of the town, the occupation of its inhabitants, or the persons who were important to the place. Such expressions as "the name of the Lord" or "in the name of Christ" mean "by his authority." "For his name's sake" means "according to his nature." *Genesis 25:25-26; 27:36; 32:28; 35:18; 1 Samuel 4:21; 25:25; 1 Chronicles 4:9; Psalms 8:1; 76:1; Jeremiah 14:7; Matthew 6:9; Mark 3:17; Acts 3:16; 4:12; Philippians 2:9-10; and many other references.*

NAMING OF JOHN

NAOMI

(nay-OH-mee)
One of the leading characters in the book of Ruth. Naomi returned to Bethlehem after the death of her husband, accompanied by her faithful daughter-in-law Ruth, also a widow. Naomi encouraged Ruth to accept the protection of their kinsman Boaz, whom Ruth later married. *Ruth 1:1–4:22.*

NAPHTALI

(NAF-tuh-lee)
One of the twelve sons of Jacob from whom the tribe of Naphtali was descended. It was also the name of their territory which lay west of the Jordan River from Lake Huleh to the southern end of the Sea of Galilee. *Exodus 1:4; Numbers 1:42-43; Joshua 19:32-39; 20:7; Isaiah 9:1; Matthew 4:13, 15.*

NARD

(nahrd)
An expensive fragrant ointment prepared from the roots and stems of the spikenard which grows in India, Nepal, Bhutan, and the valleys of Tibet. The Romans used the ointment to anoint the head. One pound cost three hundred denarii. A denarius was a day's wages for a laborer. *Song of Solomon 1:12; 4:13-14; Mark 14:3; John 12:3.*

NATHAN

(NAY-thuhn)
A prophet in the time of David and Solomon. He was the friend and counselor of King David. After David committed his great sin Nathan went to him to accuse him of his crime. This took great courage as kings in those times could have those who displeased them put to death. Nathan also played an important part in having Solomon made king after David's death. According to 1 Chronicles 29:29 and 2 Chronicles 9:29, Nathan kept records about the acts of David and Solomon, but these have never been found. *2 Samuel 7:1-17; 12:1-15, 24-25; 1 Kings 1:5-48.*

NATHANAEL

(nuh-THAN-ee-uhl)
Mentioned only in the Gospel of John as one of the disciples of Jesus. Many believe him to be the apostle called Bartholomew in the other three Gospels. (See *Bartholomew.*) *John 1:45-49; 21:2.*

NATIONS

In biblical times "nations" referred to the whole of mankind divided into kinship groups, not into countries or states as we know them today. Genesis 10 lists seventy different groups of people. Among them were the ancestors of the Hebrews. These peoples were scattered throughout the ancient Near East, and their boundaries constantly changed throughout OT times as they conquered neighboring nations or were conquered by them. Israel felt its importance among the nations because of its covenant with God. This made the Hebrews a holy people among all the nations of the earth.

NAOMI AND HER DAUGHTERS-IN-LAW

Genesis 10:1-32; 12:1-3; Exodus 19:3-6; Psalm 106:41; Matthew 24:9; 28:19; Luke 21:24; Revelation 7:9.

NAVE

(nayv)

The main room of the temple between the vestibule and the inner room. *1 Kings 6:3, 5, 17; 7:50; 2 Chronicles 3:4-5, 13; 4:22; Ezekiel 41:1-4, 23-26.*

NAZARENE

(NAZ-uh-reen)

A native of Nazareth. A NT title for Jesus because he came from the village Nazareth. Early Christians may have been called Nazarenes by Jews who wished to make fun of them. Possibly the members of a Jewish sect whose beliefs were not the traditional Jewish beliefs were also called Nazarenes. *Matthew 2:23; Mark 14:67; Acts 24:5.*

NAZARETH

(NAZ-uh-reth)

The village where Jesus lived as a child and where he grew to manhood. It is about fifteen miles from the Sea of Galilee and twenty miles from the Mediterranean. In Jesus' day Nazareth was a small, insignificant village located on a hillside. Modern Nazareth is an important city of nearly twenty thousand people and has a large Christian population. *Matthew 2:23; 21:11; Mark 1:9, 24; 10:47; Luke 2:4-5, 39, 51; 4:16, 34; John 1:45-46; 18:5, 7; 19:19; Acts 2:22; 3:6.*

NAZARITE

(NAZ-uh-rite)

In the OT a person who took a vow of dedication to serve God by following certain rules. For example, a Nazarite did not cut his hair or take wine and strong drink. At first the vow was for life, but later one could become a Nazarite for a temporary period. When the vow had been fulfilled, his hair was cut and burned on the altar as an offering. The Nazarite was not a priest but was looked upon as a holy man. *Numbers 6:1-21; Judges 13:5, 7; 16:17; Amos 2:11-12.*

NEBO, MOUNT

(NEE-boh)

A mountain opposite Jericho twelve miles east of the mouth of the Jordan River. In Deuteronomy 32 is recorded a song of Moses, spoken before he climbed this mountain for a view of Canaan. He died there. *Deuteronomy 34:1-5.*

NEBUCHADNEZZAR, NEBUCHADREZZAR

(neb-uh-kuhd-NEZ-ur, nebuh-kuhd-REZ-uhr) (Spelled Nebuchadrezzar in the books of Jeremiah and Ezekiel)

King of Babylonia 605–562 B.C., whose empire succeeded that of the Assyrians. His marriage to Amyitis of Media united the Medes and the Chaldeans. During his long reign gates and temples were built in Babylon, and enormous walls were constructed around the city. He conquered Syria and Judah. He destroyed Jerusalem and took a large number of Jews into captivity in Babylon. *2 Kings 24:1-17; 25:1-30; 2 Chronicles 36:6-21; Ezra 2:1; Jeremiah 21:2-10; 22:24-25; 27:6-8; and other places in Jeremiah; Ezekiel 26:7; 29:18-19; Daniel 1:1.*

NECO

(NEK-oh)

An Egyptian pharaoh who reigned from 609 to 594 B.C. Neco felt the time was right to expand the Egyptian Empire into Palestine because the power of the Assyrians who had held it so long was weakening. When Neco entered Palestine with his army, Josiah, the king of Judah, tried to stop him but was killed in the effort. Neco seized control of Judah. However, a few years later Nebuchadnezzar, the king of Babylon, defeated Neco and drove him back into Egypt. *2 Kings 23:29-35; Jeremiah 46:2.*

NECROMANCY

(NEK-ruh-man-see)

In OT times a form of reading the future by communicating with the dead. Such practice was forbidden to the Hebrews. *Deuteronomy 18:10-11.*

NEGEB, THE

(NEG-eb)

A region of the southern part of Canaan with numerous cities and good pastureland. The original inhabitants were the Amalekites. David incorporated the entire Negeb into the kingdom of Judah. After biblical times, due to the devastation of war and the neglect of the vegetation (which helped to hold the moisture in the soil), the Negeb became a desert. Now as a part of modern Israel the land is being restored. *Genesis 12:9; 13:1-3; Numbers 13:29; 1 Samuel 27:10; Psalm 126:4; Jeremiah 32:44.*

NEHEMIAH

(nee-uh-MYE-uh)

A Jew living in exile in Persia. He was cupbearer to the Persian king Artaxerxes I, who reigned from about 465 to 424 B.C. Nehemiah was grieved at the news that Jerusalem was still in ruins a century and a half after the first exiles had returned there. He received permission from the king to go to Jerusalem to help in the rebuilding of the city and its wall. (See *Nehemiah, Book of.*)

NEHEMIAH

NEHEMIAH, BOOK OF

Originally the book of Ezra and the book of Nehemiah were a single book. They tell of the work of restoring Jerusalem. *See the book itself; the book of Ezra.*

NETTLE

(NET-uhl)

A wild plant which grows rapidly and is noted for its stinging effect when touched. At least four species are known in Bible lands. Nettles quickly grow up in neglected fields. OT writers often used the word to indicate extreme poverty and the destruction and desolation of an area. *Job 30:7; Proverbs 24:31; Isaiah 34:13; Hosea 9:6; Zephaniah 2:9.*

NETS

Mesh traps woven of twine or cord and used for catching fish, birds, and animals. In Bible times fishing nets were of two types. One was a cone-shaped net with lead weights around the mouth to pull it down under the surface of the water. It was cast by hand. The other was a large dragnet fitted with floats and sinkers that was let out from the beach and hauled ashore in wide semicircles. *Psalm 9:15; Isaiah 51:20; Ezekiel 12:13; Mark 1:16-19; Matthew 13:47; John 21:6-8.*

NETWORK

In the OT a bronze grating on the altar of burnt offering before the tabernacle. Also, a bronze grill or latticed work used in connection with the pillars of Solomon's temple. *Exodus 27;4-5; 38:4; 1 Kings 7:18, 20, 41-42; Jeremiah 52:22-23.*

NEW MOON

The beginning of the month. It was observed as a holy day of rejoicing, special feasting, and sacrifices. *1 Samuel 20:24; Ezra 3:5; Nehemiah 10:33; Isaiah 1:13-14; 47:13; Hosea 2:11; Amos 8:4-5; Colossians 2:16.*

NICODEMUS

(nik-uh-DEE-muhss)

A member of the Jewish Sanhedrin. He came to Jesus secretly at night to ask questions and hear more of Jesus' teachings. He became a secret follower of Jesus. *John 3:1-9; 7:50-52; 19:38-41.*

NILE

(nighl)

The principal river of Egypt, nearly 3,500 miles long. It rises in the highlands of east central Africa and empties into the Mediterranean Sea. The life of Egypt has always been dependent upon the annual flooding of the river valley which spreads a rich, muddy soil over the flatlands on both sides of the riverbanks. In ancient times the annual flood was greeted with celebrations, and the Egyptians considered the river to be a god. *Genesis 41:1-3; Exodus 1:22; Isaiah 23:10; Ezekiel 29:9; Amos 9:5; Nahum 3:8.*

NINEVEH
(NIN-uh-vuh)

Capital city of the Assyrian Empire, located on the east side of the upper Tigris River. One of the oldest and greatest cities of Mesopotamia. Nineveh dates back to prehistoric times. It reached its greatest fame in the eighth century B.C. The Israelites feared and hated Nineveh because it represented the constant threat and oppression of the Assyrians. The Hebrew prophets Nahum and Zephaniah saw its wickedness and proclaimed its destruction. Nineveh was captured and destroyed by the Babylonians in 612 B.C. *Genesis 10:11-12; 2 Kings 19:36; Jonah 1:2; 3:2-9; 4:11; Nahum 1:1 2:8; 3:7; Zephaniah 2:13; Luke 11:30, 32.*

NOAH
(NOH-uh)

Hero of the OT story of the Flood. Because of the wickedness and violence of men God purposed to destroy the earth. He told Noah to build an ark (boat) large enough to hold his entire family and a pair of each kind of animal. Those in the ark were the only survivors of the Great Flood which covered the world. *Genesis 6:5–9:29.*

NUMBERS, BOOK OF
(NUHM-burz)

The fourth book of the OT. It continues the history of the people of Israel begun in the book of Exodus. The title refers to a census, or counting, of the tribes described in the opening chapters. *See the book itself.*

NOAH BUILDS THE ARK

OAK

A tree noted for its size and strength. In the OT it was often associated with a sacred place, an important event, or a person. *Genesis 12:6; 13:18; 35:4, 8; 2 Samuel 18:9-10; Isaiah 6:13; 44:14; Hosea 4:13.*

OATH
(ohth)

A solemn statement made by an individual and often accompanied by formal words and actions as a guarantee that what he has said or promised is true. The oath was very important in the life of the Hebrew community. Often God was called upon as a witness to an oath (see Psalm 7:3-5), and some symbolic act such as putting a hand on one's head or raising the hands toward heaven was performed. If the statements made with an oath were not true or if the promises made were not kept, it was a most serious

matter. The name of God had been dishonored. Jesus urged that all oaths be omitted and that a person take care to mean what he said in every situation (see Matthew 5:33-37). *Genesis 26:28-29; Leviticus 5:4; 2 Chronicles 6:22-23; Ezekiel 10:5; James 5:12.*

OBADIAH
(oh-buh-DYE-uh)

A prophet whose visions and oracles are in a book of the OT. (See *Obadiah, Book of.*)

OBADIAH, BOOK OF

A book of prophecy, the shortest in the OT. The date is uncertain, but it was probably written after the destruction of Jerusalem in 586 B.C. It describes the suffering of Jerusalem and the revengeful behavior of the nation of Edom toward Judah at the time of this disaster. The prophet foretold the doom of Edom as punishment for rejoicing in her neighbor's grief. The restoration of Judah is also predicted. *See the book itself.*

OBED

(OH-bid)
Son of Ruth and Boaz and grandfather of King David. According to the Gospels of Matthew and Luke he became an ancestor of Jesus. Several men named Obed are mentioned in the OT. *Ruth 4:17, 21-22; 1 Chronicles 2:12; Matthew 1:5; Luke 3:32.*

OBEISANCE

(oh-BEE-uhns)
In the OT the word means "to bow down" or "to touch one's face to the ground" as a sign of submission or as an act of worship or honor. *Genesis 43:28; 1 Samuel 24:8; 2 Samuel 15:5; 1 Chronicles 21:21; 2 Chronicles 24:17.*

ODOR

(OHD-er)
Scent or fragrance. In the morning and evening services of worship in OT times the sacrifices and offerings were burned so that the smoke could rise as a pleasant odor before

God. In the NT one's acts of love are spoken of in a figure of speech as a fragrant offering to God in the name of Christ (see Ephesians 5:2). *Exodus 29:18, 25, 41; Leviticus 1:9; Numbers 15:24; and other places in Leviticus and Numbers; Ezekiel 6:13.*

OFFERING

In the OT a gift to God given as an act of worship. Gifts included food, drink, incense, money, and animals. These objects represented the worshiper's offering of himself. In the NT, love and service to one's neighbors in the name of Christ are spoken of as offerings. In the early church, offerings of money were often made by Christians of one city to aid Christians in another. *Exodus 35:5-9; Leviticus 3:1-2; Numbers 7:10; and many other references in Leviticus and Numbers; Mark 12:33; Hebrews 7:27; 10:18; 1 Peter 2:5.*

OFFERING

OFFICER

In biblical use a servant or minister of the king, the army, or the temple. The men sent by the high priest to arrest Jesus were officers of the temple. *Numbers 11:16; Deuteronomy 16:18; 20:5; 29:10; 1 Chronicles 23:4; Ezra 7:28; Jeremiah 20:1; 41:1; John 7:32, 45-46; 18:3, 18, 22.*

OG
(og)

King of the land of Bashan, east of the Jordan River; remembered in the old traditions as a giant. His defeat by the Israelites was an important step toward their gaining possession of the land of Canaan. The territory of Bashan became the territory of the tribe of Manasseh. *Numbers 32:33; Deuteronomy 1:4; 3:1-11, 13; Joshua 12:4; 13:2, 30-31; Nehemiah 9:22; Psalms 135:11; 136:20.*

OIL

A liquid substance containing much fat. Oil was one of the necessities of life in Palestine and was looked upon as a gift from God. Most Palestinian oil was made by pressing olives. The first oil, obtained by putting crushed olives into a basket through which the oil would drain, was the purest and most precious. It was used in many ways in divine worship. The oil that was forced out by a second, stronger pressure was used for fuel, food, and medicine. When King Solomon paid the servants King Hiram sent from Tyre to help build the temple, he sent Hiram twenty measures of pure oil. *Exodus 27:20; 29:2, 40; Numbers 11:7-8;*

Deuteronomy 7:13; 1 Samuel 10:1; 1 Kings 5:11; 17:12; Ezra 3:7; Jeremiah 31:12; Hosea 2:8; Joel 2:19; Matthew 25:3-8; Mark 6:13; James 5:14.

OLIVE TREE

An evergreen tree with gray-green leaves and fruit that is good for eating and rich in oil. Numerous references to the tree, its wood, fruit, and oil, indicate the importance of the olive tree to the life of ancient Israel. It grew well in the rocky soil of the Holy Land. The tree is mentioned also in the poetry and promises of the prophets, often as a figure speech. From early Bible times until today, the olive branch has been seen as a symbol of peace and prosperity. *Genesis 8:11; Exodus 23:11; Deuteronomy 6:11; 8:8; 24:20; 1 Samuel 8:14; Job 15:33; Psalm 128:3; Jeremiah 11:16; Hosea 14:4-7.*

OLIVES, MOUNT OF, OR OLIVET

A hill east of Jerusalem across the Valley of Kidron. It is part of the main range of mountains that runs through central and southern Palestine. Some of the activities of Jesus during the last week of his life took place on the Mount of Olives. The garden of Gethsemane is located there. It may have been the scene of Jesus' last meeting with his disciples after the Resurrection, when he ascended into heaven. *2 Samuel 15:30; Zechariah 14:4; Matthew 21:1; 24:3; Mark 11:1-2; 14:26; Luke 19:37; 21:37; Acts 1:12.*

OMEGA

See *Alpha and Omega.*

OMER

(OH-mur)

In the OT a measure for dry substances equal to a little more than two quarts. *Exodus 16:13-36.*

OMRI

(OM-ree)

Ruler of the northern kingdom of Israel about 885–874 B.C.; successor of Zimro. Omri was the first of a family called the Omride Dynasty that ruled Israel for many years. He changed the capital from Tirzah to Samaria, which he had built. The name Samaria came to be applied to all the northern kingdom. Several other people mentioned in the OT have the name Omri. *1 Kings 16:16-28; Micah 6:16.*

ONESIMUS

(oh-NES-i-muhss)

A runaway slave probably belonging to Philemon, a member of the church at Colossae. His story is told in Paul's letter to Philemon. Not only had Onesimus run away from his master, he may have robbed him also. However, after he met Paul and heard the gospel, he was converted and became a most useful (the meaning of his name) servant. The letter expresses Paul's hope that the slave will be freed. Later there was a bishop of the church in Ephesus by the name of Onesimus, and many scholars think that this was the same man. *Colossians 4:7-9; Philemon 1:1-25.*

OPHIR

(OH-fihr)

A region of uncertain location chiefly known for its production of fine gold and for a fine-grained, heavy timber from its almug trees. The wood was also called red sandalwood and was used in the making of musical instruments. The scent of the wood was pleasing, and a dye made from it gave a rich red color to silks and woolens. *1 Kings 9:28; 10:11; 1 Chronicles 29:4; 2 Chronicles 8:18; 9:10; Job 22:24; 28:16; Psalm 45:9; Isaiah 13:12.*

OLIVE PRESS

ORACLE
(OR-uh-kuhl)
In the OT a speech or a pronouncement given by an inspired prophet, king, or priest as a message from God. An expression used often by the prophets was "Thus says the Lord." *2 Samuel 23:1; 2 Chronicles 24:27; Isaiah 15:1; Nahum 1:1; Malachi 1:1; Romans 3:2.*

ORDINANCE
A law or rule for governing social and religious customs. The term has the same meaning as "commandment." *Exodus 12:14; Leviticus 5:10; 1 Kings 9:4-5; Psalm 19:9; Isaiah 58:2; Luke 1:6; Ephesians 2:15.*

ORPAH
(ORH-puh)
A sister-in-law of Ruth and daugher-in-law of Naomi. When Naomi returned to Bethlehem, she urged Orpah and Ruth, who were widows, to remain in their own land of Moab because of the difficulties they would face in a strange land. Orpah obeyed and stayed in Moab while Ruth, in loyal devotion to Naomi, went with her to Bethlehem. *Ruth 1:4-18.*

OVEN
In biblical times an outdoor baking device. It was a large round jar of burnt clay with the fire built on pebbles at the bottom. Flat cakes of dough were stuck against the hot inner wall or laid on the pebbles after the fire was down. The fuel was usually dried grass, bushes, or dung. *Exodus 8:3; Leviticus 2:4; Psalm 21:9; Hosea 7:4; Matthew 6:30.*

OVERLAY
In OT times a layer of metal laid over various objects. Part of the tabernacle, the temple, and the holy furnishing were overlaid with gold, silver, or bronze. King Hezekiah of Judah had to strip away the overlays of precious metal to pay tribute to the king of Assyria. *Exodus 25:11; 1 Kings 6:20-32; 10:18; 2 Kings 18:16; 1 Chronicles 29:4; 2 Chronicles 3:4, 10; 4:9; 9:17; Isaiah 40:19; Habakkuk 2:19.*

OVERSEER
(OH-ver-see-er)
A taskmaster, supervisor, or foreman of a work gang, a household, or a group performing some special task. *Genesis 39:4-5; 41:34; 2 Chronicles 2:18; 34:17; Nehemiah 11:9; Isaiah 60:17.*

OX
(oks)
A domestic animal used in Bible times to pull plows, carts, and threshing sledges. Oxen were used to tread the kernels of grain out from the straw. They were sometimes used in sacrifice. *Exodus 24:5; 1 Samuel 11:7; Job 1:14; Psalm 106:20; Luke 14:5, 19; 1 Corinthians 9:9.*

OX GOAD
(oks gode)
A pointed stick used for driving or guiding cattle, especially oxen when plowing. Sometimes it was tipped with iron. *Judges 3:31; 1 Samuel 13:21; Ecclesiastes 12:11; Acts 26:14.*

OXEN AND OX GOAD

P p

PADDAN-ARAM
(pad-eh-AIR-uhm)

In the OT the homeland of the patriarch Abraham, who settled there with his kinsmen after they left Ur. It was located in northern Mesopotamia (now south central Turkey) and included the city of Haran. *Genesis 25:20; 28:2.*

PALESTINE
(PAL-uh-styhn)

In modern usage the name for the territory occupied in OT times by the twelve tribes of Israel. The name "Palestine" does not appear in the Bible, and the common Hebrew name for the land was Canaan. This term, however, did not include Transjordan, the land east of the Jordan River. The area referred to as Palestine is bordered roughly by the Mediterranean Sea on the west, the Arabian Desert on the east, the Anti-Lebanon Mountains on the north, and the Negeb and the Sinai Peninsula on the south. This was the Promised Land given by God to Abraham (see *Canaan*), but it was a challenging land which offered no soft, easy life. The Hebrews were continually aware that God had chosen this place for them to dwell in, and the OT is the record of their response to their surroundings. Their life was influenced by the physical features of the land. These are so varied that almost every kind of terrain can be found somewhere within the 10,000 square miles of territory that make up Palestine. There are rugged mountain ranges, fertile coastal plains, and dry desert regions. Mt. Hermon rises more than 9,000 feet while the surface of the Dead Sea lies 1,300 feet below sea level. The land is set between the sea and the desert but has no favorable harbors on the Mediterranean. The climate is generally one of summer drought and winter rain. The temperatures range from 100 degrees in summer to an average of 40 degrees in Jerusalem in winter. However, there is frequent frost. The west wind from the sea brings cooling wind and evening dew so that where there is enough soil crops flourish even in summer. The dreaded sirocco, or east wind that comes scorching from the desert, generally occurs in the fall. The Jordan River flows through the deep Rift Valley and cuts Palestine in half. The gorge is so steep that no cities have ever been built along the river. Palestine also forms a natural passageway between the kingdoms that grew up in the valleys of the Nile and of the Tigris-Euphrates rivers. For this reason Israel and Judah were caught in the constant warfare that went on between these kingdoms as well as those of Asia Minor. All these features combined to produce a vigorous and forceful people whose influence has been felt throughout the world.

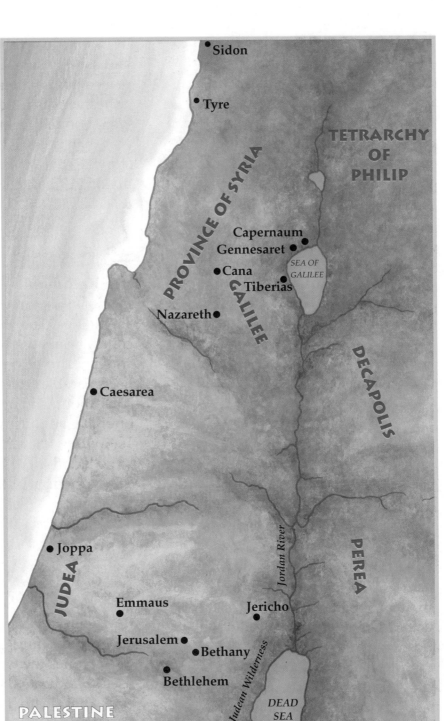

PALM TREE

A tall, slender tree with a tuft of branches or leaves at the top. In Bible times it was very useful for its fruit. Dates were an important source of food. Mats were woven from its leaves, and palm fibers provided thread and rigging for boats. In the ancient Near East the palm had religious associations. Carvings on the walls, doors, and other parts of Solomon's temple represented the palm. The palm tree often appears in the OT as a symbol of the rulers of Israel and as a figure of speech indicating righteousness. Palm Sunday, a Christian festival, received its name from the palm branches waved by the people during Jesus' triumphal entry into Jerusalem. *Exodus 15:27; Leviticus 23:40; Deuteronomy 34:3; Judges 1:16; 1 Kings 6:29, 32, 35; 7:36; 2 Chronicles 28:15; Nehemiah 8:15; Psalm 92:12; John 12:13; Revelation 7:9.*

PAMPHYLIA
(pam-FIL-ee-uh)

An area along the southern coast of Asia Minor about eighty miles long and twenty miles wide. In NT times it was a Roman province. Paul and Barnabas visited Perga, one of its leading cities, on their first missionary journey. *Acts 2:10; 13:13; 27:5.*

PAPYRUS
(puh-PYE-ruhss)

A tall red plant that grows in watery places. It was abundant in lower Egypt and was an important item of export for many centuries. Paper was made from the pith of the inner stalk. It was cut into thin strips that were laid side by side. Other strips were placed across them side by side. An adhesive was used, and the strips were bonded together by pressure. It was then polished with a shell or stone. Papyrus was also used in the making of baskets and small boats. *Job 8:11; Isaiah 18:2.*

PARABLE
(PAIR-uh-buhl)

A brief story forcefully illustrating a single idea. The word "parable" comes from a verb meaning "to be similar," "to be comparable." Jesus used parables to teach important lessons about God and his kingdom. He often began them with such phrases as "With what can we compare . . ." or "The kingdom of heaven is like . . ." or "The kingdom of heaven may be compared to. . . ." (See *Allegory, Fable, Myth.*) *Matthew 13:3-52; Mark 4:30-32; Luke 12:13-21.*

PARADISE
(PAIR-uh-dise)

A word meaning "park" or "garden." In NT times the word "paradise" was used to indicate the place of the righteous after death. *Luke 23:43; 2 Corinthians 12:1-4; Revelation 2:7.*

PARAPET
(PAIR-uh-pet)

A railing or low wall built around the edge of a roof to prevent people from falling off. *Deuteronomy 22:8.*

PARCHED GRAIN

Grain prepared by roasting the kernels in a pan or by holding a small bundle of wheat in the fire. In OT times this food was eaten by all people from the highest to the lowest. *Leviticus 2:14; 23:14; Joshua 5:11; Ruth 2:14; 1 Samuel 17:17; 2 Samuel 17:28.*

PARCHMENT

A writing material made from the skins of sheep or goats. Gradually it replaced papyrus since it was most lasting. *2 Timothy 4:13.*

PASCHAL LAMB

(PAS-kuhl)

The lamb sacrificed at the Passover festival. Paul used this term to refer to Christ's death and relate it to the Jewish Passover. (See *Passover.*) *1 Corinthians 5:7.*

PASSION, THE

A term used for the suffering and death of Jesus. It refers to the last days of Jesus' life and includes such events as the Last Supper, the agony in Gethsemane, the arrest, trial, crucifixion, death, and burial. In the Christian calendar Passion Sunday is the fifth Sunday in Lent. *Acts 1:3.*

PASSOVER, THE

The first of the three great religious festivals in the Jewish year. The Passover and Feast of Unleavened Bread were celebrated in the spring to mark the deliverance of the Israelites from Egyptian slavery. The week-long festival began on the eve of the first day with a family meal of roast lamb (called the Paschal lamb), unleavened bread, and other especially prepared foods. Unleavened bread was eaten for the following seven days. As a boy, Jesus went with his parents to observe the Passover in Jerusalem. The Feast of Unleavened Bread may originally have been a separate celebration which was later combined with the Passover. *Exodus 12:1-20; 2 Chronicles 30:1-22; 35:1; Ezra 6:19-22; Matthew 26:1-2, 17-19; Mark 14:12; Luke 22:7-8; John 11:55; 12:1; 13:1.*

PASSOVER FOODS

PASTOR

(PAS-tur)

Meaning "shepherd." In the NT a leader in the early church whose work was closely connected with teaching. *Ephesians 4:11.*

PATMOS

(PAT-muhss)

A Greek island about ten miles long and six miles wide composed of rocky, volcanic hills, just off Miletus. The Romans banished political prisoners to small islands such as this. John "the Seer," who wrote the book of Revelation, was exiled on Patmos during a period when the Roman authorities were persecuting Christians. *Revelation 1:9.*

PATRIARCHS

(PAY-tree-arks)

Meaning "fathers." NT term referring to the ancestors of the Israelites. It refers most frequently to Abraham, Isaac, and Jacob. *Acts 2:29; 7:8; Romans 9:5; Hebrews 7:4.*

PAUL THE APOSTLE

(pawl)

A first-century Jew who was changed from a persecutor of Christians into the leading missionary of the early Christian church. He called himself an "apostle to the Gentiles" and was the founder of churches in Asia Minor and Greece. His letters to these churches form an important part of the NT. The Book of Acts tells of Paul's life and missionary career. "Paul" is the Greek form of his Jewish name "Saul." He was born in Tarsus (in modern Turkey) and inherited Roman citizenship from his family. By trade he may have been a weaver of materials used in making tents, though some scholars think he was a leatherworker. It is not known what happened to Paul after his last journey and imprisonment in Rome. Tradition says that he was put to death by the Emperor Nero about A.D. 64. *Acts 8:1-3; 9:1-25; 13:9-50; 16:9-39; and other places in Acts; Romans 1:1; 1 Corinthians 1:1; Galatians 1:1; and other references.*

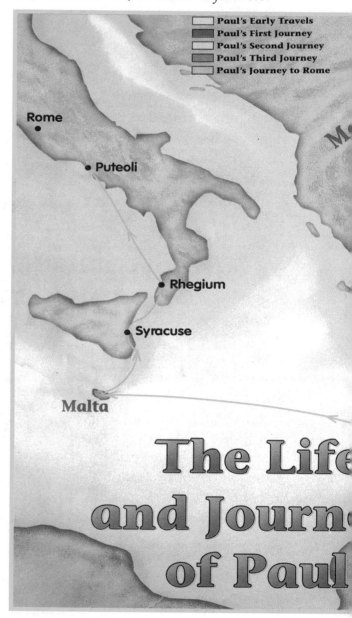

Paul's Early Travels
Paul's First Journey
Paul's Second Journey
Paul's Third Journey
Paul's Journey to Rome

Rome
Puteoli
Rhegium
Syracuse
Malta

The Life and Journeys of Paul

PEKAH
(PEE-kuh)

King of the northern kingdom of Israel about 740–732 B.C. He succeeded to the throne by murdering King Pekahiah with the assistance of Rezin, king of Syria. Later Tiglath-pileser, the Assyrian emperor, attacked Syria and Israel, put to death both Rezin and Pekah, and deported the people to other parts of the Assyrian Empire. *2 Kings 15:25-37; 16:5; Isaiah 7:1.*

PEKAHIAH
(pek-uh-HYE-uh)

King of the northern kingdom of Israel about 742–740 B.C.; son and successor of Menahem. He continued his father's policy of paying tribute to the emperor of Assyria. He was murdered by Pekah with the backing of Rezin, king of Syria. *2 Kings 15:23-26.*

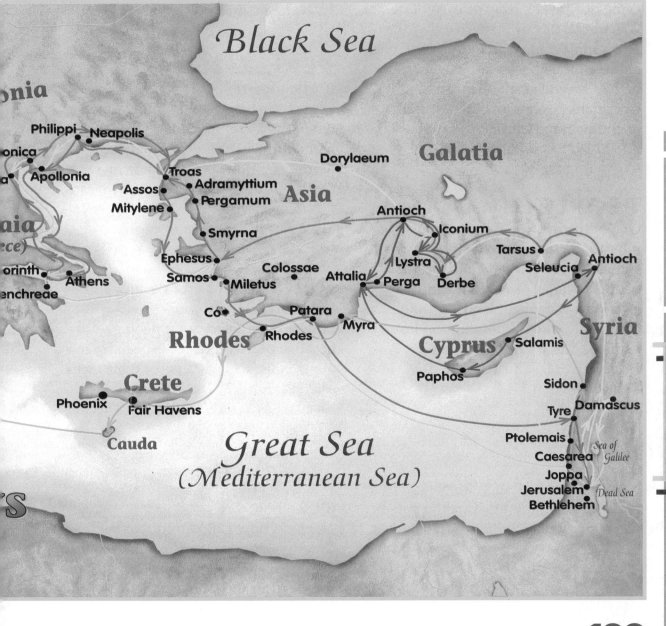

PENNY

A roman coin of OT times, probably equal to about one fourth of a cent. *Matthew 5:26; 10:29; Mark 12:42; Luke 12:6.*

PENTECOST
(PENT-uh-kost)

Meaning "fiftieth." It was the Greek term for the Jewish Feast of Weeks held fifty days after the Passover. It marked the beginning of the offering of the first fruits of the harvest and came during late May or early June. It was on the day of Pentecost that the Holy Spirit came upon Jesus' disciples gathered together in Jerusalem after he had ascended into heaven. Christians celebrate Pentecost as the birthday of the Christian church. *Acts 2:1; 20:16; 1 Corinthians 16:8.*

PEOPLE OF GOD

One of the many OT expressions that refer to the special covenant relationship existing between God and the people of Israel. The NT meaning identifies "people of God" with the church grounded upon faith in Jesus Christ. *2 Samuel 14:13; Psalm 47:9; Hebrews 4:9; 11:25; 1 Peter 2:9-10; Revelation 21:3.*

PEOR
(PEE-ohr)

Name of a mountain in Moab and of a god worshiped by the Moabite people. *Numbers 23:28; 25:18; 31:16; Joshua 22:17.*

PERDITION
(pur-DISH-uhn)

In the Bible a word which refers to death and destruction. *2 Samuel 22:5; Psalm 18:4; John 17:12; Revelation 17:8, 11.*

PERFUME

In Bible times sweet-smelling substances used in cosmetics, in preparing the dead for burial, in scenting furniture and clothing, and in incense for worship. *Exodus 30:25; 2 Chronicles 16:14; Proverbs 27:9; Isaiah 3:20-24.*

PERIZZITE
(PAIR-uh-zite)

One of the tribes living in Palestine when the Israelites came. They are named in lists of the population, but no information about them is given. *Genesis 13:7; 15:20; 34:30; Deuteronomy 7:1; Joshua 3:10; 17:15; 24:11; Judges 1:4-5; 1 Kings 9:20; 2 Chronicles 8:7.*

PERSECUTION
(pur-si-KYOO-shuhn)

Suffering inflicted upon people because of their beliefs, especially religious beliefs, or because of their race. *Matthew 5:10-12; 13:21; Mark 10:30; Acts 8:1; 2 Corinthians 12:10; 2 Timothy 3:11.*

PERSIA
(PUR-zhuh)

The land now called Iran that lies roughly between the Caspian Sea on the north and the Persian Gulf on the south. After the Persians' defeat of the

Babylonians in the sixth century B.C., the great Persian Empire was established from India to Greece, and King Cyprus proclaimed himself "king of the world." His policy of tolerance toward the exiled Jews in Babylon permitted them to go back to Jerusalem and rebuild the walls of the city. Kings of Persia mentioned in the Bible are Cyrus, Darius, and Artaxerxes. (See also *Medes, Cyrus.*) *2 Chronicles 36:20, 22-23; Ezra 1:1-2, 8; 3:7; 4:3, 5, 7; 6:14; Nehemiah 12:22; Daniel 5:25-28; 6:8.*

PESTILENCE
(PES-te-lunses)
Infectious diseases usually associated with a military siege and probably brought on by a contaminated water supply. In Bible times such disasters were seen as divine punishment. *Exodus 5:3; Leviticus 26:25; Numbers 14:12; Deuteronomy 28:21; Jeremiah 14:12; 27:13; 42:17; 44:13; Luke 21:11.*

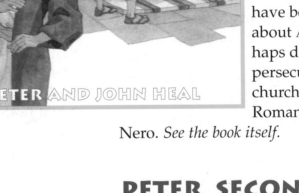
PETER AND JOHN HEAL

PETER
(PEE-tur)
Also called Simon, Simon Peter, and Cephas. The most outstanding of Jesus' twelve apostles. His natural leadership qualities made him the spokesman for the Twelve. To Peter, Jesus gave the responsibility of leading the disciples after the

Resurrection. Peter was a witness to the Resurrection and became a strong leader of the early church. *Matthew 4:18-20; 10:2; 14:28-29; 16:16-18; Mark 1:29-30; 14:54, 66-72; Luke 18:28; John 1:41-42; 18:10; Acts 2:14, 37-38; 3:1-12; 1 Corinthians 9:5; Galatians 2:7-9; 2 Peter 1:1; and many other references.*

PETER, FIRST LETTER OF
A book of the NT written by or in the name of Peter, the apostle. The letter was probably written for Gentile Christians who were being persecuted in Asia Minor. The letter declares the greatness of the Christian faith and gives instruction for sharing in the suffering of Christ. The letter may have been written about A.D. 70, perhaps during the persecution of the church by the Roman emperor Nero. *See the book itself.*

PETER, SECOND LETTER OF
The author of this NT book took the name of the apostle Peter to emphasize the importance of his letter. The letter was probably written in the second century A.D. to settle the doubts and false teachings that were confusing the churches. *See the book itself.*

PHARAOH
(FAIR-oh)

A title given to the king of Egypt. It meant "the Great House" and referred to the palace until about 1500 B.C., when it became a title for the person who lived in the royal palace. The pharaoh was considered by the Egyptians to be a god. The land and the people of Egypt belonged to him. The pharaohs in the time of Joseph and of the Exodus cannot be identified with certainty. *Genesis 41:42; Exodus 2:5; 7:10; 12:29-30; 1 Kings 3:1; 23:29; 2 Chronicles 12:2-9; Nehemiah 9:10; Psalms 135:9; 136:15; Jeremiah 44:30; Acts 7:13, 21; Romans 9:17.*

PHARISEES
(FAIR-uh-seez)

A powerful religious party among the Jews in NT times. These men were not priests but laymen who were trained in the law. Their belief in the resurrection after death and their strict way of following the law made them different from the Sadducees, another religious party (see *Sadducees*). The Pharisees expected the royal line of David to be restored and with it the political power of Jerusalem and Israel. The Pharisees opposed Jesus because he did not insist on keeping the law as strictly as they did, and because he did not keep away from sinners. Paul, who became an apostle after the Resurrection, was a member of the Pharisees. After he became a Christian, he saw that the law of love as taught by Jesus was more important than the strict law of the Pharisees. This party continued to oppose Christians and the early church throughout NT times. *Matthew 9:11-13; 12:2-8; 22:15-22; Mark 2:16-17; Luke 11:37-44, 53; John 11:46-48, 57; 18:3-6; Acts 15:5; 23:6-9.*

PHILEMON, LETTER TO
(fye-LEE-muhn)

The eighteenth book of the NT. It was a short letter written by Paul to Philemon, a Colossian Christian, about Philemon's runaway slave, Onesimus. The letter was probably written from Rome about A.D. 62. (see *Onesimus.*) *See the book itself.*

PHILIP
(FIL-ip)

1. Philip the apostle came from Bethsaida, which was also the home of Andrew and Peter. It was Philip who brought Nathanael to Jesus. Philip is a Greek name, and this, together with the fact that some Greeks who came looking for Jesus approached him for help, suggests that he probably spoke that language. *Matthew 10:3; Mark 3:18; Luke 6:14; John 1:43-48; 6:5-7; 12:20-22; 14:8-9.*
2. Philip the evangelist. He was one of the Greek-speaking Christians who was given special duties to assist the apostles in the early church in Jerusalem. Following the martyrdom of Stephen, Philip fled to Samaria, where he preached the gospel. *Acts 6:5; 8:4-13; 21:8-9.*

PHARAOH

PHILIPIANS, LETTER TO THE

(fi-LIP-ee-uhnz)

The eleventh book in the NT; a letter written by Paul to the church he had started in Philippi. This was his first Christian church in Europe, and his letter shows his loving personal concern for the members. He gave them encouragement and counsel. The letter was probably written when Paul was a prisoner in Rome about A.D. 60–63. *See the book itself.*

PHILISTINES

(fi-LIS-teenz)

The people who occupied Philistia on the southwestern coast of Palestine. Their name came from an Egyptian word meaning "people of the sea." They may originally have come from the island of Crete. Their chief cities were Gath, Gaza, Ashkelon, Ashdod, and Ekron. The Philistines were often at war with the Israelites. They had large armies well equipped with chariots and weapons of iron. *Exodus 15:14; 23:31; Judges 3:3; 14:1-4; 16:23; 2 Samuel 21:15-19; Psalm 60:8; Isaiah 2:6; Jeremiah 25:20; 47:4.*

PHOENICIA

(fuh-NEE-shuh)

A long, narrow country on the east coast of the Mediterranean Sea, north of Palestine (modern Lebanon). The irregular coastline provided good harbors, and the people became colonizers and traders and operated ships in the Mediterranean. The cities of Tyre and Sidon were centers of industry and trade (see Ezekiel 27:1-36). The history of Phoenicia goes back very far, and from ancient times Phoenicia was famous for its purple dye. Probably the term "Canaanites" in the OT included the people of Phoenicia, since the word "Canaan" means "the land of the purple." Their worship of Baal influenced the religion of the Israelites when they settled in Canaan. Jesus crossed over to Tyre and Sidon in his ministry (see Matthew 15:21; Mark 7:24). Some of the early Christians settled in Phoenicia to escape persecution. *Obadiah 1:20; Acts 11:19; 15:3; 21:2.*

PHRYGIA

(FRIJee-uh)

In NT times a large area of Asia Minor in what is now Turkey. The Roman authorities divided the area into two parts to be governed by the provinces of Galatia and Asia. Many Jews lived in Phrygia. Paul frequently visited the Phrygian cities of Antioch and Iconium, and Christianity, although persecuted, became strong in Phrygia. *Acts 2:10; 16:6; 18:23.*

PHYLACTERIES

(fi-LAK-tur-eez)

Small leather boxes that were worn bound to the foreheads and arms of the Jewish men at daily prayer. They contained verses from the OT. The head phylactery had four small compartments which contained copies of Exodus 13:1-16 and Deuteronomy 6:4-9; 11:13-21. The hand or arm phylacteries had one compartment. Strips attached to the arm phylacteries were wound seven times around the arm,

PILATE

forming two "shins," an abbreviation of the name of God; then the ends were twisted three times around the palm and three times around the second finger. The Greek word for phylactery meant "safeguard," "means of protection." *Matthew 23:5.*

PIGEON

See *Dove.*

PILATE, PONTIUS
(PYE-luht, PON-shus)

The Roman governor of Judea A.D. 26–36, and therefore judge in the trial and execution of Jesus. *Matthew 27:2, 11-26, 58-65; Mark 15:1-15; Luke 3:1; 13:1; 23:13-16; John 19:19; Acts 3:13; 4:27; 13:28; 1 Timothy 6:13.*

PILLAR

In the Bible rough, uncut stone with a round top set up as a monument to commemorate an important event or as an object of worship; also, a support column for a roof. *Genesis 28:18; Exodus 23:24; 2 Samuel 18:18; 2 Kings 17:10; 2 Chronicles 14:3; Hosea 3:4; 10:1-2; Micah 5:13.*

PLANE TREE

Tall, stately tree with smooth bark; wide-spreading branches; glossy, vine-like leaves; and spiky, round seed-pods. Jacob used branches of this tree in his plot to deceive his uncle Laban. *Genesis 30:37-43; Ezekiel 31:8.*

PLEIADES
(PLEE-uh-deez)

A cluster of seven stars. Because of its brillance it is mentioned in the literature of many peoples throughout the world. *Job 9:9; 38:31; Amos 5:8.*

PLOW, PLOWSHARE

An implement for breaking up the ground. In Bible times the plowshare was a forked stick with a pointed metal tip. It did not dig deep but served only to scratch the ground. Plows with shafts attached were drawn by oxen. *1 Samuel 13:20-21; 1 Kings 19:19; Proverbs 20:4; Isaiah 2:4; Luke 9:62.*

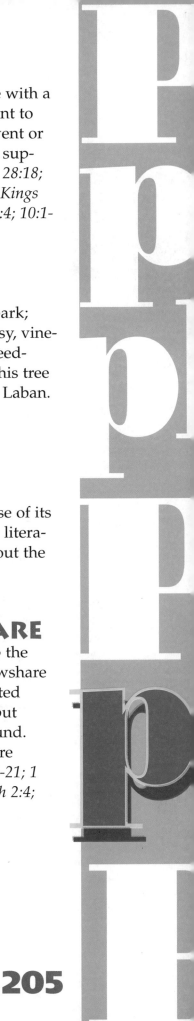

PONTUS
(PON-tuhss)
In NT times an area in northern Asia Minor (now in Turkey) that bordered on the Black Sea (then called Euxine Sea). Under Roman rule Pontus became part of the new province of Bithynia and was known as Bithynia and Pontus. Jews from Pontus were in Jerusalem on the day of Pentecost when the Holy Spirit came upon the disciples. *Acts 2:9; 18:2; 1 Peter 1:1.*

POTIPHAR
(POT-uh-fur)
The Egyptian officer who bought Joseph when he was sold into slavery. Later he had Joseph put into prison. *Genesis 37:36; 39:1.*

POTSHERD
(POT-Shurd)
A piece of broken pottery. Potsherds were sometimes used for writing brief notes as we might use a scrap of paper. Potsherd was also a symbol of dryness and utter worthlessness. *Job 2:8; 41:30; Psalm 22:15; Jeremith 19:2.*

POTTER
A man who made vessels and dishes from clay. He often used a wheel for shaping the clay into bowls, jars, laps, and plates. The Hebrews learned to make pottery in Canaan. *1 Chronicles 4:23; Isaiah 41:25; Jeremiah 18:1-6; Romans 9:21.*

POUND
In NT times a weight of about twelve ounces; also, a unit of money. *Luke 19:11-27; John 12:3, 19:39.*

PRAETORIUM
(pray-TOHR-ee-uhm)
In the NT the official residence or palace of a Roman governor. Possibly it was also the barracks and judgment hall. Pilate's temporary residence in Jerusalem during the trial of Jesus may have been Herod's praetorium. The term "praetorian guard" refers to the bodyguard of the Roman emperor. *Matthew 27:27; Mark 15:16; John 18:28, 33; 19:9; Acts 23:35.*

PRAYER
Any attempt to communicate with God. Prayer may be spoken or silent. It may include praise, confession, thanksgiving, repentance, or meditation on behalf of oneself or of another person. The word appears frequently in both OT and NT. Prayer has been at the center of the worship of God from the earliest times. *2 Chronicles 7:15; Psalms 65:2; 84:8; 102:1; Proverbs 15:8; Lamentations 3:8; Matthew 6:5-13; 21:22; Mark 12:40; Luke 2:37; Acts 3:1; Philippians 4:6; James 5:15-16; 1 Peter 4:7.*

PRIESTS AND LEVITES
(preests, LEE-vites)
Those who stand before God as his servants. Under the covenant of Moses the whole nation of Israel was to be a "kingdom of priests." They were to be a holy people fit to serve

God. Their holiness proved to be very imperfect in actual practice. However, the idea of holiness was symbolized in the official priesthood. Among the Israelites the priesthood developed into three divisions—high priest, priest, and Levite, each having its own distinctive functions and privileges. The high priest represented all the people of Israel before God in the sanctuary. He alone could enter the holy of holies once a year to make atonement for the nation's sin. The priests took care of the sanctuary, taught the law, and took part in the sacrifices. The Levites assisted the priests and were responsible for the care of the temple, cleaning the sacred vessels, preparing the cereal offerings, and carrying out the service of praise. They represented the people of Israel as substitutes for the firstborn sons who belonged, by right, to God. In the OT the priesthood began with Moses. He consecrated his brother Aaron and Aaron's sons to be priests. These men were of the tribe of Levi, the traditional priestly tribe. *Exodus 19:6; 28:1, 40-43; 1 Samuel 1:9; 5:5; 1 Chronicles 15:14; 2 Chronicles 34:14; Ezra 3:2; Nehemiah 3:1; Luke 1:5; Acts 4:1, 6; Hebrews 7;23-24; 1 Peter 2:9.*

PRAYER

PRINCE
A ruler. In the Bible the word was used for a king, military officer, leader, chief of a tribe or of the temple, or any man of noble birth, one worthy of honor. *1 Samuel 2:8; 9:15-16; 13:14; 2 Kings 20:5; Nehemiah 9:32; Isaiah 9:6; Jeremiah 1:18; Hosea 3:4.*

PROCONSUL
(proh-KON-suhl)
In the Roman Empire the administrator of a province. The proconsul usually held office for one year under the authority of the Senate in Rome. *Acts 13:7-8, 12; 18:12-13; 19:38.*

PROFANE

To treat a holy person, place, or institution as if it were not holy; to make unclean or defile a holy name. The Hebrews took great care never to speak the name of God for a foolish or useless purpose. To use it so was to profane or defile God's name. *Exodus 20:25; Leviticus 19:12; 21:6; 22:6; Jeremiah 19:4; Malachi 1:12; Matthew 12:5; Acts 24:6; 1 Corinthians 11:27.*

PROPHET
(PROF-uht)

In the Bible a spokesman for God. One who was inspired to speak God's message of God's purpose and judgment to the people. The prophets saw God at work in all things, even the misfortunes of Israel, and used specific events to proclaim God's will and purpose. Prophecies were often in poetry, parables, stories, or pantomime, which was acting out the prophecy. *Deuteronomy 18:15-18; 1 Samuel 3:20; 9:9; 1 Kings 18:1-40; 2 Kings 19:2-7; Isaiah 37:2; Jeremiah 18:18.*

PROSELYTE
(PROS-uh-lite)

In the NT a person who was converted to the Jewish religion, accepting all its customs and requirements. *Matthew 23:15; Acts 2:10; 6:5.*

PROVERBS, BOOK OF
(PRAH-vurbz)

The twentieth book of the OT. It belongs to the Hebrew writings called "wisdom literature." The book is made up of brief, wise sayings that give advice on how to live a good and happy life. These sayings were probably collected and some written during the fifth and fourth centuries B.C. King Solomon may have composed some of the proverbs. *See the book itself.*

PROVINCE
(PRAHV-uhns)

A division of an empire ruled by an appointed official. Judah, for instance, was a province of the Babylonian and Persian Empires after the fall of Jerusalem. Under the Romans in NT times the province was called Judea. All the territory of Asia Minor, Syria, Palestine, Egypt, and other countries, was divided into provinces by the Roman government. *Ezra 4:10; Esther 3:12-14; Acts 23:34; 25:1.*

PRUNING HOOK

In the OT a curved blade attached to a handle and used for removing surplus twigs and trimming vines. *Isaiah 2:4; 18:5; Joel 3:10; Micah 4:3.*

PSALMS
(sahlmz)

The nineteenth book of the OT. It is a collection of poems, prayers, and hymns for use in public and private worship. These 150 psalms were collected over a long period of time and divided into five sections by the end of the third century B.C. The psalms speak of all the experiences of life. They tell of joy and sorrow, sin and suffering, evil and righteousness. The meanings of the titles are not clear to us today. They may contain directions for the musical performance of these pieces. Jesus often quoted from the psalms. *See the book itself.*

PURIFICATION
(pyur-i-fuh-KAY-shuhn)
The act of cleansing by washing or by offering a sacrifice after contact with something unclean under Jewish law. *Nehemiah 12:45; Luke 2:22-24; John 2:6; Acts 21:26.*

PURIM
(POO-rim)
A two-day Jewish festival celebrating the deliverance of the Jews in Persia from Haman's plot to kill them. The story is told in the book of Esther. *Esther 9:23-32.*

PURPLE
A color associated with royalty and wealth. It was the most valuable of ancient dyes and was obtained from a secretion of mollusks found in the Mediterranean Sea. Both Crete and Phoenicia have been associated with the discovery of purple dye. (See *Phoenicia.*) *Exodus 25:4; Lamentations 4:5; Ezekiel 27:7; Luke 16:19; John 19:2, 5; Acts 16:14.*

THE PROPHET ELIJAH BEING FED BY RAVENS

QUAIL
(kwayl)
A reddish-brown bird with dark-brown markings and light-brown underparts. Used in Bible times for food. Quail were eaten by the Hebrews on their journey from Egypt to Canaan. *Exodus 16:12-13; Numbers 11:31; Psalm 105:40.*

QUEEN OF HEAVEN
A foreign goddess; an object of worship, particularly for women, in Judah in the time of Jeremiah. It may possibly refer to the goddess Ishtar, who was identified with the Venus star. Jeremiah condemned the Jewish refugees in Egypt for burning incense to the Queen of Heaven. *Jeremiah 7:18; 44:17-19, 25.*

QUIRINIUS
(kwi-RIN-ee-uhss)
The Roman governor of Syria in NT times. He was appointed by the emperor in A.D. 6. *Luke 2:2.*

QUIVER
A container for carrying arrows. It was usually made of leather, decorated with metal or paint, and carried hung over the shoulder. *Genesis 27:3; Job 39:23; Isaiah 22:6; 49:2; Jeremiah 5:16; Lamentations 3:13.*

QUAIL

RAAMSES

(ray-AM-seez)
See *Rameses* (city).

RABBAH

(RAB-uh)
Ancient capital city of the Ammonite kingdom, located about twenty-three miles east of the Jordan River. Today it is called Amman and is the capital of the modern country Jordan. Og, the giant king of Bashan, was said to have had his big iron bedstead in Rabbah. David captured Rabbah and organized the Ammonite people into a labor force to work for him. *Deuteronomy 3:11; Joshua 13:25; 2 Samuel 11:1; 12:27, 29; 17:27; 1 Chronicles 20:1; Jeremiah 49:2-3; Ezekiel 21:20; 25:5; Amos 1:14.*

RABBI

(RAB-eye, reh-BOH-nigh)
Hebrew word meaning "master." In the NT rabbi was a title of respect for a teacher. In modern Judaism a rabbi is ordained, and his or her office is similar to that of a minister. *Matthew 23:7-8; John 1:38, 49; 3:2, 26; 4:31; 6:25; 9:2; 11:8; 20:16.*

RACHEL

(RAY-chuhl)
Younger daughter of Laban, second wife of Jacob, and the mother of Joseph and Benjamin. Jacob worked for Laban seven years as a marriage payment for Rachel. At the end of the time Laban tricked Jacob by giving him Leah, the older daughter. Jacob worked seven more years to get Rachel. *Genesis 29:15–30:24; 33:1-2; 35:16-20; Ruth 4:11; 1 Samuel 10:2; Jeremiah 31:15; Matthew 2:18.*

RAHAB
(RAY-hab)

1. A woman living in Jericho at the time of the Israelite invasion of Canaan. She hid Joshua's spies in stalks of flax on the roof of her house and allowed them to escape. Joshua spared her life when he took Jericho. *Joshua 2:1-21; 6:17, 23-25; Hebrews 11:31; James 2:25.*

2. The name of a mythical beast representing disorder and chaos. *Job 9:13; 26:12; Psalm 89:10; Isaiah 30:7; 51:9.*

RAINBOW

Called "bow" in the OT. A rainbow is the reflection and refraction of sunlight caused by a curtain of falling rain. It is often seen against a backdrop of retreating clouds and indicates that the storm is over. It is mentioned in the Bible as a sign of God's promise that a flood would never again destroy the world. *Genesis 9:13; Lamentations 2:4; Ezekiel 1:28; Habakkuk 3:9-11; Revelation 10:1.*

RAISIN-CAKES

In Bible times a common food prepared by pressing dried grapes. Because it did not spoil, it was suitable for travelers and for military provisions. *2 Samuel 6:19; Isaiah 16:7; Hosea 3:1.*

RAMAH
(RAY-muh)

Also called Ramathaim-Zophim, this was a town in the hill country of Ephraim northwest of Jerusalem. It was the home of Samuel and one of the places where he administered justice to Israel. It was to Ramah that the elders of Israel came to ask Samuel for a king. Several other towns with this name are mentioned in the OT. Ramoth-Gilead is also called Ramah. (See *Ramoth-Gilead.*) *1 Samuel 1:19; 2:11; 7:17; 8:4; 15:34; 28:3.*

RAMESES (CITY)
(RAM-uh-seez)

The name of one of the Egyptian store-cities built by the Israelites when they were slaves in Egypt. It is also spelled "Raamses." Ramses II (1290–1224 B.C.) founded and named the city. It is located in the Egyptian Delta. This was the starting point from which the Israelites began the Exodus. *Exodus 1:11; 12:37; Numbers 33:3-6.*

RABBI

RAMOTH-GILEAD
(RAY-moth-GIL-ee-ad)
Any important fortress in Gilead, located in the eastern part of the territory of Gad. It was a city of refuge. It is often called Ramah. (See *Cities of Refuge.*) *Deuteronomy 4:43; Joshua 21:38; 1 Kings 4:13; 2 Kings 8:28; 9:1, 4, 14.*

RAMPART
(RAM-part)
Outer fortification encircling a city, consisting of a broad, sloping embankment usually made of earth. *2 Samuel 20:15; Psalm 48:13; Lamentations 2:8; Nahum 3:8; Zechariah 9:3.*

RAVEN
A large, crowlike bird mentioned in both the OT and NT. It is purplish black and travels in flocks. The raven is a scavenger, eating dead flesh and also attacking small, helpless animals. For this reason it was unclean to the Hebrews and was not to be used for food. *Genesis 8:7; Leviticus 11:15; 1 Kings 17:4-6; Job 38:41; Psalm 147:9; Proverbs 30:17; Song of Solomon 5:11; Isaiah 34:11; Zephaniah 2:14; Luke 12:24.*

REAP
To harvest grain. In OT times the worker grasped a few stalks and cut them off halfway up the stalk. He used a small sickle made with a head of flint set in a wooden or bone handle. Later the worker probably used a small, curved blade like the sickle of today. *Leviticus 19:9; 23:10, 22; 25:5; 1 Samuel 8:12; Matthew 6:26; Romans 1:13.*

REBEKAH (NT, REBECCA)
(re-BEK-uh)
Wife of Isaac and mother of Jacob and Esau. Rebekah plotted with Jacob to cheat Esau out of the blessing Isaac intended for him. *Genesis 24:15-67; 25:20-28; 26:7; 27:5-17, 42-46; 29:12; 49:31; Romans 9:10-12.*

RECONCILE, RECONCILIATION
To bring agreement; agreement and harmony between persons who have had a quarrel or a misunderstanding. In the Bible it refers to the restoration of harmony and love between humans and God. The NT emphasizes that God in God's divine love has brought about a new harmony through the life and death of Jesus Christ. (See *Atonement.*) *1 Samuel 29:4; Matthew 5:24; Romans 5:10-11; 2 Corinthians 5:18-20.*

RECORDER
An official in the royal court of Israel. He advised the king and probably was in charge of keeping the historical records. *2 Samuel 8:16; 2 Kings 18:18, 37; 2 Chronicles 34:8.*

REBEKAH AT THE WELL

RED SEA

The arm of the sea that separates Egypt from Arabia. In ancient times the Red Sea included the Indian Ocean, the Persian Gulf, the Gulf of Suez, and the Gulf of Aqabah. The words "sea" and "lake" had the same meaning for the Israelites. The "Red Sea" that the Israelites crossed when fleeing the Egyptians may have been a marshy area or a small lake north of the Gulf of Suez, called the Sea of Reeds. *Exodus 10:19; 15:22; 1 Kings 9:26; Psalm 136:13-15; Acts 7:36; Hebrews 11:29.*

REDEEM, REDEEMER, REDEMPTION

Redeem means to reclaim, to get back, or to buy back. Redeemer is the person who performs these acts. Redemption is the act of reclaiming or liberating or getting back. In OT times firstborn children were considered to belong to God, and a provision was made in Hebrew law to "redeem" them by payment of a fixed sum. It was family law for the nearest relative to buy back, or redeem, a person who had been sold into slavery or to reclaim, buy back, a piece of property lost because of debts. The word "redeem" was used also in reference to God's delivering the Israelites from their slavery in Egypt. "Redeemer" was one of the prophet Isaiah's favorite names for God. In the NT the word "redemption" always implies deliverance or liberation from the power of sin and its effects. Jesus' death was a redemptive act, a deliverance for God's people. *Genesis 48:16; Exodus 6:6; 34:20; Leviticus 25:25, 48-49; Numbers 3:48-49;* *18:15-16; Ruth 4:6; Job 19:25; Psalms 19:14; 25:22; 26:11; 107:2-3; 130:7-8; Isaiah 43:1, 14; Jeremiah 32:7-8; Luke 24:21; Galatians 3:13; Ephesians 1:7.*

REED

The flowering stalk of any of several tall grasses that grow in marshy places. Reeds are sometimes called rushes. The reed had many uses. Measuring rods, pens, baskets, mats, and other things were made of reed. *Genesis 41:2; 1 Kings 14:15; 2 Kings 18:21; Job 40:21; Isaiah 42:3; Ezekiel 29:6; 40:5-7; Matthew 11:7; 12:20; 27:29-30; Mark 15:19, 36; Luke 7:24.*

REFINE, REFINING

To strain or filter out impurities or dross from metals by melting them in large earthenware containers in a hot furnace; the act of purifying. Archaeologists have found Solomon's copper and iron ore furnaces at Ezion-geber. In the Bible "refine" is sometimes used as a figure of speech to describe the way God cleanses or purifies God's people. *1 Chronicles 28:18; 29:4; Job 28:1; Psalm 12:6; Isaiah 48:10; Jeremiah 9:7; Zechariah 13:9; Malachi 3:3.*

REFUGE

A place of escape, a stronghold. The word is used to describe God's protection. (see also *Cities of Refuge.*) *Ruth 2:12; Psalms 5:11; 16:1; 36:7; Proverbs 30:5; Jeremiah 16:19; Nahum 1:7.*

REHOBOAM
(ree-huh-BOH-uhm)

King of Judah from about 931 to 913 B.C., a son and successor of Solomon. Rehoboam was the first king of the southern kingdom after the united kingdom was divided. *1 Kings 11:43–12:27; 14:21-31; Matthew 1:7.*

RELIGION

Found in the NT only, this word refers to service and worship of God through an approved system of beliefs, practices, and patterns of behavior. *Acts 26:5; 1 Timothy 2:10; James 1:26-27.*

REMNANT
(REM-nuhnt)

In the Bible that part of a community that is left after a calamity and that is responsible for the future of the community. The word is used specifically to refer to those Jews who returned to Jerusalem after the Exile. In more general use the word may refer to the small number of people who remained faithful to God when the large number deserted. *Genesis 45:7; Ezra 9:8, 14-15; Isaiah 10:20-22; 11:11, 16; 28:5; 37:31-32; Amos 5:14-15; Micah 5:7-8; Haggai 1:12-14; Zechariah 8:6.*

RENEWAL

The act of reforming completely, being made new spiritually. In the NT it is the process by which one changes the direction of one's life. The idea is implied in many of Jesus' sayings, but the word occurs only one time. It indicates a complete break with an old way of life and acceptance of Jesus' way. Paul speaks of being a new person in Christ. *Titus 3:5.*

PAUL PREACHES RENEWAL

REPENT, REPENTANCE

In biblical usage to turn away from sin and back to God; the act of doing this. It marks the beginning of a new religious or moral life. In the OT Israel as a nation owed obedience to God, fell under God's judgment when it disobeyed, and could come back into God's favor only by turning away from sin. In the NT repentance and faith in God's love and mercy go together. In the early church repentance was considered basic to faith. *Job 42:6; Ezekiel 14:6; Matthew 3:8-11; Luke 3:3; 5:32; 24:47; Acts 2:38; 5:31; 13:24; 19:4; 20:21; 2 Corinthians 7:10.*

REPHAIM, VALLEY OF

(REF-ay-im)
A broad valley or plain near Jerusalem named for the people who lived in Canaan before the Israelites came. They were thought to be a race of giants. The valley is described as being rich in grain. *Deuteronomy 2:11, 20-21; 3:11; Joshua 15:18; 18:16; 2 Samuel 5:18, 22; 1 Chronicles 11:15; 14:9; Isaiah 17:5.*

RESURRECTION, THE

(rez-ur-EK-shuhn)
In the NT the Resurrection is the central fact of the Christian gospel. It is the reality that Jesus was alive after the Crucifixion. This was the event that the apostles preached to the world to show that Jesus was the Christ, the Son of God. Not only did the Resurrection demonstrate Jesus' defeat of death, it also held out to all believers a lively hope for personal resurrection. (See *Everlasting Life, Immortality.*) *Matthew 22:23-32; Luke 14:14; John 11:23-27; Acts 1:22; 2:24; 4:2; 24:15; Romans 1:4; 6:5; 1 Corinthians 15:12-22; 1 Peter 1:3.*

REUBEN

(ROO-buhn)
First of the twelve sons of Jacob and the ancestor of the tribe of Reuben. *Genesis 29:32; 37:22-30; 46:8-9; Exodus 6:14.*

REUBENITES

(ROO-buhn-ites)
The descendants of Reuben who lived in the land east of the Jordan River. *Joshua 1:12; 12:6; 13:15-23; 1 Chronicles 5:6, 18.*

REVELATION

(rev-uh-LAY-shuhn)
Making known the nature and will of God. In the Bible, God is represented as becoming known to us by God's actions in history and especially in Jesus Christ. The Bible is a record of this revelation and also one of the ways in which God becomes known to humans. *2 Samuel 7:27; Luke 2:32; Romans 16:25; 1 Corinthians 14:26; Galatians 1:12; Ephesians 1:17; 3:3; 1 Peter 1:13; Revelation 1:1.*

REVELATION, BOOK OF

The last book in the NT, written probably toward the end of the first century A.D. It was written by an early

Christian church leader named John who was concerned for seven churches in Asia Minor that were probably under his care. It was a time of persecution, and John himself was imprisoned on the Isle of Patmos in the Mediterranean Sea just off Miletus. John wrote his letter in dramatic form using symbols and visions to reassure his readers of God's purpose, God's saving power, and God's final victory over evil. *See the book itself.*

with friends, parents, teachers, and others, and with God. Each relationship makes demands on persons. When God or human fulfills those demands, then he or she is, according to the OT, righteous. In the NT righteousness has to do with a "right relationship" with God. God, through Christ, is considered the source of all righteousness. *Genesis 15:1-6; Psalm 118:19; Proverbs 10:2; Isaiah 26:10; Jeremiah 23:6; Matthew 3:15; 5:6; Romans 4:3; 2 Corinthians 6:4-7; Philippians 3:9; James 1:20; 2 Peter 2:21.*

REZIN

(REE-zin)

A king of Damascus in the eighth century B.C. With King Pekah of Israel he attacked Judah. (See *Pekah.*) *2 Kings 15:37; 16:5-9; Isaiah 7:1, 8.*

RHODES

(rohdz)

A Greek island and city in the southeastern part of the Aegean Sea. Paul's ship stopped there on his last journey to Jerusalem. *Ezekiel 27:15; Acts 21:1.*

RIGHT-EOUSNESS

Godliness; being free from wrong or sin; doing what is right. Every person has many relationships

JOHN WRITES REVELATION

ROCK

Stones or a stone mass or cliff; a place of shelter of safety formed by caves and rocky crags. Often used in the psalms to indicate being safe in God's care. One of the parables of Jesus deals with building on a solid foundation of rock. *Psalms 94:22; 95:1 and other psalms; Matthew 7:24-27.*

ROD

A stick cut from the branch of a tree; a staff. Shepherds and travelers who journeyed by foot used staffs. Rods were also used as poles for carrying burdens and as measuring sticks. A shorter staff, knobbed at one end and often studded with nails or bits of flint, was used as a weapon by soldiers and shepherds. *Exodus 4:2-5, 20; Psalms 2:9; 23:4; 89:32; Proverbs 10:13; 13:24; 1 Corinthians 4:21; 2 Corinthians 11:25; Revelation 2:27; 11:1; and many other references.*

ROMANS, LETTER TO THE

(ROH-muhnz)

In the NT a letter written by Paul to the Christian church in Rome, probably between A.D. 54 and 57. In the letter Paul wrote a complete and clear account of his understanding of the gospel of Jesus Christ. *See the book itself.*

ROME, CITY OF

(rohm)

Capital of the world in NT times, located halfway down the west coast of Italy and ten miles up the Tiber River. From there developed the mighty Roman Empire that included the whole Mediterranean world. Christianity came to Rome before A.D. 50. Paul visited the Christian church in Rome, and later he was imprisoned there. There is a strong tradition that Peter visited Rome and that he and Paul were martyred there. *Acts 2:10; 18:2; 19:21; 28:14-16; Romans 1:7, 15; 2 Timothy 1:17.*

ROOF

The covering of a building. In ancient Middle Eastern homes the roof was flat and covered with a smooth clay. An outside staircase led up to the roof where the family spent a good amount of time. *Joshua 2:6; 1 Samuel 9:25; 2 Kings 4:8-10; Mark 2:4.*

RUE

(roo)

A strong-smelling shrub with clusters of yellow flowers. Rue was gathered and used as an herb in seasoning, in medicines, as a disinfectant, and as a charm. *Luke 11:42.*

RULER OF SYNAGOGUE

(ROO-ler, SIN-uh-gog)

In NT times the leader or president of a synagogue who took charge of the arrangements for the services. *Mark 5:22-42; Luke 13:10-17; Acts 13:14-15; 18:8.*

RUTH

(rooth)

Meaning "friend, companion." In the OT a Moabite woman who married a Hebrew. At the death of her husband she chose to go with her mother-in-law Naomi instead of returning to her own people. She is mentioned in the genealogy of Jesus in Matthew 1:5. (See *Ruth, Book of.*)

RUTH, BOOK OF

The eighth book of the OT, probably written sometime between 450 and 250 B.C. It is a short story of human kindness and devotion. The story is a good example of the possibility of goodwill and respect for others no matter what their nationality of religion. *See the book itself.*

RUTH

SABBATH

(SAB-uhth)

From a word meaning "to cease" or
"to be at an end." The Ten
Commandments provided that the
last day of the seven-day week be a
day of rest. From sundown on the eve
of the sabbath until sundown on the
sabbath all ordinary work and activities stopped. The Hebrew laws setting
forth what things could and could not
be done were very strict. For example,
only very limited travel was permitted (see *Sabbath Day's Journey*).
However, the sabbath was a day of
joy for the privilege of worshiping
God, and there was no fasting on the
sabbath. During the times when the
temple stood, the official beginning of
the sabbath was announced by a
trumpet blast. Then special services of
worship with prayer and sacrifices
were held. Changing the bread of the
Presence was a part of the sabbath ritual. After the Exile, services came to
be held in the synagogues also. Prayer
and readings from the Pentateuch and
the prophets were the main features
of these services. After the final
destruction of the third temple in A.D.
70 the synagogue sabbath services
became the most important part of
Jewish public worship. During his
ministry Jesus took part in these synagogue services. He also gave a new
teaching: "It is lawful to do good on
the sabbath." *Exodus 20:8-11; 34:21;
35:2-3; Leviticus 19:3; 25:2-7; 26:34-35;
Nehemiah 10:31; Jeremiah 17:19-27;
Ezekiel 20:12; 46:1-4; Matthew 12:1-14;
Mark 1:21-23; John 19:31; Acts 13:27;
18:4.*

SABBATH DAY'S JOURNEY

In NT times the distance that one was allowed to travel outside a city on the sabbath, probably about three-fifths of a mile. This interpretation of the OT law (see Exodus 16:29) had been made by the scribes. *Acts 1:12.*

SACKCLOTH

Coarse cloth made of goats' and camels' hair and used for bags. Sackcloth was worn as a sign of mourning, of national disaster, or of repentance. *Genesis 37:34; 2 Samuel 3:31; 2 Kings 19:1-2; Nehemiah 9:1; Esther 4:1-4; Psalm 69:11; Isaiah 15:3; 20:2; 37:1-2; 50:3; Jeremiah 4:8; Joel 1:13; Jonah 3:8; Matthew 11:21.*

SACRIFICES AND OFFERINGS

(SAK-ri-fi-sez)

In the OT something presented to God. A sacrifice involved the killing, burning, and sometimes eating, of an animal at the altar. An offering could be made of grain, ground flour, fruit, or vegetables. Such things were presented with symbolic gestures such as waving, lifting up, or burning. A sacrifice could be offered for various reasons—as a "gift" to God when asking for protection or for a favor, as an act of thanksgiving, as a tribute or act of devotion to God for God's greatness, as a sign of one's repentance for sin, and also as payment of vows or promises made to God. Often the rite of sacrifice was carried out in such a way that it bound God and human together in a sacrificial meal. Part of the animal was offered to God, part eaten by the priests, and part eaten by the worshiper. There were extra offerings on sabbaths, seasonal festivals, and holy days. Some of the prophets declared that the people placed too much emphasis on the ritual of the sacrifices and did not realize that the offering represented the worshiper. *Exodus 3:18; 40:29; Leviticus 2:1-2; 3:1-5; 7:11-15; 16:5-6, 11, 15-16; 22:21, 23; Numbers 15:3; 28:2-3; 31:50; Deuteronomy 12:5-6; Psalms 50:12-15, 23; 51:16-17; Isaiah 1:11-14; Jeremiah 17:26; Micah 6:6-9.*

SACRIFICE

SACRILEGE

(SAK-reh-lij)

The abuse or defiling of something sacred or holy. This might involve using holy things for one's own purposes or bringing pagan vessels and idols into the place kept apart for the worship of God. In the second century B.C. a Greek ruler over the Jews set up altars to Greek gods in the Jerusalem temple. *Matthew 24:15; Mark 13:14.*

223

SADDUCEES
(SAJ-eh-seez)
In NT times a priestly religious party of the Jews. The high priest in the temple was chosen from among this group. Well educated and aristocratic, the Sadducees were in the majority in the high council in Jerusalem. The big difference between the Sadducees and the Pharisees, another religious party, was in their interpretation of the law. The Sadducees differed with the Pharisees over the question of the resurrection of the dead (see *Pharisees*). The Sadducees did not believe in the resurrection of the dead, probably because it was not found in the law. Jesus told them they were wrong and that they did not understand the scriptures or the power of God. *Matthew 3:7; 16:1-12; 22:23; Mark 12:18-27; Luke 20:27-40; Acts 4:1-2; 5:17; 23:6-10.*

SAINT
Meaning "holy" or "set apart" for God's use. In the OT the term is used to describe Israel as God's holy people. In the NT the term is used for members of the Christian church. They were considered the new people of God under the lordship of Jesus Christ. The word was particularly associated with the love Christians showed to one another. *2 Chronicles 6:41; Psalms 16:3; 31:23; 37:28; 145:10; Proverbs 2:8; Daniel 7:18; Acts 9:13; 26:10; Romans 1:7; 16:15; 1 Corinthians 1:2; 6:1-2; Ephesians 2:19; 1 Timothy 5:10.*

SALAMIS
(SAL-uh-miss)
A principal city of Cyprus situated on the east coast. In the sixth century B.C. the city came under Greek rule. In NT times it was under Roman rule. Paul and Barnabas visited a Jewish colony there. According to tradition, Barnabas was martyred at Salamis. *Acts 13:5.*

SALOME
(suh-LOH-mee)
1. A Galilean woman who was a follower of Jesus. She was probably the wife of Zebedee and the mother of James and John. She was present at the Crucifixion and was one of the women who brought spices to anoint Jesus' body for burial. *Mark 15:40-41; 16:1.*
2. The daughter of Herodias who danced for King Herod Antipas and demanded the head of John the Baptist as her payment. Sources outside the Bible report that her name was Salome. *Matthew 14:6; Mark 6:22.*

SALT
A mineral mined in Bible times from the area around the Dead Sea, or evaporated from its waters. Salt was used as a seasoning and for preserving food and was sprinkled on sacrifices in the temple. It was eaten to seal a covenant, or agreement, which bound two people together in loyalty to each other. In OT times it was custom for any army to sow the land they had conquered with salt to prevent any growth of crops. The term is often used in the Bible in figures of speech

that reflect both the destructive and life-giving qualities of salt. *Leviticus 2:13; Numbers 18:19; Judges 9:45; Ezra 4:14; 6:9; Job 6:6; Jeremiah 17:6; Matthew 5:13; Mark 9:50; Colossians 4:6.*

SALT SEA

In very early biblical history a name for the lake later called the Dead Sea. It is fed by the Jordan River, but it has no outlet. This lake is over 1,200 feet below sea level and has the highest percentage of salt in any water in the world. Today it is a rich source of valuable minerals; however, there is no plant or animal life in the Dead Sea. Some excavation is at present going on in search for cities that may be under its waters. (See *Sodom, Gomorrah.*) *Genesis 14:3; Numbers 34:3; Deuteronomy 3:17; Joshua 3:16.*

SALVATION, SAVIOR

(sal-VAY-shuhn, SAYV-yor)
Meaning the "saving," "redeeming," or "delivering" of something; the person who does this. Salvation is the central theme of the whole Bible. In the OT the history of the people of God, the Hebrews, is the story of their salvation by the acts of God from destruction and ruin.

The high point and most important event in this salvation history is the deliverance of the people of Israel from Egypt and God's care for them through the wilderness journey. In the NT, Jesus—whose name means "savior"—is announced as the fulfillment of God's saving of God's people. Through Jesus a new people, those who believe that he is the Christ, are saved from the power of sin and death, and a new saving history is begun in the church. *Exodus 14:13; 2 Samuel 22:3, 36, 47; Nehemiah 9:27; Psalms 27:1; 96:2; Isaiah 12:2-3; Luke 1:47-77; 2:11; John 4:42; Romans 1:16; Ephesians 1:13; Philippians 2:12; 1 Timothy 4:10; Hebrews 1:14; 2 Peter 1:1.*

SADDUCEES AT THE BAPTISM OF JESUS

SAMARIA
(suh-MAIR-ee-uh)

In OT times the capital of the northern kingdom Israel. The city was built by King Omri, and King Ahab continued to enlarge and beautify the city. It was located on a hill in central Palestine about forty-two miles north of Jerusalem. It was a well-planned city with strong fortifications. However, in 722 B.C. it fell to the Assyrians after a siege of three years. The Assyrian king brought people from many other lands to settle in Samaria. The northern kingdom was often called the territory of Samaria. Archaeological excavations have uncovered evidences of many buildings of Omri and Ahab. Potsherds from the time of Jeroboam have also been discovered. On these are written receipts and orders for oil, wine, and barley. *1 Kings 16:24, 32; 20:1; 22:10; 2 Kings 6:24-25; 14:23; 17:1-6, 24-26; 23:19; Ezra 4:8-24; Nehemiah 4:1-9; Jeremiah 31:5; Micah 1:1-7; Acts 1:8; 9:31; 15:3.*

SAMARITANS
(suh-MAIR-i-tuhnz)

The mixed peoples of Samaria. Many of them did not follow the law and worship of the Hebrews. The Samaritans established their center for worship on Mt. Gerizim rather than at Jerusalem. The Jews who returned to Judah from their exile in Babylon found the leaders in Samaria against the rebuilding of Jerusalem and the temple. This was one of the causes of the ill feeling that existed between the Jews and Samaritans in NT times. *2 Kings 17:29; Matthew 10:5; Luke 9:52; 17:16; John 4:2-42; Acts 8:25.*

SAMSON
(SAM-suhn)

A judge of the Israelite tribe of Dan. He was famous for his great strength. Samson was dedicated as a Nazarite from birth and kept the vow of not cutting his hair. His long hair was considered to be the secret of his strength. The collection of stories about Samson is based on Hebrew folklore, probably told over and over for generations. The stories give a colorful picture of life in the period of the judges. *Judges 13:2–16:31; Hebrews 11:32.*

SAMUEL
(SAM-yoo-uhl)

Meaning "name of God." A prophet of the eleventh century B.C. who, as a child, was dedicated to the service of God. He lived in Ramah and was the last judge of Israel. As a prophet Samuel called the Israelites to repent of their idol worship. When the people wished to have a king like other nations, Samuel anointed Saul and later David as king over Israel. *See the first book of Samuel; 1 Chronicles 6:28; 9:22; 29:29; Jeremiah 15:1; Acts 13:20; Hebrews 11:32.*

SAMUEL, FIRST AND SECOND

The ninth and tenth books of the OT. They report the events of the period from the birth of Samuel through the reigns of Saul and David. Originally the two were one book. The books probably contain the records of several writers who got their material from folklore, historical records, and prophecies. In several instances there are different versions of the same story. The materials were probably compiled into the books in the seventh or sixth century B.C. *See the books themselves.*

SANCTIFICATION, SANCTIFY

(sangk-ti-fi-KAY-shuhn, SANGK-ti-fye)
The setting apart of something so that it might belong to God; being made clean or acceptable to God. In the OT a person, a priest, or the temple was made holy or set apart for a sacred use. In the NT Christians were sancti-fied by their faith in Christ and set apart for God by the action of the Holy Spirit. *Exodus 29:43; 31:13; Joshua 3:5; 2 Kings 10:20; 1 Chronicles 15:14; 2 Chronicles 29:17-19; Job 1:5; Isaiah 29:23; Ezekiel 37:28; Joel 1:14; Romans 6:19, 22; 1 Thessalonians 5:23; Hebrews 2:11; 9:13; 1 Peter 1:2.*

SANCTUARY

See *High Place.*

SAMUEL

SANDALS, SHOES

Flat soles of leather or wood bound to the feet by thongs. Sandals were the usual shoes of people of Bible times. Going without sandals was considered a sign of mourning or poverty. Taking off one's shoes at a holy place was an act of respect. Putting on one's shoes indicated readiness for a journey. Presenting a shoe legally confirmed a business transaction. Shoes were removed at the door of a house and the feet were washed to remove dust and dirt and thus keep the house clean. *Exodus 3:5; 12:11; Ruth 4:7; Amos 8:6; Mark 1:7; 6:9; Luke 10:1, 4; 15:22; Acts 7:33.*

SANHEDRIN
(san-HE-drin)

The supreme Jewish council in Jerusalem following the Exile. It was presided over by the high priest and consisted of seventy-one members chosen from among the priests, scribes, Sadducees, and Pharisees. The Sanhedrin had the authority to make laws for the Jews and to judge lawbreakers. Jesus, Peter, John, Stephen, and Paul appeared before this council. *Matthew 26:59; Mark 14:55-63; 15:1; Luke 22:66; John 11:47-53; Acts 4:13-20; 5:17-29; 6:8-15; 22:30; 24:20.*

SARAH, SARAI
(SAIR-uh, SAIR-eye)

Meaning "princess." The wife of Abraham, who in her old age became mother of Isaac. This birth fulfilled God's promise to Abraham. Her name was changed from Sarai to Sarah at the time God gave Abraham his covenant name. *Genesis 11:30; 17:15-21; 18:6-15; 21:1-3; and many other places in Genesis; Isaiah 51:2; Romans 4:19; 9:9; Hebrews 11:11; 1 Peter 3:6.*

SARDIUS
(SAR-di-uhs)

A deep orange-red, semiprecious stone; a variety of chalcedony. It was used in the priest's breastplate. *Exodus 28:17; 39:10.*

SARGON
(SAR-gon)

The name of two kings of Assyria. Little is known about the first, but Sargon II was an able military leader who headed the Assyrian Empire from about 722 to 705 B.C. Shalmaneser V of Assyria began the attack on the city of Samaria. The siege lasted for three years, and apparently he died in the middle of it. Sargon II took over and conquered the city in 722 (see 2 Kings 17:1-6). He deported most of the people into faraway provinces in Media, where they disappeared. *Isaiah 20:1.*

SATAN
(SAY-tuhn)

The chief of the devils, the rival of God. In the OT he was the one who accused humans and brought them to trial before God. Satan acted only with God's consent and orders. In late OT times Satan was thought to be a destructive angel, taking part in a struggle between good and evil. Satan plays an important part in the poetic drama of Job. In the NT Satan appears as a distinct being. He is represented as the enemy of God who enters into the minds and hearts of humans and is responsible for their evil deeds. Other names or expressions for Satan are "the evil one," "the tempter," "the enemy," "the prince of demons," "the ruler of this world," "the accuser," "the devil," "the obstructor," "Belial," "prince of the power of the air," "Beelzebul," and "the great dragon." He also appears as the tempter and opponent of Jesus. *1 Chronicles 21:1; Job 1:12–2:7; Zechariah 3:1-2; Matthew 4:1-11; 12:24-28; Mark 1:13; 4:15; Luke 4:1-15; 10:17-18; 22:3, 31; John 13:27; Acts 5:3; Romans 16:20; 1 Corinthians 7:5; 1 Thessalonians 2:18.*

SATRAP
(SAY-trap)
A governor of a province in the Persian Empire. *Ezra 8:36; Esther 3:12; 8:9; 9:3; Daniel 3:2, 3; 6:1-7.*

SAUL
(sawl)
1. The first king of Israel (from about 1020 to 1000 B.C.). At the request of the people, Saul was chosen and anointed by Samuel. Saul was a handsome and commanding figure who was also a good military leader. He challenged and weakened the power of the Philistines and stopped their advance into the central highlands of Israel. In the later years of his reign, as the

young David gained fame and favor, Saul was tormented by jealousy and fear until he finally went mad. *1 Samuel 9:21; 11:5-15; 13:8-14; 18:6-9; 31:1-6; and many other places in 1 Samuel; 1 Chronicles 10:2-14; Isaiah 10:29; Acts 13:21.*
2. The Jewish name of the apostle Paul. (See *Paul.*) *Acts 9:1-25.*

SAVIOR
See *Salvation.*

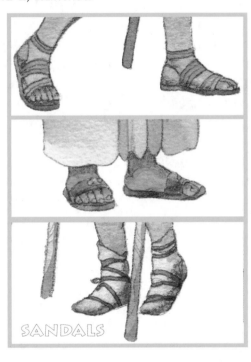

SANDALS

SCEPTER
(SEP-tuhr)
A rod or staff carried by a king as a sign of his authority and power. Two types of scepters were common in OT times: one a long, slender staff or rod with a decorated head; the other a short-handled club with a heavy head similar to a military weapon. This symbolized the king's striking power. The word is also used as a figure of speech to mean "rule" or "ruler." *Genesis 49:10; Numbers 21:18; Esther 4:11; Psalms 45:6; 110:2; 125:3; Isaiah 14:5; Jeremiah 48:16-17; Ezekiel 19:14; Amos 1:5, 8; Hebrews 1:8.*

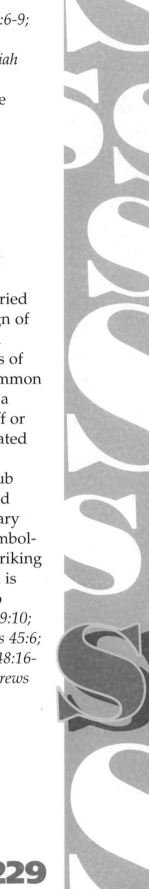

SCRIBE

Originally a person who could write. The scribe was important to a king because he could write messages and keep records. The OT scribes became a professional class of men during the Exile. They studied, interpreted, and taught the Jewish law. They came from the families of priests and were probably responsible for gathering together and setting down many of Israel's sacred writings which make up the OT of today. The scribes of NT times were a professional group defending and teaching the law and were important in the Sanhedrin, which was the high council in Jerusalem. Some were members of a religious party called the Pharisees. *1 Chronicles 27:32; 2 Chronicles 34:13; Ezra 4:8-10; 7:6, 11-12, 21; Nehemiah 8:1, 4, 9, 13; 12:26, 36; Psalm 45:1; Jeremiah 8:8; 36:32; Matthew 2:4; 8:19; 13:52; Mark 2:6, 16; 7:1; Luke 20:1, 19; Acts 6:12; 23:9.*

SCRIPTURE
(SKRIP-chur)

Meaning "a writing." As it is used in the NT, "scripture" refers to the sacred writings of the Jews, or what is now the OT. Today the Christian Bible, which contains OT and NT, is often called the Scriptures. "Scripture" is sometimes used to refer to a verse or passage from the Bible. *Matthew 22:29; Mark 12:10, 24; Luke 4:21; 24:27, 44-45; John 2:22; 5:39; 19:24, 28; Acts 18:24, 28; Romans 15:4; Galatians 3:8; 1 Timothy 4:13; 2 Timothy 3:15-17; 2 Peter 3:15-16.*

SCROLL

Meaning "book," a roll of papyrus or parchment, sometimes called the "roll of a book." The scroll was made by fastening the sheets together and rolling them around a rod. Such a roll was usually nine to eleven inches wide and thirty feet long. Writing was done in columns, and the scroll was rolled from right to left as it was read. In 1947 at Qumran, near the Dead Sea, about five hundred scrolls were found in caves. Some of the scrolls contained copies of parts of the OT. One of a complete scroll of Isaiah. The scrolls were the library of a religious group that had lived at Qumran. When the members were forced to leave Qumran about A.D. 70, they stored their parchment scrolls in pottery jars and hid them in the caves. The dry air of the Dead Sea region kept them in good condition. These scrolls are still being examined and studied today. *Ezra 6:2; Isaiah 34:4; Jeremiah 36:2-32; Revelation 5:1-9.*

SCYTHIANS
(SITH-ee-uhnz)

An ancient wandering tribe of people who came on horseback from the area around the Black Sea. At one time they were allies of Assyria. In the OT they are referred to under the name of Ashkenaz. The threat of their savage raids may have been the reason Zephaniah wrote his book of prophecies and Jeremiah made some of his pronouncements. Paul used the word "Scythian" to mean wild, uncivilized people. *Genesis 10:3; Jeremiah 51:27; Colossians 3:11.*

SCROLL

SEA, MOLTEN

Also called the "bronze sea" and "the sea." It was a large basin about fifteen feet in diameter, made of bronze three inches thick with a brim turned out as a cup. It rested upon twelve bronze oxen set in four groups of three, facing north, east, south, and west. It was located at the entrance of the temple close to the altar. It was a storage place for the water needed by the priests for cleansing the sacrificial vessels and for washing themselves before and after a sacrifice. When the Babylonians captured Jerusalem in 586 B.C., the sea was broken up and carried off to Babylon. *1 Kings 7;23-44; 2 Kings 16:17; 25:13, 16; 2 Chronicles 4:2-15.*

SEA OF THE ARABAH

(AR-uh-buh)

A name used in the OT for the Salt Sea, now called the Dead Sea. *Deuteronomy 3:17; 4:49; Joshua 3:16; 12:3; 2 Kings 14:25.*

SEA OF GALILEE

See *Galilee, Sea of.*

SEA OF GLASS, GLASSY SEA

A sea-like crystal in God's throne room; seen in a vision of John, the seer. This was a symbolic way of showing God's judgment on humanity's sin and of God's way of purifying and cleansing humans from sin. The vision may have been inspired by the molten sea that had been in the first temple. (See *Sea, Molten.*) *Revelation 4:6; 15:2.*

SEALS

In ancient times bone, metal, stone, or precious gems that had been carved with a design. This design was pressed into a clay or wax to serve as a person's signature. Seals were used to close letters or official documents. A king's seal was one of the signs of his authority. *1 Kings 21:8; Nehemiah 9:38; Esther 8:8; Job 38:14; 41:15; Jeremiah 32:10; Daniel 6:17; John 3:33; Ephesians 1:13.*

SEER

Meaning "one who sees." In the OT it usually referred to a person who had visions and could predict the future. Prophets were sometimes referred to as seers in everyday language. However, prophecy was a more lasting and dependable gift. *1 Samuel 9:9-12, 18-19; 2 Chronicles 12:15; 16:7-10; Isaiah 30:10.*

SEIR

(SEE-ur)

The chief mountain range of Edom. It became the home of Esau and his descendants, the Edomites. "Seir" is also used as a name for the Edomite nation. *Genesis 32:3; 33:14, 16; 36:8-9; Numbers 24:18; Joshua 24:4; Judges 5:4; 2 Chronicles 25:11-14.*

SELAH

(SEE-luh)

A word of uncertain meaning. Probably a musical direction to the choir or to the musicians. It occurs seventy-one times in thirty-nine psalms. *Psalm 3:2, 4, 8; Habakkuk 3:8, 13.*

SELEUCIA

(suh-LOO-shee-uh)

A coastal city in Syria, it was the port on the Mediterranean for Antioch. From here Paul and Barnabas sailed on their first missionary journey. The modern city of Seudiah stands on this site. Excavations of recent times have uncovered houses, a market gate, a Doric temple, and an early fifth-century church. *Acts 13:4.*

SENNACHERIB

(suh-NAK-uh-rib)

King of Assyria and Babylonia from 705 to 681 B.C. He attacked the southern kingdom of Judah and took several of the cities. King Hezekiah of Judah paid heavy tribute to Sennacherib so that Jerusalem would be spared. When the Assyrians invaded Judah a second time, there was a miraculous deliverance when a plague broke out among the Assyrian troops, killing many of them. Sennacherib was murdered in his capital city, Nineveh. *2 Kings 18:13–19:37.*

SERAPHIM

(SER-uh-fim)

Six-winged heavenly beings seen by the prophet Isaiah in a vision. Like the cherubim they are associated with the glory of God. *Isaiah 6:2-6.*

SERPENT, BRONZE

The figure of a snake made by Moses during the wilderness journey from Egypt to Canaan. There was an invasion of the Israelites' camp by poisonous snakes. This was understood by the people as a judgment from God for their impatience and discontent. Moses put the image of a snake on a pole so that the people could see it. It was a symbol of God's healing power, and those who looked up to it were healed of their bites. *Numbers 21:8-9; John 3:14.*

SERVANT OF THE LORD, THE

One who serves God, as a devoted slave or servant works for a master. In the OT the title was given to the patriarchs, prophets, and some kings. Israel, the nation, was often called the servant of the Lord. In the book of Isaiah the writer speaks of a suffering servant, a servant whose labors cost him pain and humiliation. The servant accepts the suffering willingly and because of this accomplishes the salvation of others. Down through the centuries Christians have recognized in the prophets' descriptions the likeness of Jesus Christ. *Genesis 26:24; Exodus 14:31; Deuteronomy 34:5; Judges 2:8; 2 Samuel 3:18; 2 Kings 9:7; Ezra 9:11; Job 1:8; Psalms 89:20; 105:42; Isaiah 41:8; 49:1-6; 52:13–53:10; Amos 3:7; Mark 10:43-45; Philippians 2:5-8.*

JESUS AS SERVANT

SHADES

In the OT a word referring to the ghosts, or spirits, of the dead. Throughout the ancient Near East the spirits of the dead were thought to have power to do harm. The biblical view is that the shades have no power to do good or evil. *Job 26:5; Psalm 88:10; Isaiah 14:9.*

SHADRACH, MESHACH, ABEDNEGO

(SHAD-rak, MEE-shak, uh-BED-nuh-goh)

Three young men who were companions of Daniel in the court of Nebuchadnezzar in Babylon. Their names are Babylonian court names given them when they became favorites of the king. The story was probably written in the second century B.C. when the Jews were suffering under Greek rule. It tells of the blameless lives of these young men, lived according to Hebrew law even in a foreign court, and of their courage and faith, which made it possible for them to face death rather than worship the pagan image set up by Nebuchadnezzar. They were put in a fiery furnace but were not harmed by the fire. *Daniel 1:7; 2:49; 3:12-30.*

SHALLUM

(SHAL-uhm)

King over the northern kingdom of Israel for one month in the year 752 B.C. He gained the throne by murdering King Zechariah, and in turn was murdered by Menahem. The prophet Hosea was preaching in Israel about this time. Several other persons with the name Shallum are mentioned in the OT. *2 Kings 15:10, 13-15.*

SHALMANESER

(shal-muh-NEE-zur)

There were five Assyrian kings with this name, but only two are connected with biblical events. Shalmaneser III (858–824 B.C.) was the first Assyrian king to come in contact with the kings of Israel. Though he is not mentioned in the OT, he tried to conquer Israel when Ahab was king and later when Jehu ruled. Shalmaneser V (727–722 B.C.) laid siege to Samaria and forced Hoshea, king of Israel, to pay tribute. Shalmaneser apparently died or was murdered during the siege, and the Assyrian army retreated quickly. His brother, Sargon II, completed the conquest of Samaria. *2 Kings 17:3-6; 18:9-10.*

SHAPHAN

(SHAY-fuhn)

Secretary and financial officer to King Josiah. Shaphan brought the "book of the law" that had been found in the temple to the king. Shaphan and his sons helped in the great reform that King Josiah led in the kingdom of Judah in the seventh century B.C. *2 Kings 22:3-13; 2 Chronicles 34:8-20.*

SHARON

(SHAIR-uhn)

A plain about ten miles wide and fifty miles long along the eastern Mediterranean shore extending approximately from Joppa in the south to Mt. Carmel in the north. It was known for its marshes and forests during early Israelite history. Today it is a fertile agricultural area. Recent excavations show that there were some small settlements in Sharon as early as 1200 B.C. The rose of Sharon was a type of crocus growing in the region. *1 Chronicles 27:29; Song of Solomon 2:1; Isaiah 33:9; 65:10.*

SHAVING

Removing hair with a razor. Shaving the face and head was not practiced among the Hebrews except in special cases. It was a sign of mourning or shame. It was also done at the completion of a Nazirite vow (see *Nazirite*) or when leprosy of the head was discovered. It was, however, considered proper for Joseph, while living in Egypt, to follow the customs of the Egyptians and to appear before the pharaoh clean-shaven. *Genesis 41:14; Leviticus 13:33; 14:8-9; Numbers 6:18-19; 2 Samuel 10:4-5; 1 Chronicles 19:4; Job 1:20.*

SHADRACH, MESHACH, ABEDNEGO

SHEATH

The case or covering for a sword or bow. Also called a scabbard. The judgment of God is likened to a sword drawn from the sheath. *1 Samuel 17:51; 2 Samuel 20:8; Jeremiah 47:6; Ezekiel 21:3-5; Habakkuk 3:9; John 18:11.*

SHEBA
(SHEE-buh)

In OT times an area in southwestern Arabia that was the center of caravan trade. The visit of the queen of Sheba to Solomon may well have been for the purpose of making trade agreements. *1 Kings 10:1-13; Psalm 72:15; Jeremiah 6:20; Ezekiel 27:22.*

SHECHEM
(SHEK-uhm)

An ancient Canaanite city in the hill country north of Jerusalem. It was associated with the patriarchs and after the conquest of Canaan became an important political and religious center for the Israelites. Later in its history it served for a time as the capital of the northern kingdom Israel under its first king, Jeroboam. *Genesis 12:6-7; 33:18-20; Numbers 26:31; Joshua 21:21; 24:1, 32; Judges 9:6; 1 Kings 12:1, 25; Jeremiah 41:5; Hosea 6:9.*

SHEEP, SHEPHERD

An animal raised for its wool, meat, and milk; the keeper of sheep. Sheep and goats were the main domestic animals of the Hebrews. Sheep represented the chief wealth of early Bible people. The wool and skin were used for cloth, clothing, and sometimes tent coverings. Sheep were important in sacrifices and were burned upon the altar. The shepherd's care of the sheep was often used in the Bible as a figure of speech to show God's love, God's mercy, and God's compassion for God's people and also to indicate the care religious teachers and leaders should have toward their people, who are like flocks. *2 Samuel 12:1-14; Psalm 23:1; Isaiah 40:11; 43:23; 53:6-7; Jeremiah 23:1-4; Ezekiel 34:1-31; Mark 6:34; Luke 15:3-6; John 10:1-18.*

SHEKEL
(SHEK-uhl)

See *Money.*

SHEM
(shem)

A son of Noah. According to Genesis, Shem is the ancestor of the Hebrews and of other people who, like the Hebrews, are called Semites (from Shem). *Genesis 6:10; 10:21-32; 1 Chronicles 1:4; Luke 3:36.*

SHEOL
(SHEE-ohl)

In the OT a name often used to indicate the place under the earth where the spirits of the dead were supposed to dwell. (See *Abaddon, Gehenna, Hades.*) *Genesis 37:35; 44:29; Deuteronomy 32:22; 1 Samuel 2:6; Psalm 49:14-15; Isaiah 14:9, 11, 15; Ezekiel 31:15-17.*

SHEPHELAH
(shuh-FEE-lah)

Meaning "lowland." In OT times the name for a region of low hills and valleys between the Mediterranean coastal plain and Judean hill country. It was an important agricultural area with an abundance of grain, olives, and grapes. The Shephelah, with well-fortified cities, served as the first line of defense against the Philistines and others attacking the Israelites from the west. *1 Kings 10:27; 1 Chronicles 27:28; 2 Chronicles 1:14; 9:27; 26:10; 28:18; Jeremiah 32:44.*

SHIBBOLETH
(SHIB-oh-leth)

A word meaning "river" or "ear of grain" or "branches." In the OT story of Jephthah it was the password used by the Gileadite sentries at the fords of the Jordan to distinguish between their own people and the enemy Ephraimites. If a man mispronounced the word as "siboleth," he was recognized as an Ephraimite. *Judges 12:4-6.*

SHEPHERD

SHILOH
(SHYE-loh)

A city of OT times situated in the hill country north of Bethel and east of the main road that ran from Shechem to Jerusalem. At the time of the conquest of Canaan the area was unoccupied. Its remoteness may have been the reason for Joshua's choosing Shiloh as his headquarters. It became an important religious center for the Israelites. Samuel was dedicated there as a child. The ark of the covenant and the tabernacle remained there until the time of Samuel. It was one of the cities of refuge. (See *Cities of Refuge.*) *Joshua 18:1, 8-10; 19:51; 22:9, 12; Judges 21:19; 1 Samuel 1:3, 24; 4:4; 14:3; Psalm 78:60; Jeremiah 7:12, 14.*

SHINAR
(SHY-nar)

OT name for the territories which came to be known as Babylonia. According to biblical tradition the tower of Babel was built in Shinar. (see *Babel.*) *Genesis 11:2; 14:1, 9; Isaiah 11:11; Daniel 1:2; Zechariah 5:11.*

SHIPS, SAILING

Waterborne vessels; transportation by water using wind power. Because there were no good harbors on the Mediterranean coast of Palestine, and because for a long time the coastal plane was held by the Philistines, the Hebrews did not naturally turn to sea trade as a means of livelihood. In the time of Solomon, however, a fleet of galley ships was built and sailed out of Ezion-geber on the Gulf of Aqabah. Hiram, king of Tyre, sent Phoenician sailors to train the men for Solomon's fleet. In OT times the Hebrews' contact with ships and sailing was chiefly through the Phoenicians (see Ezekiel 27:1-36). Ships were powered by the force of the wind in sails or by the rowing of teams of slaves. In NT times Paul's missionary journeys were often made by ship. *1 Kings 9:26-28; 2 Chronicles 9:21; Acts 27:6-44; 28:11-16.*

SHITTIM
(SHIT-im)

Meaning "acacia trees." It was a place in the Plains of Moab, northeast of the Dead Sea. It was the last camping spot of the Israelites before crossing the Jordan into Canaan. Shittim was known for its acacia trees, called shittim wood, from which the ark of the covenant was made. *Numbers 25:1; 33:49; Joshua 2:1; 3:1; Hosea 5:2; Micah 6:5.*

SHOWBREAD

See *Bread of the Presence.*

SHROUD
(shrowd)

A linen sheet wound around a dead body in preparing it for burial. *Matthew 27:59; Mark 15:46; Luke 23:53.*

SICKLE

A tool for reaping grain. In early Bible times the blade was made of flint inserted into a curved wooden frame; later it was made of metal with a wooden handle riveted on. *Deuteronomy 16:9; 23:25; Joel 3:13; Mark 4:29.*

SIEGE OF JERUSALEM

SIDON

(SYE-don)

An ancient Phoenician city on the shores of the Mediterranean about twenty-five miles north of Tyre. These two cities are often mentioned together. Today the city that was Sidon is called Saida. In Bible times it was a commercial city famous for its purple dye industry. Jesus visited the area of Tyre and Sidon during his ministry. Paul stopped there on his way to Rome. *Genesis 10:19; 49:13; Joshua 19:28; Judges 1:31; 10:6; 2 Samuel 24:6; Jeremiah 25:22; 27:3; 47:4; Ezekiel 28:20-23; Joel 3:4; Matthew 11:21-23; Mark 3:8; Luke 4:26; 6:17; Acts 12:20; 27:3.*

SIEGE

(seej)

A military blockade. In OT times this method of warfare was used to capture a city or territory. The attackers attempted to cut off a city's water and flood supply and to weaken the city walls by tunneling under them or by smashing them with battering rams mounted on siege mounds. A city's ability to withstand a siege depended in large part on its water supply. The siege of Rabbah is the first recorded siege by the Israelites. *Deuteronomy 28:52-53; Joshua 10:31; 2 Samuel 11:1; 20:15; 2 Kings 17:5; 25:2; Jeremiah 32:24; 52:4.*

SIEVE

(siv)

An implement for sifting or cleaning grain after it has been winnowed. In the OT the word was often used as a figure of speech in referring to the day of judgment, when the Lord would "sift the nations." *Isaiah 30:28; Amos 9:9.*

SIGNS AND WONDERS

A combination of words used in the Bible in referring to the acts of God throughout Hebrew history. In the OT the phrase is found mostly in connection with the events surrounding the Israelites' escape from Egypt. In the NT the phrase refers to the miracles of Jesus Christ and the works of the apostles which revealed God's will and purpose. In his ministry Jesus did not use wonders to convince unbelievers, but the wonders were signs to those who did believe. In the faith of the church God's mightiest act was the Resurrection. *Deuteronomy 6:20-24; 26:8; Nehemiah 9:10; Psalm 135:9; Jeremiah 32:20; Matthew 24:24; Luke 11:29; John 2:11; 6:26; 11:47; Acts 2:22, 43; 6:8; 14:3; 15:12; Romans 15:19; 2 Corinthians 12:12; Hebrews 2:4.*

SILAS, SILVANUS
(SYE-luhss, sil-VAY-nuhss)
A leading member of the church in Jerusalem. Both the Aramaic form of his name (Silas) and the Latin form (Silvanus) are found in the NT. He was associated with both Paul and Peter in the mission of the early church. *Acts 15:22; 16:19; 17:4, 10, 14; 2 Corinthians 1:19; 1 Thessalonians 1:1; 1 Peter 5:12.*

SILOAM
(sye-LOH-uhm)
A pool in Jerusalem that was part of a network of canals, reservoirs, tunnels, and aqueducts built by Hezekiah to supply Jerusalem with water. When Sennacherib's Assyrian armies laid siege to Jerusalem, King Hezekiah kept the water flowing into the city by means of this water system, and Sennacherib failed at the time to capture Jerusalem. By this pool in NT times Jesus healed a man born blind. In 1880 a school boy crawled into Hezekah's tunnel on a hot day to cool off. He kept on crawling until he came to the spring with which it connected. He fell into the water and found on a wall an inscription which he reported to his schoolmaster. Scholars translated it and found that it explained how the tunnel was dug. *2 Kings 20:20; 2 Chronicles 32:4; Isaiah 7:3; 22:11; John 9:7.*

SILVERSMITH
One who works with silver. In OT times the smith was usually a "founder" who refined the ore and cast it by pouring the liquid metal into casts or molds (see Jeremiah 10:9). He also shaped the silver by beating it. He made musical instruments, decorations, and utensils for the tabnernacle and temple. Paul ran into trouble with a guild of silversmiths in Ephesus. *Judges 17:4; Acts 19:24.*

SIMEON
(SIM-ee-uhn)
1. One of the twelve sons of Jacob and the head of the tribe of Simeon, called Simoneonites. The Simeonites at one time occupied territory in central Canaan, but later they merged with the tribe of Judah. *Genesis 29:33; 42:24; Joshua 19:9; Judges 1:3, 17; 1 Chronicles 2:1; 12:25.*
2. A devout man of Jerusalem who took the baby Jesus in his arms and blessed him when Joseph and Mary brought the child to the temple to present him to the Lord. *Luke 2:25-35.*

SIMON
(SYE-muhn)
1. One of the twelve apostles. Jesus named him "Peter," or "Cephas," meaning "rock." (See *Peter.*) *Matthew 4:18; 10:2; 16:16; Mark 3:16; Luke 6:14; 7:36-50; 22:31; John 1:42; Acts 10:32.*
2. Simon the Cananaean or the Zealot was another of the twelve apostles of Jesus. (See *Cananaean.*) *Matthew 10:4; Mark 3:18; Luke 6:15; Acts 1:13.*

SIN, TRANSGRESSION, TRESPASS
(tranz-GRE-shuhn, TRESS-pass)
Distrust or disobedience of God that causes separation from God. In the

OT, acts which broke Hebrew law; acts of idol worship, hatred, disobedience, dishonesty, revolt, and the like were sins against God. They were looked upon as defiance of God and rebellion against God's rule. The prophets emphasized that their nation's sin brought suffering, military defeat, and finally the exile in Babylon. In the OT relief for the Hebrew nation lay in casting itself completely on God's mercy. The people were urged to repent of their transgressions and to keep God's law more carefully in the future. The NT emphasized that Christ conquered the power of sin through his death on the cross. He preached repentance and, in his life, demonstrated God's forgiveness. The NT made clear that a sinner can come to God through Christ, be judged and forgiven, and be given power to become a new person in Christ. *Genesis 18:20; Exodus 34:6-9; Leviticus 5:14-19; 16:15-16, 21-22; 1 Kings 8:34-35, 46-51; 2 Kings 17:7-18; Psalms 51:1-4; 85:2; Isaiah 1:18; Amos 5:12; Matthew 6:14-15; 9:5-6; Mark 2:15; Romans 4:15; 7:15-25; 1 Corinthians 15:3; Galatians 1:3-5.*

SINAI, MOUNT
(SYE-nye)
Also called Horeb. The mountain near which the Israelites camped on their way from Egypt to Canaan and on which God revealed himself to Moses and entered into a covenant relationship with the Israelites. The exact location of the mountain is uncertain. Tradition identifies it with Jebel Musa in the high mountains of the southern Sinai Peninsula. Some scholars think it was in northwestern Arabia. *Exodus 19:1-25; 24:16; 34:32; Leviticus 25:1; Nehemiah 9:13; Psalm 68:8.*

SIMEON SEES BABY JESUS

SLAVERY

The ownership of one person by another. In OT times, slavery was a common practice. The main source of a supply of slaves was captives taken in war. Children were sometimes sold into slavery to pay a family's debts, or a man might sell himself into slavery to pay his debts. Among the Hebrews, slaves were used mostly as domestic servants in the households of the rich. The laws of the Hebrews provided for the release of debtors—slaves—every seven years. Slavery continued in NT times and was practiced throughout the Roman Empire. The term "slave" is used in the OT and NT as a figure of speech for those who are owned by or controlled by sin. *Exodus 21:2-6, 20-21; Leviticus 25:39-46; Deuteronomy 16:12; 1 Kings 9:20-21; Matthew 8:9; Romans 6:17-18; Colossians 3:11; Philemon 1:15-16.*

SLEDGE, THRESHING
(SLEJ, THRESH-ing)

A machine made of two planks turned up slightly at the front. Sharp stones were set in holes in the bottom, and the machine was weighted with stones or with a driver. These machines were pulled over grain by animals, and the sharp stones collected the straw and separated it from the grain. *2 Samuel 24:22; Job 41:30; Isaiah 28:27-28; 41:15; Amos 1:3.*

SLING

A weapon for hurling small stones or clay pellets. It was made of two narrow strips of leather or woven cloth joined by a broader middle section and attached at the center to a pouch-shaped piece of leather for holding a stone. One end was tied to the wrest and the other end held by the hand so that it could be released and the stone thrown after being swung over the head in a circular motion. It was used as a weapon by shepherds as they protected their sheep from wild animals and by soldiers in war. The stones were carried in a bag slung over the shoulder. *Judges 20:16; 1 Samuel 17:40; 25:29; 1 Chronicles 12:2; Proverbs 26:8.*

SLOTHFUL, SLUGGARD
(SLOTH-fuhl, SLUG-uhrd)

Lazy, idle; one who is lazy or idle. In the OT wisdom books there are many wise sayings about the foolishness of living a lazy and idle life. Jesus used the same thought in his parable about the "wicked and slothful servant." *Proverbs 6:6; 10:26; 12:24, 27; 13:4; 15:19; 19:15, 24; 20:4; 21:25; 22:13; 24:30-34; 26:13-16; Ecclesiastes 10:18; Matthew 25:26.*

SNOW

Crystals of frozen water formed from the water vapor of the air. Snow is rare in Palestine. In the hills there are usually three days of snow each year, and there are many snow-capped mountains. There are imaginative passages in the OT telling where snow was stored in nature and describing the cold winds that caused ice, snow, and hail as God's breath. The coldness, cleanness, and beauty of snow were a wonder to the people of Bible times. *2 Samuel 23:20; Job 38:22; Psalms 51:7; 147:16-17; Proverbs 25:13; Isaiah 1:18; Jeremiah 18:14.*

SODOM
(SOD-uhm)

A city in the time of Abraham that is today thought to be under the waters of the southern end of the Dead Sea. This city and its neighboring city, Gomorrah, were known for their wickedness. They were destroyed by fire, and their destruction was often referred to as a warning for other wicked cities. Scientists, speculating about the cause of the fire, have suggested an earthquake, a volcanic eruption, an explosion of gas, or a stroke of lightning setting fire to oil seeping from the earth. The name Sodom has come to be used for any wicked place. *Genesis 10:19; 13:10-13; 18:16–19:29; Deuteronomy 29:23; Isaiah 1:9; 13:19; Jeremiah 23:14; Amos 4:11; Matthew 10:15.*

SOJOURNER
(SOH-jurn-er)

In the OT a person living in a community and among people not that person's own. A sojourner's position is between that of one who is native-born and one who is a stranger passing through. Among the Hebrews a sojourner had the same rights, privileges, and responsibilities as others in the community but could not own land. The Hebrews had laws that protected the rights of sojourners (and which recalled that the Hebrews themselves had been sojourners, first in Canaan and then in Egypt). *Genesis 23:4; Exodus 2:22; Leviticus 19:10; 24:22; Numbers 9:14; 35:15; Deuteronomy 10:19; 26:11; 1 Chronicles 29:15; Psalms 39:12; 119:19; Malachi 3:5; Ephesians 2:19.*

SOLOMON
(SOL-eh-mehn)

Son of David and Israel's third king (965–931 B.C.). He was famous far and wide for his wisdom. Solomon created a strong central government and undertook an extensive building program. He built the temple in Jerusalem, created a large army, developed a navy, and increased Israel's trade with foreign countries. He taxed the people to support his luxurious court and used forced labor for his building projects. This eventually led to revolt in Israel. He permitted his many foreign wives to worship other gods in Jerusalem. *2 Samuel 12:24; 1 Kings 1:1–12:19; 2 Chronicles 1:1–9:31; Nehemiah 13:26; Matthew 12:42; Luke 12:27; Acts 7:47.*

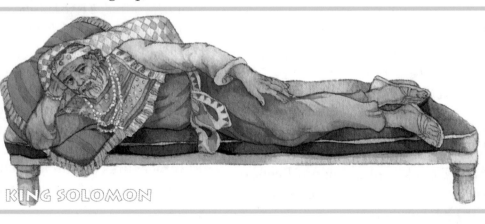

KING SOLOMON

SON OF GOD

In the OT a phrase, usually in the plural, used to mean divine beings, angels, or godlike persons. Israel was also called God's son in a special way because God had chosen the nation to be God's own people. Just as a son is dependent on and obedient to his father, so Israel was to be dependent on and obedient to God. In the NT the term refers to Jesus as the special or unique Son of God. The plural "sons (also translated *children*) of God" in NT use refers to believers in Jesus, whose faith in the Son of God makes them "children" also. *Genesis 6:2; Deuteronomy 14:1-2; Job 1:6; 38:7; Matthew 4:3, 6; 5:43-45; 27:40, 43; Mark 1:1; 3:11; 5:7; 15:39; Luke 1:35; 4:3, 9, 41; 20:36; John 1:34, 49; 3:16-18; Romans 1:4; 8:14-23.*

SON OF MAN

In the OT a term for a man or human being. In the NT it is a title for Jesus, one that he often used for himself. It refers to Jesus as one who was a son of man but who also was the Son of God, that is, a man but also the Christ. Before the time of Jesus there were writings that used "Son of man" to indicate the coming Messiah. *Numbers 23:19; Job 35:8; Psalms 8:4; 80:17; 144:3; Isaiah 51:12; Ezekiel 2:1, 3; 4:1; 6:1; Matthew 8:20; 12:8, 32, 40; 13:37; 16:13-16, 27-28; 26:63-64; Mark 2:10; 8:31; 9:12; 14:61-62; Luke 22:67-70; 24:7; John 1:51; Acts 7:56.*

SONG OF SOLOMON

An OT book containing a collection of love poems, some of which were intended for use in Hebrew weddings. It is also known as Song of Songs. Biblical scholars agree that Solomon was not the author of this book, though it may have been dedicated to him or have belonged to him (see Song of Solomon 1:1). It was probably edited in the fifth century B.C. *See the book itself.*

SOOTHSAYER

One who predicts future events by observing various kinds of signs. (See *Divination.*) *2 Kings 21:6; Isaiah 2:6; Jeremiah 27:9; Micah 5:12; Acts 16:16-19.*

SORCERY
(SOR-sur-ee)

The use of power that was supposedly gained through the use of charms, magic, or divination. The Israelites were forbidden to practice this sort of witchcraft. (See *Divination.*) *Deuteronomy 18:10; 2 Kings 17:17; Isaiah 19:3; Galatians 5:20.*

SOUL

In biblical use "soul" meant "life," the "self" or "person." The soul was not considered to be separate from the body. *1 Samuel 18:1; Psalms 42:1-11; 49:15; 116:8; 119:81; Isaiah 55:3; Mark 12:30; Acts 2:43; 1 Peter 2:11, 25.*

SPAN

A measure based on the distance between the end of the thumb and the little finger when the hand is spread. It measures a little more than eight inches. "Span" sometimes refers to length of life. *Exodus 28:16; 39:9; 1 Samuel 17:4; Isaiah 40:12; Ezekiel 13:13; Luke 12:25.*

SPARROW

In the Bible a perching, seed-eating bird of the finch family that may have been similar to our house sparrow. These birds were sold as food in the marketplace but were not of much value. *Psalm 84:3; Proverbs 26:2; Matthew 10:29-31; Luke 12:6-7.*

SPICE

The sweet-smelling leaves, roots, and gums of certain vegetables and herbs that were prized for use in cosmetics, sacred oil, incense, perfume, and in preparing a body for burial. In Bible times spices were not generally used in cooking as they are today. *Exodus 25:6; 1 Kings 10:2; 2 Chronicles 2:4; 16:14; Ezekiel 27:22; Mark 16:1; John 19:40.*

SPICES

SPIRIT

(SPIHR-it)

In the Bible a term applied to God, gods, bodiless beings, and to the divine element in humans. It was sometimes used to indicate God's power in humans. Originally meaning "movement of air" or "breath of God," it came to mean also the living force in human or creature. The phrase the "Spirit of God" referred to God's activity and God's power in the world. In the OT it was thought of as inspiring the prophets and leaders. In the NT the Holy Spirit was thought of as God's power in those who had faith in Christ. (See *Holy Spirit*.) *Genesis 1:2; Exodus 35:21; Judges 3:10; 1 Samuel 10:6-10; 2 Samuel 13:39; Job 10:12; 27:3; 33:4; Psalms 51:10; 104:30; Isaiah 42:5; Micah 3:8; Zechariah 12:1; Matthew 3:16; 5:3; 12:28, 43-45; Acts 8:7; Romans 8:10; Galatians 4:6.*

SPIT

To expel saliva from the mouth. Among the Hebrews spitting was a sign of contempt. However, saliva was thought to be useful in healing, and Jesus followed a Jewish belief and practice in the use of saliva to heal. *Numbers 12:14; Deuteronomy 25:9; Job 17:6; Mark 7:33; 8:23; 14:65.*

SPOIL

Loot or plunder taken as a right of conquest. In Bible times warfare involved the right to possess anything belonging to the conquered enemy such as cattle, clothing, metals, and the people themselves. There were rules for dividing the spoil. *Numbers 31:9-11; 1 Samuel 30:22-25; 2 Samuel 12:30; 1 Chronicles 26:27; Psalm 119:162; Proverbs 16:19; Isaiah 3:14; 9:3; 53:12.*

SPONGE

The skeleton of a type of marine animal. The sponge can absorb liquids without losing its own toughness. The word is used three times in the New Testament when Jesus, on the cross, is offered a sponge full of sour wine, or gall, to quench his thirst. *Matthew 27:48; Mark 15:36; John 19:29.*

STACTE
(STAK-ti)

Drops of spicy, gum substance from a number of shrubs and trees used in the holy incense. Flowers of stacte, or the storax shrub, are like snow drops in shape and are fragrant. *Exodus 30:34-35.*

STAFF

A long pole used by shepherds and travelers for climbing and for defense. (See *Rod.*) *Psalm 23:4; Isaiah 10:15; Zechariah 8:4; Matthew 10:10; Mark 6:8; Hebrews 11:21.*

STANDARD

In OT times a banner or sign of a tribe or an army troop. It was often used as a rallying signal. (See *Banner.*) *Numbers 2:2-3; 10:14; Isaiah 31:9; Jeremiah 4:6.*

STEADFASTNESS

Patient endurance. In the NT usually related to enduring afflictions, persecutions, and even martyrdom. *Romans 15:4-6; 2 Thessalonians 1:3-4; James 1:3-4.*

STEPHEN
(STEEV-uhn)

One of the seven men in the early Christian church selected to serve tables and supervise the giving of help to the poor. These men, called deacons, were chosen at the command of the Twelve, who prayed over them and laid hands on them, to appoint them to this work. Stephen became an evangelist, and later he was stoned to death as a result of the opposition of Greek-speaking Jews. He was the first Christian martyr. *Acts 6:5–8:2; 11:19; 22:20.*

STEPPE
(step)

In the Bible "steppe" refers to level, unforested land found on and along the edge of the desert east of the Jordan. It received eight to sixteen inches of rain per year. *1 Chronicles 6:78; Job 39:6.*

STEWARD
(Stoo-urd)

In the Bible an official who was responsible for the affairs of a large household. He directed servants, oversaw meals, and controlled household expenses on behalf of his master. In the NT Christians were spoken of as stewards of God's affairs. Their stewardship involved the use of time, talent, possessions, and themselves in behalf of God. *Genesis 43:19; 44:4; 1 Chronicles 27:31; 28:1; Isaiah 22:15; Daniel 1:11, 16; Matthew 20:8; Luke 8:3; 16:1-8; John 2:8-9; 1 Corinthians 4:1; Titus 1:7; 1 Peter 4:10.*

STIFF-NECKED

A word used in the OT to mean rebellious, stubborn, unteachable. It was originally taken from the way the ox stiffens his neck when he refuses direction. It was used to refer to Israel's refusal to listen to the word of God as delivered by the prophets. *Exodus 32:9; 33:3, 5; 34:9; 2 Chronicles 30:8; Acts 7:51.*

STOICS

(STOH-iks)

In NT times followers of a school of philosophy of the Greek-Roman world, founded in the fourth century B.C. It takes its name from a porch, a "stoak," which in Athens was an open colonnade where Zeno, the first teacher of this philosophy, taught. Stoic philosophy held that reason can rule all of life. *Acts 17:18.*

STONING

Among the Hebrews a method of execution. Death by stoning was required by OT law for such offenses as adultery, the worship of other gods, and blasphemy. Stoning took place outside the city. Two witnesses to the crime had to cast the first stone. If this first blow did not kill the criminal, all the people joined in the stoning. *Leviticus 24:14; Deuteronomy 17:2-7; 1 Kings 12:18; 21:13; Matthew 21:35; John 8:5-7; 10:31-33; Acts 7:58-60; 14:5-7.*

STORE-CITIES

Locations where in ancient times warehouses were built for the storage of government supplies of various kinds. Store-cities have been excavated in several places in Egypt. *Exodus 1:11; 1 Kings 9:19; 2 Chronicles 17:12-13; 32:27-29; Malachi 3:10.*

THE STONING OF STEPHEN

STRONGHOLD

A fortress chiefly for refuge or defense against military attack. In the Bible "stronghold" is used figuratively to mean God as a refuge for the righteous. *Judges 9:46-49; 1 Samuel 24:4; 2 Samuel 5:7; Psalms 9:9; 144:2; Amos 1:10; 6:8.*

SUCCOTH
(SOOK-oth)

1. Succoth is mentioned as the first stop on the flight of the Israelites from Egypt. *Exodus 12:37; 13:20.*
2. A city in eastern Palestine not far from the Jordan Valley. This town refused to supply bread for Gideon's army. After his military victory Gideon returned to punish the elders of the city for being so inhospitable. *Judges 8:5-17.*

SURETY
(SHUR-i-tee)

In OT times a person who made himself legally responsible for repaying the debts of another. The same term is used figuratively in the Bible, speaking of the relationship of God and Jesus to people. *Genesis 43:9; 44:32; Job 17:3; Proverbs 6:1; Hebrews 7:22.*

SURNAME
(SIR-naym)

A name added to a person's given name. In Bible times it might indicate the family connection, the occupation, or the qualities of a person. *Isaiah 44:5; 45:4; Mark 3:16-17; Acts 1:23; 4:36.*

SWADDLING

A square of cloth used chiefly to wrap a newborn baby to keep the child from moving his or her arms and legs. This custom was followed throughout the period of the OT and the NT. *Job 38:9; Luke 2:7.*

SYCAMORE
(SIKuh-mohr)

In Palestine a strong, tall tree with dense clusters of mulberry figs smaller and not so sweet as the fruit of the fig tree. This tree is not connected at all with the American sycamore. A "dresser of sycamore trees" pierced the unripe fruit with a sharp instrument to make it edible by pollinating the fruit so it would ripen. The wood of the tree is porous but enduring. Mummy cases made of it have lasted three thousand years. *1 Kings 10:27; 1 Chronicles 27:28; Psalm 78:47; Isaiah 9:10; Amos 7:14-15; Luke 19:4-7.*

SYNAGOGUE
(SIN-uh-gog)

Place of assembly for worship used by Jewish communities. The word does not appear in the OT, but it is believed that synagogues were first built in the Babylonian exile to give the Jews a place for prayer and instruction. The NT was used by the Jews chiefly for public worship but also for teaching the Scriptures and the law. The reading of the scripture was the most important part of the service, which included a brief talk and prayers. Scrolls of the law and the prophets were kept in the "ark" in the synagogue. In the first century A.D. most cities and towns had a synagogue. The buildings were rectangular and faced toward Jerusalem. Boys went to the synagogue to school. *Matthew 12:9; 13:54; 23:1-6; Mark 5:36; Luke 4:14-39; John 6:59; 16:2; 18:20; Acts 9:2; 13:5; 14:1; 17:1; 18:1-4.*

SYRIA, SYRIANS

(SIR-ee-uh, SIR-ee-uhnz)

In OT times the same as Aram, an area northeast of Palestine. The Syrians, or Arameans, were an important Semitic people living throughout the area in many scattered tribes and settlements. Damascus was the capital and the center of Syrian power. About 300 B.C. Syria stretched from the Mediterranean to the borders of India. Syria was often at war with the Israelites until it was conquered by the Assyrians. In NT times Syria was a small Roman province. *Judges 10:6; 2 Samuel 8:5-6; 10:6; 1 Kings 15:18; 2 Chronicles 16:2-3, 7; 18:30; 24:23-24; 28:23; Isaiah 7:1-8; Jeremiah 35:11; Amos 1:5; Matthew 4:24; Luke 2:2; Acts 15:23; 18:18; Galatians 1:21.*

INSIDE VIEW OF SYNAGOGUE

JESUS READING IN THE SYNAGOGUE

TABERNACLE

(TAB-ur-nak-uhl)

Meaning "tent" or "dwelling." The tabernacle was also called the "tent of meeting." It was a portable sanctuary for the worship of God. The tabernacle was carried by the Israelites during their wilderness journey from Egypt to Canaan. The ark of the covenant was kept in it, and for the Israelites it was a symbol of the presence of God. The tabernacle was probably kept in several different places in Canaan after the Israelites settled there. It finally was replaced by Solomon's temple. The tabernacle may have been more simple than the description in Exodus, which was written at a later time. *Exodus 25:1–27:21; 36:1–40:38 (a later description); Numbers 1:50, 53; 3:23-26; 7:1; 9:15, 22; 10:1-28; 1 Chronicles 6:48; 21:29.*

TABERNACLES, FEAST OF

See *Booths, Feast of.*

TABLE

A piece of furniture made with a flat surface fixed on legs. Several kinds of tables are mentioned in the Bible.
1. The most common use of the table was for eating, though usually only by the wealthy or by royalty. In NT times it was the custom to eat from tables while reclining on couches. For a banquet the tables were often arranged in a U-shape. *2 Kings 4;10; Psalm 23:5; Isaiah 21:5; Matthew 15:27; Luke 7:36-38; 22:14-27.*
2. Tables were used in connection with worship in the temple. The bread of the Presence was set out on a table. *Exodus 25:23-30; Ezekiel 40:39-43; Malachi 1:7.*

3. Money changers in the temple court used tables in their business. *Matthew 21:12.*

4. The "tables" of the testimony or covenant were two stone tablets on which the Ten Commandments were written. *Exodus 24:12; 31:18; 32:15-16; 34:1-4; Deuteronomy 9:9-17; 10:1-5; 1 Kings 8:9; Hebrews 9:4.*

TABLET

In Bible times a writing surface made from any of a number of materials: stone, wood, metal, or wax. A writing tablet was also made from clay which had been moistened, kneaded, and shaped. Sometimes the word was used in a figure of speech such as the "tablet of your heart." *Proverbs 3:3; 7:3; Isaiah 8:1; 30:8; Jeremiah 17:1; Habakkuk 2:2; Luke 1:63; 2 Corinthians 3:3.*

TABOR, MOUNT

(TAY-bor)

A hill in the Valley of Jezreel about twelve miles southwest of the Sea of Galilee. It is mentioned in connection with the judges in Israel. It is traditionally identified with the Mount of Transfiguration, but this is uncertain. Helena, the mother of Constantine, built a church on Mt. Tabor in A.D. 326. A modern road to the top of Mt. Tabor makes it possible to take a bus trip for a view of the valley. It is possible that Jesus came here from nearby Nazareth to see this view. *Joshua 19:22; Judges 4:6, 12, 14; 8:18; Psalm 89:12; Jeremiah 46:18.*

STONE TABLETS

TALENT
(TAL-ent)

In OT times the standard large weight used for payment before coins were made. It probably weighed about seventy-five pounds. Other nations throughout the ancient Near East used talents. In Jesus' parable of the talents, a talent is worth more than fifteen year's wages of a soldier or a laborer. *Exodus 25:39; 38:24; 2 Samuel 12:30; 2 Kings 5:23; 18:14; 2 Chronicles 36:3; Matthew 18:23-24; 25:18-28.*

TAMARISK
(TAM-uh-risk)

A desert shrub or tree with small, scale-like leaves pressed close to feathery branches. Some species have a gumlike substance, thought by some to be similar to the manna which the Israelites ate as they journeyed through the wilderness. *Genesis 21:33; 1 Samuel 22:6; 31:13.*

TANNER, TANNING

One who prepared leather from the skins of animals by using lime, juices from certain plants, or the bark or leaves of certain trees; the process of tanning skins. Because tanners handled the skins of dead animals—which according to Hebrew law were unclean—they were unpopular among the Hebrews and had to live outside the cities. The fact that Peter was willing to stay in the house of Simon the tanner indicates that he was ready to change his views about people who were considered outsiders. *Exodus 25:5; 26:14; 35:7; Acts 9:43; 10:6, 32.*

TARSHISH
(TAHR-shish)

A faraway port of uncertain location, perhaps Spain. In the OT "ships of Tarshish" referred to large, seagoing ships regardless of their origin or ports of call. Tarshish also appears in the OT as a personal name. *Genesis 10:4; 1 Kings 10:22; 22:48; Esther 1:14; Psalm 72:10; Isaiah 2:16; 23:1, 10, 14; 66:19; Jeremiah 10:9; Ezekiel 27:12; Jonah 1:3; 4:2.*

TARSUS
(TAR-suhss)

In NT times the capital of the Roman province of Cilicia, located on the southeastern coast of Asia Minor. Tarsus was a prosperous city set in a fertile coastal plane. It was well known for its schools and industries, which included the weaving of linen and the making of tents. Tarsus had a mixed population of Greeks, Romans, and Jews. Because Tarsus was a free Roman city, Paul, who was born there, had Roman citizenship even though he was a Jew. The history of Tarsus dates back to about 3000 B.C. In the modern city of Tarsus in Turkey in 1947 archaeologists excavated a Roman building decorated with mosaics. *Acts 9:11, 30; 11:25; 21:39; 22:3.*

TASKMASTER

See *Overseer.*

TAX

Payment which people are forced to make to support the government, local, national, or foreign. The tax in Bible times was paid in money, treasure, farm products, hours of labor, and so on. In the OT story of Joseph in Egypt there is the report of a tax taken in grain during the seven years of plenty (see Genesis 41:34-35, 47-48). In Israel during the time of the judges there was no army or royal court to support, and therefore no taxes were required. Saul and David supported their armies and courts with tribute and loot taken from the defeated Canaanites around them. Solomon was probably the first to collect a state tax to support the expending kingdom. He used forced labor to complete the temple (see 1 Kings 5:13). He also collected toll from caravans and traders passing through his territory (see 1 Kings 10:14-15). Throughout their history the Hebrews were often forced to pay tribute to foreign conquerors such as the Assyrians and Babylonians. This tax was usually collected from the defeated king. The Persians developed a system for collecting tax from individuals. In NT times Palestine was under the authority of Rome. There was apparently a systematic enrollment of individuals for the purposes of a head, or poll, tax (see Luke 2:1-3). Under King Herod the Great there was a tax on farm products, a sales tax, and in Jerusalem a house tax. Aside from government taxes the Hebrews throughout their history and into NT times paid a half-shekel fee to support the sanctuary (see Exodus 30:11-16). This tax was called "atonement money." *2 Chronicles 24:6-11; 2 Kings 23:35; Nehemiah 5:4; Ezra 4:13; Matthew 17:24; 22:17, 19; Mark 12:14; Luke 3:12; 19:2; Romans 13:6-7.*

TAX COLLECTOR, TAX OFFICE

An official who collects and keeps account of taxes; the table or booth set up at the gate of the city, on a caravan route, or in the marketplace for collecting taxes. Tax collectors are never popular, and to the Jews of NT times they were especially despised because they represented the foreign authority of Rome. Very often these revenue officers charged too much in order to keep some part of the money for themselves. *Matthew 9:9-11; 11:19; 18:17; Mark 2:14-16; Luke 5:27-30.*

TEACHER

Anyone who instructs. In the OT usually anyone who instructed in and explained the law. King Jehoshaphat sent his princes out as teachers of the law. Part of the duty of the Levites was to explain the meaning of the law (see Nehemiah 8:7-8). In the NT "teacher" is chiefly a title of respect meaning "master" or "rabbi." It was often applied to Jesus. Some leaders of the early church were also called teachers. *2 Chronicles 17:7-9; Isaiah 30:20-21; Luke 2:46; 3:12; 5:17; John 1:38; 3:10; Acts 13:1; 1 Corinthians 12:28-29; Ephesians 4:11; 2 Timothy 1:11; James 3:1.*

TEKOA

(te-KOH-uh)

A city in the hill country of Judah about six miles south of Bethlehem. It was the home of the prophet Amos. It also appears in the OT as a personal name. *2 Samuel 14:2-4; 2 Chronicles 11:5-6; 20:20; Jeremiah 6:1; Amos 1:1.*

TEMPLE, JERUSALEM

(juh-ROO-suh-lem)

The great sacred building constructed in Jerusalem as the religious center of the life of the community of the Hebrews. It was also called the house of the Lord, or the house of God. There are three temples mentioned in the Bible, all built on the same spot. This location is absolutely certain and is occupied today by the famous Muslim "Dome of the Rock." The first temple was built by King Solomon on the land chosen by his father David. He brought in skilled builders from Phoenicia to supervise the work. The building took seven years, and Solomon spared no expense. This first temple was probably completed around 950 B.C. It was destroyed by the Babylonians in 586 B.C. When the people returned to Jerusalem after their exile, they rebuilt the temple, following the basic plan of the original but in a much simpler way. The temple stood for five hundred years. Around 20 B.C. King Herod built a third temple. This is the temple mentioned in the NT and the one that Jesus knew. This was a much-enlarged building set in a complex of other royal houses and surrounded by a system of porches in the Greek style. This building was destroyed about A.D. 70. The basic ground plan for all three temples was the same. Each one had three rooms: the porch or vestibule; the holy place where the golden candlestick, the table holding the bread of the Presence, and the altar of incense were kept; and the holy of holies, where the presence of God among God's people was symbolized. In this innermost room, the most holy place, there were two enormous cherubim and, until the Exile, the ark of the covenant. In the courtyard outside the temple was the great altar of burnt offering and a spectacular brass basin, called the molten sea, which contained water for the priests to wash themselves and the offerings and vessels. *1 Kings 6:1-38; 2 Chronicles 36:18-19; Ezra 5:14-16; Jeremiah 7:4; 50:28; Habakkuk 2:20; Matthew 4:5; 12:5-6; 21:12-16, 23; Mark 11:11, 15-16; 12:35; John 2:14-21; 10:23-24; Acts 3:1-10; 4:1; 21:28-30; 25:8; 26:21.*

TEN COMMANDMENTS

Meaning "ten words." They summarize the covenant between God and God's people, making clear to the Hebrews their duty to God and to others. In the account in Exodus, Moses receives this law directly from God, who writes on two tables of stone. This great occasion at Mt. Sinai when God revealed God to the Hebrews was important in their understanding of themselves as God's people. The longer explanations of the law found in Deuteronomy were probably added at a later time. *Exodus 20:1-17; 34:28; Deuteronomy 4:13; 5:6-22; 10:4.*

TENT OF MEETING

Another name for the tabernacle. (See *Tabernacle.*)

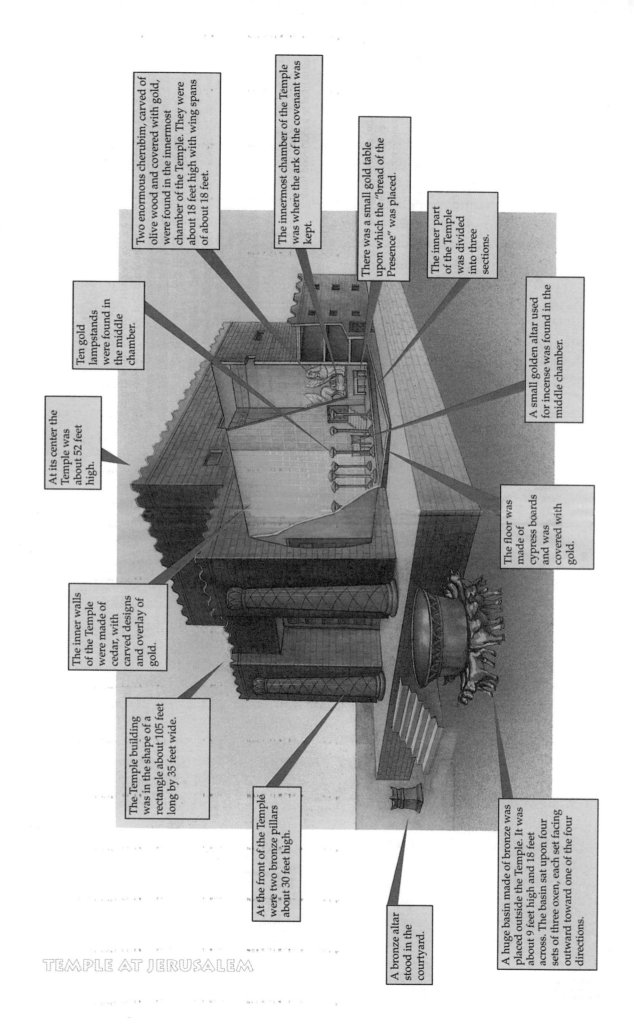

Two enormous cherubim, carved of olive wood and covered with gold, were found in the innermost chamber of the Temple. They were about 18 feet high with wing spans of about 18 feet.

The innermost chamber of the Temple was where the ark of the covenant was kept.

There was a small gold table upon which the "bread of the Presence" was placed.

The inner part of the Temple was divided into three sections.

Ten gold lampstands were found in the middle chamber.

A small golden altar used for incense was found in the middle chamber.

At its center the Temple was about 52 feet high.

The floor was made of cypress boards and was covered with gold.

The inner walls of the Temple were made of cedar, with carved designs and overlay of gold.

The Temple building was in the shape of a rectangle about 105 feet long by 35 feet wide.

At the front of the Temple were two bronze pillars about 30 feet high.

A bronze altar stood in the courtyard.

A huge basin made of bronze was placed outside the Temple. It was about 9 feet high and 18 feet across. The basin sat upon four sets of three oxen, each set facing outward toward one of the four directions.

TEMPLE AT JERUSALEM

TENTMAKER

Weaver of a feltlike cloth usually made of goats' hair for use in making tents. Some of this cloth was produced in Cilicia, the province in which Tarsus, Paul's native city, was located. It was a tradition among the Jews that every boy should learn a trade no matter what his profession or wealth. Paul's trade may have been tentmaking. Wherever he traveled, he earned his living by working at his trade. Sometimes he lived and worked with others who had the same trade, as in the home of Aquila and Priscilla in Corinth. *Acts 18:3.*

TERAH
(TAIR-uh)

Father of Abraham. *Genesis 11:26-32; Joshua 24:2; Luke 3:34.*

TERAPHIM
(TER-uh-fim)

In OT times small idols made of clay or wood and kept as household gods. *Judges 17:5; 18:14-18; 2 Kings 23:24; Ezekiel 21:21; Hosea 3:4; Zechariah 10:2.*

TEREBINTH
(TER-uh-binth)

A strong, study tree of the desert with spreading branches, a heavy trunk, and boughs thick enough to make a good shade from the hot sun. The leaves are coppery green, and red berries hang in clusters. It is sometimes called the turpentine tree. *Isaiah 6:13; Hosea 4:13.*

TERTIUS
(TUR-shuhss)

A friend of Paul to whom the apostle's letter to the Romans was dictated. He gives his own name and greeting in the letter. *Romans 16:22.*

TERTULLUS
(tur-TUHL-uhss)

The prosecutor of Paul before the Roman governor of Judea. He charged that Paul had been a disturber of the peace, a public nuisance, and the leader of the Nazarenes (Christians), who were dangerous extremists. *Acts 24:2-8.*

TESTIMONY
(TES-teh-moh-nee)

In the Bible, evidence given by a witness to the action and demands of God. In the OT it is often used in connection with the ark or the tabernacle and refers to the Ten Commandments, the special testimony of God's statutes and judgments. In the NT this word refers especially to evidence given by the witnesses to the mighty acts which revealed God's action through Jesus Christ. *Exodus 25:16, 21; 30:36; Numbers 1:50; 17:4-10; Deuteronomy 6:17; Psalms 19:7; 119:2, 24, 36, 59, 125, 152; Isaiah 8:16, 20; Matthew 10:18; Mark 14:55; Luke 21:13; John 1:7, 19; 3:11, 32-33; 5:31; 8:14; Acts 4:33; 2 Timothy 1:8.*

TETRARCH
(TET-rark)

Originally the ruler of a fourth part of an area. This exact meaning was lost however, and in NT times it was the title for a ruler of a part of a Roman province. This title was lower than king and did not indicate the same authority. The tetrarch is called a king, however, as Herod is in Matthew 14:9. *Matthew 14:1; Luke 3:1; 9:7; Acts 13:1.*

THADDAEUS
(tha-DEE-uhss)
One of Jesus' twelve apostles. Possibly this name was given to Judas the son of James to avoid confusion with Judas Iscariot, who betrayed Jesus. According to tradition Thaddaeus helped carry the gospel to Armenia. *Matthew 10:3; Mark 3:18.*

THEOPHILUS
(thee-AH-fil-uhss)
The person to whom the Gospel of Luke and the Book of Acts are addressed. Who he was no one knows, but he is the only person to whom NT writings have been dedicated. *Luke 1:3, Acts 1:1.*

LIVING IN TENTS

THESSALONIANS, FIRST AND SECOND LETTERS TO THE

(thess-uh-LOH-nee-uhnz)
Two letters written by Paul to the church at Thessalonica. This was a struggling young church which he had started. The first letter was written about A.D. 50 or 51 after Timothy had returned from a visit to Thessalonica and had reported on the church. In the letter Paul expressed his love and concern for the church and gave instructions for these new Christians. The second letter probably was written shortly after the first. It was written to encourage the Thessalonians to stand firm in the face of persecution, to correct a misunderstanding some of them had about the expected return of Christ, and to advise the church on how to discipline lazy members. These two letters are regarded as the earliest writings in the NT. *See the books themselves.*

THESSALONICA

(thess-uh-loh-NYE-kuh)
In NT times an important trading city and chief seaport of the Roman province of Macedonia. Today it is known as Salonica and is the second largest city of Greece. In spite of a riot stirred up against him by Thessalonian Jews, Paul established a Christian church largely made up of Gentiles. *Acts 17:1-13; 27:2; Philippians 4:16; 1 Thessalonians 1:1; 2 Thessalonians 1:1; 2 Timothy 4:10.*

THISTLES, THORNS

Wild plants with sharp briers or spines on their stems and leaves. In the hot, rocky soil of Palestine this type of plant could thrive best. The blossoms of one type were a pink-lavender with silvery green leaves; another had golden yellow blossoms. Thistles and thorns were used in figures of speech as symbols of worthlessness. Since ancient times thorny bushes have been used as hedges between pieces of ground. Dried thorn bushes have also been used for fuel down through the centuries in Bible lands. *Genesis 3:18; Job 31:40; Proverbs 26:9; Isaiah 9:18; 34:13; Hosea 10:8; Matthew 7:16; 13:7, 22; Mark 4:7, 18; 15:17; John 19:2, 5; Hebrews 6:8.*

THOMAS

(TOM-ehs)
Meaning "twin," one of the twelve apostles. He was also known as Didymus among Greek-speaking Christians. Thomas was not present when Jesus appeared to the disciples on the day of the Resurrection. Thomas said that he could not believe what the others told him without proof. Later he did see the risen Jesus with his own eyes, but he became most famous for his doubting. However, he was also courageous as was proved by his willingness to accompany Jesus to Jerusalem when he was certain that death awaited them. *Matthew 10:2-3; Mark 3:18; Luke 6:15; John 11:16; 20:24-29; Acts 1:13.*

THRESHING

The process of separating the kernels of grain from the straw. In Bible times the sheaves of grain were laid out on the threshing floor on a flat surface of rock or earth pounded hard—usually in an open place outside a town. The stalks of grain were beaten with a stick or trampled by oxen or by a donkey pulling a threshing sledge over them. *Genesis 50:10-11; Leviticus 26:5; Numbers 15:20; Ruth 3:2; 1 Samuel 23:1; 1 Kings 22:10; 1 Chronicles 21:15-28; Job 41:30; Isaiah 28:27; Jeremiah 51:33; 1 Corinthians 9:9-10.*

THRONE

In the Bible the ceremonial chair or seat of a king from which he performed his royal duties. The throne was actually the symbol of the kingship. In the OT the ark of the covenant represented the throne of God the king. Sometimes Jerusalem or the temple or the nation was called the "throne of God." *2 Samuel 3:10; 7:16; 1 Kings 10:18-20; 22:19; 1 Chronicles 22:10; 28:5; Psalms 9:4; 11:4; 47:8; 122:5; Isaiah 6:1; Jeremiah 3:17; 43:10; Matthew 5:34; 25:31; Luke 1:32; Acts 2:30; Hebrews 1:8; Revelation 1:4; and other places in Revelation.*

THUNDER AND LIGHTNING

The loud vibrations and electrical flashes which often accompany storms. In Palestine these natural occurrences are usually in the spring and autumn. They are always awe-inspiring, and the people in Bible times could see divine power demonstrated in them. Some passages in the Bible mention thunder as the voice of God and lightning as the spear or sword of God. Storms often came from the direction of their enemies and suggested to the Israelites the power of God. *Exodus 9:23-34; 19:19; 20:18; 1 Samuel 12:17-18; Job 26:14; 37:2-5; Psalms 29:3; 104:7; Jeremiah 10:13; John 12:29; Revelation 6:1; 10:3-4.*

THRONE

TIBERIAS

(tye-BIHR-ee-uhss)

In NT times a city on the west coast of the sea of Galilee. It was built by the tetrarch Herod Antipas about A.D. 25 and was the capital of the tetrarchy of Galilee and Perea. The name Tiberias honored the emperor Tiberius Caesar. During this period it was a name for the Sea of Galilee. *John 6:1, 23; 21:1.*

TIBERIUS CAESAR

(tye-BIHR-ee-uhss SEE-zur)

The second emperor of the Roman Empire. The adopted son of Augustus, he was named by the Roman Senate to succeed his father. He came to the throne in A.D. 14. In the Gospel of Luke the beginning of the ministry of Jesus is dated as the fifteenth year in the reign of Tiberius. In other places in the Gospels he is mentioned only by title as Caesar. *Matthew 22:17-21; Mark 12:14-17; Luke 3:1; 20:22-25; 23:2; John 19:12-15.*

TIGLATH-PILESER (III), TIGLATH-PIL-NESER

(TIG-lath-pi-LEE-zur, TIl-gath-pil-NEE-zur)

King of Assyria from 745 to 727 B.C. He was a strong ruler and a skillful military leader. His reign ended a time of weakness for Assyria and laid the groundwork for the Assyrian Empire. His conquests included much of Israel and Judah. He deported many of the people to other parts of his empire and exacted tribute from their kings. After a campaign against Babylonia he made himself king of the city of

Babylon, taking the name of Pul. *2 Kings 15:19-20, 29; 16:7-10; 1 Chronicles 5:6, 26; 2 Chronicles 28:20.*

TIGRIS

(TYE-gris)

An important river in western Asia, which originates in Armenia. It flows through the Mesopotamian plain and joins the Euphrates River forty miles north of the Persian Gulf. It empties into this gulf. Many important ancient cities such as Nineveh, the capital of Assyria, were located on the Tigris. The fertile valley between the Tigris and Euphrates river was the land where the Assyrians and Babylonians created great empires. *Daniel 10:4.*

TIMBREL

(TIM-brehl)

A musical instrument like a tambourine. *Exodus 15:20; Judges 11:34; 1 Samuel 18:6; Psalms 68:25; 150:4; Isaiah 24:8; 30:32.*

TIMOTHY

(TIM-uh-thee)

A trusted and faithful worker with Paul who often traveled with Paul on his missionary journeys. He is mentioned in many of the letters Paul wrote to the early churches. When Paul could not visit a church himself, he often sent Timothy. Paul sent Timothy to Thessalonica, for example, to encourage the Thessalonian Christians who were being persecuted. This gave Paul a direct report on how the young church was getting along. (See *Timothy, First and Second*

Letters to.) *Acts 16:1-3; 17:14-15; 18:5; 19:22; 20:4; Romans 16:21; 1 Corinthians 4:17; 16:10-11; 2 Corinthians 1:1, 19; Philippians 2:19; Colossians 1:1; 1 Thessalonians 1:1; Philemon 1:1.*

TIMOTHY, FIRST AND SECOND LETTERS TO

Two letters in the NT which along with the letter to Titus are called the Pastoral Letters. In them a chief pastor is giving practical advice about church matters. Scholars think the two letters were written in the first half of the

second century and were probably written in the name of Paul. Some fragments of Paul's writings may be in 2 Timothy. *See the books themselves.*

TIRZAH

(tihr-zuh)
An OT city in Canaan conquered by Joshua. It later became the capital of the northern kingdom Israel from the time of Jeroboam until Omri moved the capital to Samaria. Its location is uncertain. Also, a personal name. *Joshua 12:24; 1 Kings 14:17; 15:21, 33; 16:17-18, 23-24; 2 Kings 15:14, 16; Song of Solomon 6:4.*

TITHE

(tythe)
A tenth part. In Bible times a tenth of the produce of the fields, orchards, and flocks was given for the support of the priesthood, for the upkeep of places of worship, and for charity. This was the way in which the Hebrews acknowledged God's ownership of the land and all that it produced. Jesus criticized people who were careful to tithe only their material possessions but neglected to practice justice and to show love in their relationships. *Genesis 28:22; Leviticus 27:30-32; Numbers 18:21-28; Deuteronomy 12:6-17; 14:22-29; 2 Chronicles 31:5-6; Nehemiah 10:37-38; 12:44; 13:5, 12; Amos 4:4; Malachi 3:8, 10; Matthew 23:23; Luke 11:42; 18:12; Hebrews 7:4-9.*

TITUS

(tye-tuss)

A Gentile Christian and co-worker with Paul. When Paul first took Titus to Jerusalem, the Jewish Christians insisted that he could not be one of them unless he was circumcised. Paul, however, used Titus' case to demonstrate that the old Jewish law did not apply to Christians who were not Jews. Faith in Jesus Christ was the only requirement. (See *Titus, Letter to.*) *2 Corinthians 2:13; 7:6, 13-14; 8:6, 23; 12:17-18; Galatians 2:1-10; 2 Timothy 4:10.*

TITUS, LETTER TO

A letter in the NT which, like the letters to Timothy, is one of the Pastoral Letters. It is a letter from a chief pastor to the pastor of a church telling how to organize churches and the kind of people to appoint to office. It was probably written in the name of Paul in the first half of the second century. *See the book itself.*

TOMB

(toom)

In Bible times a natural or artificial cave cut into the rock of a hillside and used as a burial place for the dead. Shelves or ledges were cut into the walls of the cave, and the bodies were laid on them. In NT times tombs were often sealed with a round, flat stone which was rolled in front of the entrance. Pits, caves, and cisterns were used as tombs by the poor. Since contact with a dead body made a person ceremonially unclean, tombs were whitewashed to warn people to stay away from them. *Genesis 50:5; 2 Samuel 2:32; Isaiah 22:16; Matthew 8:28; 23:27-29; 27:52-60; Mark 5:2-3; 6:29; 16:2-8; Luke 8:27; John 11:38; 20:11.*

TONGUES, GIFT OF

Also referred to as "speaking in tongues." An emotional experience in which a person considered possessed by the Holy Spirit utters sounds that often cannot be understood. Speaking in tongues was common among the early Christians. The apostle Paul wrote that speaking in tongues was a genuine gift of the Holy Spirit, but warned that it encouraged self-centeredness and disrupted worship. He felt it should be controlled. Speaking in tongues was a part of many religions of the ancient world. *Acts 2:3-11; 10:46; 19:6; 1 Corinthians 12:20, 28, 30; 13:1; 14:2-33, 39-40.*

TOWER

A high, narrow structure, generally higher than things around it. In Bible times towers were a common sight located in cities, pastures, vineyards, and farmlands. Built of brick or stone, they served chiefly for refuge or defense against military attack. Watchtowers were built in vineyards and fields. From here the crops could be guarded against animals and against raiding parties as the crops ripened and were harvested. The word was also used symbolically in referring to God's protective power. *Genesis 11:4-5; Judges 9:51; 2 Kings 9:17; 17:9; 2 Chronicles 14:7; 26:10; 27:4; 32:5; Psalm 61:3; Proverbs 18:10; Isaiah 2:15; Micah 4:8; Matthew 21:33; Mark 12:1; Luke 13:4.*

TRADITION, ORAL; TRADITION OF THE ELDERS

(truh-DISH-uhn)

Unwritten memories, stories, customs, beliefs, laws, and other knowledge handed down from one generation to another by word of mouth. Much OT material comes from the oral traditions kept alive among the Hebrews. "Tradition of the elders" refers to the Jewish unwritten law, the purpose of which was to make clear the written law. *Matthew 15:1-6; Mark 7:1-13; Galatians 1:14.*

JESUS' EMPTY TOMB

TRANSGRESSION

Meaning "to go beyond" the limits of the law. In the Bible it means revolt, rebellion, going against the will of God. (See *Sin, Transgression, Trespass.*)

TRANSJORDAN

(trans-JOR-duhn)

The general term for the area just east of the Jordan River. The area is usually referred to in the Bible as "beyond the Jordan." It included the territories of Ammon, Bashan, Edom, Gilead, and Moab. It is roughly the same as the modern state of Jordan.

TRAPS AND SNARES

Contrivances for catching birds and animals. In Bible times nets, rope nooses, and pits covered with camouflaged nets or brush were used to trap birds and animals. The terms are also used in figures of speech to describe sudden danger, unexpected death or disaster. *Joshua 23:13; Job 18:8-10; 22:10; Psalms 18:4-5; 69:22; 91:3; 140:5; 142:3; Jeremiah 18:22; 91:3; 140:5; 142:3; Jeremiah 18:22; 48:43-44; Ezekiel 12:13; 17:20; Amos 3:5; Luke 21:34; Romans 11:9.*

TRESPASS

See *Sin, Transgression.*

TRIBE

A group of clans or families held together by bonds of blood and kinship. It was the normal social unit among Semitic nomads, especially among the Israelites before the conquest of Canaan. According to tradition the people of Israel consisted of twelve tribes who were the descen-dants of Jacob (also called Israel) and his sons. The names of the tribes were also given to the tribal territories they occupied. *Genesis 49:28; Numbers 1:1-54; Joshua 18:11–19:51; 2 Samuel 5:1; Matthew 19:28; Romans 11:1; Philippians 3:5.*

TRIBULATION

(trib-yoo-LAY-shuhn)

Suffering, distress, and affliction of various kinds. In the NT it especially refers to the suffering of Christians for their faith. *Deuteronomy 4:30-31; Matthew 13:18-21; John 16:33; Acts 14:22; Romans 8:35; 12:12; Revelation 7:14.*

TRIBUNAL

(tri-BU-nuhl)

Also called judgment seat. The official place from which the Roman governor heard and judged cases brought before him. *Matthew 27:19; John 19:13; Acts 25:6, 10, 17.*

TRIBUNE

(TRIB-un)

A Roman military officer in charge of a cohort (army division). *Acts 21:31-33; 23:17-22; 24:22; 25:23.*

TRIBUTE

(TRIB-ut)

A compulsory contribution in money, goods, or people forced upon a defeated nation by its conquerors. Sometimes a nation paid tribute to obtain military help from another nation. In the NT it is another word for tax. *Numbers 31:28-41; Judges 3:14-18; 2 Samuel 8:2, 6; 2 Chronicles 28:21; Hosea 10:6; Matthew 17:25; Luke 20:22.*

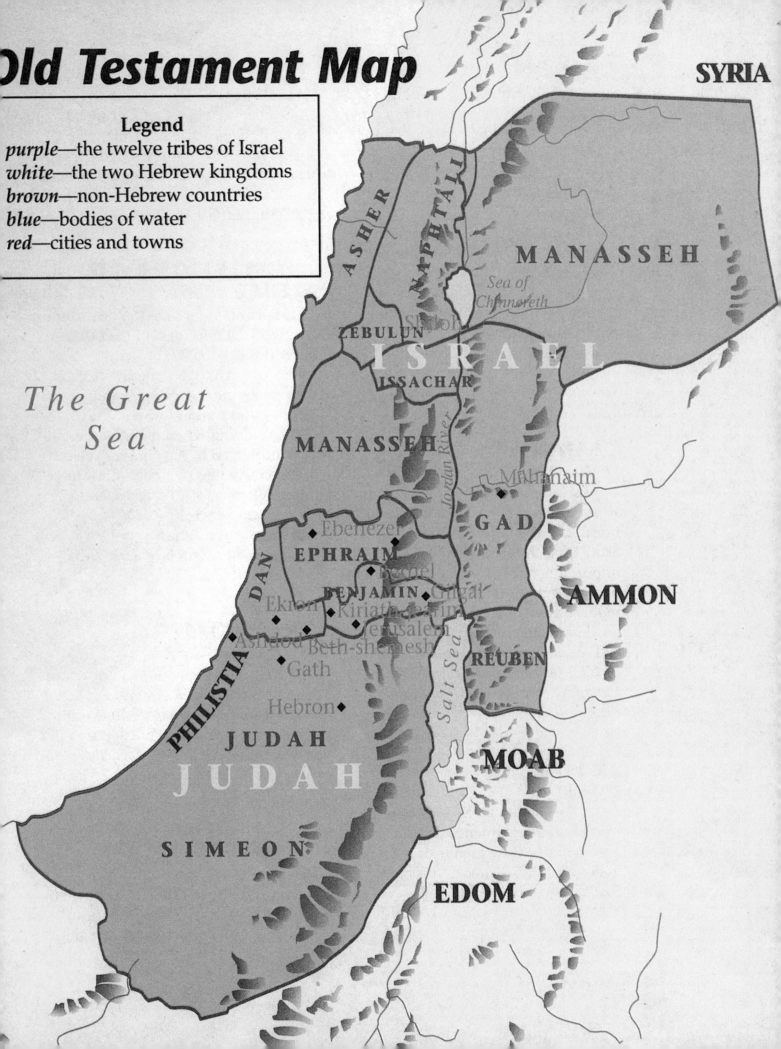

Old Testament Map

SYRIA

Legend
purple—the twelve tribes of Israel
white—the two Hebrew kingdoms
brown—non-Hebrew countries
blue—bodies of water
red—cities and towns

ASHER

NAPHTALI

MANASSEH

Sea of Chinnereth

Shiloh

ZEBULUN

I S R A E L

ISSACHAR

The Great Sea

MANASSEH

Jordan River

Mahanaim

GAD

Ebenezer

EPHRAIM

Bethel

DAN

BENJAMIN

Gilgal

Ekron

Kiriath-jearim

AMMON

Ashdod

Beth-shemesh

Jerusalem

Gath

REUBEN

Salt Sea

Hebron

PHILISTIA

JUDAH

J U D A H

MOAB

S I M E O N

EDOM

TRIGON

A musical instrument, a triangular lyre or harp. (See *Musical Instruments.*) *Daniel 3:5, 7, 10, 15.*

TROAS

(TROH-az)

In NT times a city located in north-western Asia Minor on the shore of the Aegean Sea. Paul visited and preached in Troas several times. It was here that Paul had a vision directing him to preach the gospel in Macedonia (a part of Europe). *Acts 16:8, 11; 20:5-6; 2 Corinthians 2:12; 2 Timothy 4:13.*

TRUMPET

(TRUHM-pet)

A musical instrument. In OT times trumpets were made from animals' horns and were used to muster an army or as the signal that some important occasion was about to begin or some announcement was to be made. Straight trumpets of metal were used in the temple in pairs or for special services in large numbers. (See *Musical Instruments.*) *Judges 3:27; 2 Chronicles 5:12-13; 29:26-28; Psalms 81:3; 98:6.*

TUNIC

(TU-nik)

A kind of coat. In Bible times a long, shirtlike undergarment draped over one shoulder. It was made of wool or linen. *Job 30:18; Matthew 10:10; John 19:23.*

TURBAN

(TUHR-ben)

A head covering. A cloth wrapped around the head, usually made of linen. In the OT the priest wore a special turban as part of ceremonial clothing. *Exodus 28:4, 39; Leviticus 8:9; 16:4; Job 29:14; Ezekiel 44:18; Zechariah 3:5.*

TURTLEDOVE OR DOVE

A small variety of pigeon. It was used in sacrificial offerings. In the OT two turtledoves could be brought by a poor person as a sin offering instead of a larger more expensive animal. In the NT Mary brought two turtledoves as her offering when the infant Jesus was presented in the temple. The dove has come to be a symbol of the Holy Spirit. *Genesis 15:9; Leviticus 5:7-10; 12:6-8; Numbers 6:10; Psalm 74:18-19; Song of Solomon 2:11-12; Jeremiah 8:7; Matthew 3:16; Mark 1:10; Luke 2:24; 3:22; John 1:32.*

TYCHICUS

(TIK-i-kuhss)

A Christian from the Roman province of Asia who associated with Paul on his missionary journeys. Along with Onesimus he carried Paul's letter to the church in Colossae. *Acts 20:4; Ephesians 6:21; Colossians 4:7; 2 Timothy 4:12; Titus 3:12.*

TYRE

(tire)

A very old Phoenician city located on the east coast of the Mediterranean Sea. Tyre was important as a trading and shipping center throughout Bible times. Its chief product was purple dye made from secretions of shellfish. The dye, known as Tyrian purple, was the most famous and precious of dyes in ancient times. Tyre is usually mentioned with Sidon. Today it is an Arab town named Sur. (See *Sidon.*) *Joshua 19:29; 2 Samuel 5:11; 24:7; 1 Kings 5:1; Isaiah 23:1; Ezekiel 27:2-9; Matthew 11:21-22; Mark 7:24; Acts 21:3-7.*

TURBANS

UNCIRCUMCISED
(uhn-SUR-kuhm-sized)
All people who failed to keep the law of circumcision. In the OT it referred usually to the Philistines. It was also used as a figure of speech to mean unclean or uncontrolled. In the NT it referred to all Gentiles. *Exodus 6:12, 30; Leviticus 26:41; Judges 14:3; 2 Samuel 1:20; Jeremiah 9:25-26; Acts 7:51; 11:3; Romans 4:9; 1 Corinthians 7:18.*

UNCLEAN, UNCLEANNESS
Not pure according to religious laws. OT laws declared that certain animals, foods, places, objects, and persons were unclean. To come in contact with these, with anything dead, with lepers, with someone who had a bodily discharge, made a person unclean. To be purified one had to go through a cleansing ritual. *Leviticus 5:2-3; Isaiah 6:5; Hosea 9:3; Matthew 23:27; Acts 10:9-16, 28.*

UNLEAVENED BREAD
(uhn-LEV-end)
Bread or cakes baked without yeast. Among the Hebrews the absence of leaven was a mark of holiness, so all baked grain offerings brought to the altar were baked without yeast. During the seven days of the Feast of Unleavened Bread (the Passover) unleavened bread was eaten (and still is) to remind the Hebrews of the hasty departure their ancestors had made from Egypt, not even stopping to bake leavened bread. *Deuteronomy 16:16; Judges 6:19-21; 2 Chronicles 30:13; Mark 14:1; Luke 22:1.*

UPPER ROOM

A room in the upper floor of a house or a room on the roof, usually for guests. In the NT an upper room was the place chosen by Jesus for his last meal with his disciples. *1 Kings 17:19; 2 Kings 1:2; Mark 14:14-15; Luke 22:11-12; Acts 1:12-13, 9:37.*

UR

An ancient city on the Euphrates River in lower Mesopotamia. It was at one time the capital of the Sumerian Empire. An ancient ziggurat (temple) dedicated to the moon-god Sin has been unearthed at Ur. It is mentioned in the Bible as the home of Abraham. *Genesis 11:28, 31; 15:7; Nehemiah 9:7.*

URIM AND THUMMIM
(UHR-im, THUHM-im)

In early OT times objects used to determine the will of God. They may have been precious stones or pieces of metal which the priest used in casting lots or in trying to obtain from God answers to questions. The priest kept the stones in a pocket of his breast piece, worn over the ephod, or priestly garment. He shook them in a container and cast them on the ground in the way dice are thrown. Nothing is known of their origin. *Exodus 28:8; Leviticus 8:8; Numbers 27:21; Deuteronomy 33:8; 1 Samuel 14:41-42; 28:6; Ezra 2:63.*

UZZAH OR UZZA
(UZ-uh)

There are several persons by this name mentioned in the OT. The most notable was the man who drove the oxcart when David arranged to take the ark to Jerusalem. In the story Uzzah was struck dead when he put out his hand to stead the ark. *2 Samuel 6:2-7; 1 Chronicles 13:1-10.*

UZZIAH
(uh-ZYE-uh)

King of the southern kingdom of Judah from 792 to 740 B.C., son of King Amaziah. He is also mentioned as Azariah. Azariah may have been his personal name and Uzziah his throne name. He was sixteen years old when he came to the throne. Uzziah was a strong ruler, adding to Judah's defenses and agricultural prosperity. He became a victim of leprosy, and his son Jotham ruled as regent in his stead. The prophets Isaiah, Amos, and Hosea were active during his reign. *2 Chronicles 26:1-16, 21-23; 2 Kings 15:1-3; Isaiah 6:1; Hosea 1:1; Amos 1:1.*

UPPER ROOM

VANITY, VAIN

The quality of being empty or vain; having no real value. In Bible usage, it often refers to pagan gods, which were empty and worthless. *Exodus 20:7; Psalm 89:47; Ecclesiastes 1:2; 6:12; 11:8; 12:8; and many other places in Ecclesiastes; Isaiah 49:4; Acts 14:15.*

VASSAL

(VAS-uhl)
One in a subordinate position who has promised loyalty to an overlord. In Bible times a defeated king was often appointed governor by his conquerors and allowed to rule over his own people or territory. He was required to pay tribute to the conquering nation and thus was the vassal of the victorious king. *2 Kings 17:3; Lamentations 1:1.*

VEIL

A head covering worn usually by women. It is not certain what these were like, but most scholars agree that they were more for decoration than for concealing the face or person. In the OT story of Rebekah her veil was probably a sign that she was unmarried. *Genesis 24:65; Song of Solomon 4:1; Isaiah 3:23.*

VEIL OF THE TEMPLE OR TABERNACLE

The curtain which hung at the entrance to the most holy place in the tabernacle and in the temple. In early OT times when the tabernacle was moved the veil is said to have been used to cover the ark. After the Exile the ark was never restored, and the most holy place stood empty. In the NT the veil is called the curtain. (See

Curtain of the Temple.) *Exodus 26:31-35; 30:6; 35:12; 36:35; 39:34; Leviticus 16:2, 12; 24:3; Numbers 4:5; 18:7; 2 Chronicles 3:14.*

VESTMENTS

Ceremonial garments worn by the priests conducting religious ceremonies. Among the Hebrews they included the ephod, breastpiece, breeches, robe, and turban (see these terms). *2 Kings 10:22; Ezra 3:10.*

VILLAGE

A small grouping of houses and other buildings. In OT times unlike a city a village had no wall. Villages were often located close to a city, or even built against a city wall. They were dependent upon the cities for markets and for protection in time of war. The village was governed by a council of elders or was sometimes under the control of a nearby city. *Leviticus 25:31; Numbers 32:41-42; Deuteronomy 3:5; Joshua 15:32-62; Nehemiah 12:29; Zechariah 2:4; Matthew 10:11; 21:2; Acts 8:25.*

VESTMENTS

VINEYARD
(VIN-yurd)

A planting of grapevines. In biblical times the vines were usually planted on hillsides since such land was not often used for growing grains. The workman who pruned the vines was called a vinedresser. Olives, figs, and grapes were among the most typical products of Palestine. Grapes were valued because they were the source of wine. In OT times there were various laws governing the use of vineyards. "Vine" and "vineyard" were used in the Bible as figures of speech to mean Israel. In the NT Jesus speaks of himself as a vine and of his followers as branches. Several of his stories have vineyards as their setting. *Exodus 22:5; 23:11; Leviticus 19:10; Deuteronomy 20:6; 1 Kings 21:1-18; 2 Kings 5:26; 18:32; 19:29; Nehemiah 9:25; Isaiah 5:1-10; Matthew 20:1-16; 21:28-41; Mark 12:1-9; Luke 20:9-16; John 15:1-7.*

VISION
(VIZH-uhn)

In the Bible an experience similar to a dream in which God revealed God or God's will to someone, most often a prophet. *Genesis 15:1; 46:2; Job 4:13; 7:14; Isaiah 1:1; Ezekiel 1:1; 8:3; 11:24; 12:22-24; Matthew 17:9; Acts 9:10-15; 10:3, 17, 19; 11:5; 16:9; 2 Corinthians 12:1.*

VOTIVE OFFERING
(VOHT-iv)

A gift to God as a part of a promise made in a vow. *Leviticus 7:16; Deuteronomy 12:17; 2 Kings 12:18; 2 Chronicles 15:18.*

VOW

In the Bible a promise or pledge made to God, sometimes as a bargain. In the OT there were many laws which laid down rules for carrying out different kinds of vows, for such promises were very sacred. *Genesis 28:20-22; Numbers 6:21; 21:2; 1 Samuel 1:11; Psalm 132:2-5; Jonah 1:16; Acts 18:18; 21:23.*

WAFERS

Thin, unleavened cakes made of flour, sometimes mixed with honey. In the Bible they are usually mentioned in connection with offerings to God, although one reference indicates that they were also part of the everyday diet of the early Hebrews. *Exodus 16:31; 29:2, 23; Leviticus 2:4; 8:26.*

WAISTCLOTH

An inner garment or girdle worn around the waist. It was made of leather or linen. Workmen removed outer garments and wore only the waistcloth when on the job. *Job 12;18; Isaiah 5:27; Jeremiah 13:1-11.*

WALLS

Enclosure of bricks, wood, stone, or other materials for privacy or protection. Stone walls were built around cities for defense against enemy attack. They were usually of great height and thickness with watchtowers and a gate. Sometimes a city had a double wall. The space between the two walls was used for storage or guardrooms. The city gate was the center of community life. Here people bought and sold goods, judges settled disputes, and proclamations and speeches were read. Vineyards and sheepfolds had walls made of piles of loose stones with thorns on the top to prevent thieves and wild animals from stealing the fruits or sheep. *Leviticus 25:31; Joshua 2:15; 2 Chronicles 8:5; 25:23; Ezra 4:12; Nehemiah 4:3-19; Ezekiel 38:11; Acts 9:25.*

WATCHMAN

In Bible times a sentry or guard. A watchman was placed in the fields and vineyards during the time of the ripening and harvesting of crops. He stayed in a temporary booth or watchtower to frighten away thieves, birds, or animals. The watchman of a city patrolled the walls of the city at night and from time to time called out that all was well. He was particularly valuable during a time of invasion or siege. *1 Samuel 14:16; 2 Samuel 18:24-27; 2 Kings 9:17-20; Job 27:18; Psalm 127:1; Song of Solomon 3:3; 5:7; Isaiah 21:6-12; 52:8; Jeremiah 51:12; Hosea 9:8.*

WATER

Liquid which descends from the clouds as rain and is found in springs, lakes, rivers, seas, brooks, and so on. Palestine was a hilly, rocky land where fertility depended upon the annual rainfall. Thus, the Jews came to look upon water as a special blessing from God. They often used "water" as a figure of speech to symbolize God's blessings or goodness; "living water" was fresh, running water. In the NT Jesus referred to himself as living water in a figure of speech to symbolize the new life, the life of God, springing up in believers. *Psalms 72:6; 77:17; Isaiah 35:6-7; 41:17-18; Luke 3:16; John 2:7-9; 4:7-15; 7:37-39.*

WATERSKIN

Whole goatskins with the neck and feet tied together to form a container. A poetic figure of speech to describe rain clouds. *Genesis 21:14; Job 38:37.*

WAY

A path, road, or street along which one passes to reach a destination. In the OT a word used to describe the courses of nature and of a person's life. It is also used to describe the paths of good and of evil. In the NT, Christ is referred to as the "Way," and Christianity came to be known as the "Way." *Psalm 1:6; Proverbs 16:17; 21:2; 30:18-19; Isaiah 53:6; John 14:4-6; Acts 9:2; 19:9, 23; 22:4; 24:14, 22.*

WEEKS, FEAST OF

A harvest celebration among the Hebrews ending the round of festivals that began with Passover. In Palestine, the festival was actually only one day, the fiftieth or last day of a seven-week period (a sabbath of weeks). The seven weeks were counted from the end of the wheat harvest and the beginning of the barley harvest. The first cuttings of the grain were offered in thanksgiving and in recognition that God was the source of the harvest. In NT times the festival was called by the Greek name Pentecost meaning "fiftieth." After the destruction of the temple in a.d. 70 the Feast of Weeks became a celebration of the giving of the law. For Christians the feast of Pentecost took on a special meaning as the day on which the Holy Spirit came upon the apostles and followers of Jesus as they prayed in Jerusalem. (See Pentecost.) *Exodus 34:22; Numbers 28:26; Deuteronomy 16:9-12, 16; 2 Chronicles 8:13.*

WHEAT

WELLS

A source or storage place for water. Because of the scarcity of rainfall, wells have always been important in the dry Bible lands. "Beer" was the Hebrew word for a well. It was used in the names of many towns and villages where wells were located. The depth and shape of wells varied according to the type of soil and the level of the underground water. Some wells were shallow pits and others, great shafts many feet deep. From these the water was removed in jars or waterskins attached to ropes. Ancient peoples made songs about the wells that told of spirits living in the running waters. A very old Hebrew song of the wells sings of running or living water as the power of the Lord. *Genesis 16:14; 21:30; 26:22; 29:2-3; Numbers 21:16-18; 1 Samuel 19:22; 2 Samuel 17:18-21; 23:15-16; Jeremiah 6:7; John 4:6-15.*

WESTERN SEA

A name for the Mediterranean Sea. (See Mediterranean Sea.) *Deuteronomy 11:24; 34:2; Joel 2:20; Zechariah 14:8.*

WHEAT

A grain crop which produced some of the most important foods in biblical times. It was made into flour for bread or roasted and eaten as parched grain. *Exodus 34:22; Judges 6:11; Ruth 2:33; 1 Chronicles 21:20; Isaiah 28:25; Amos 8:5; Matthew 3:12.*

WHIRLWIND

A word used in the Bible for several kinds of winds: a high destructive wind, a tornado, or whirling clouds of dust. *2 Kings 2:11; Job 38:1; 40:6; Psalm 77:18; Isaiah 17:13; Jeremiah 23:19; Nahum 1:3.*

WIDOW

A woman whose husband has died. Among the Hebrews death before old age was considered a calamity, a judgment for sin, and a wife left in this way was disgraced. She had no right of inheritance. However, if she had no children, she would remain with her husband's family and wait for his brother to marry her. She might also return to her own family and remarry (see Ruth 1:8-13). In the early Christian church special consideration was given to widows. *Deuteronomy 24:17-21; 26:12; Psalms 68:5; 94:6; 146:9; Lamentations 1:1; Matthew 22:24; Luke 4:25; 20:47; Acts 6:1; 9:39-41.*

WILDERNESS

A term often used when referring to sandy deserts, rocky plateaus, barren pasturelands, and desolate mountain regions. God's protection of the Israelites during the journey through the wilderness was one of the most important experiences in their history. *Exodus 15:22; Numbers 33:11-16; Deuteronomy 1:19; 8:2; 32:10; Judges 1:16; Isaiah 27:10; 40:3; 41:18; Matthew 3:1; 4:1; John 6:31; Acts 7:36.*

WILLOW TREE

A tree commonly found in Palestine growing in moist places by brooks and rivers. Willow branches along with other branches were used by the Jews in their celebration of the Feast of Booths. *Leviticus 23:40; Job 40:22; Psalm 137:2; Isaiah 15:7; 44:4; Ezekiel 17:5.*

WINEPRESS

A vat in which the juice was pressed from grapes. The vat was usually a hollowed-out limestock rock on a hill-wide near the vineyard. Grapes were spread over the floor, and barefooted men walked and jumped on the grapes to press out the juice. They shouted while they worked, and their jumping and stomping had a rhythm. All the people joined in their singing, and it was a joyous, happy time. A hole in the rock allowed the juice to trickle down to a lower rock-hewn vat where it was left to settle and ferment into wine. The wine was then put into jars and wineskins. The prophets used word pictures of an abundance of grapes in the winepress to symbolize God's blessing. *Deuteronomy 16:13-14;*

Nehemiah 13:15; Job 24:11; Isaiah 5:1-2; 16:10; Jeremiah 48:33; Joel 3:13; Micah 6:15; Matthew 21:33; Mark 12:1; Revelation 14:20.

WINNOW

The process of separating the kernel of the grain from the chaff by fanning or by throwing the cut stalks of grain into the air with a long-handled fork so that the grain seeds would fall back into a pile while the light straw chaff would be carried away by the wind. "Winnowing" is used as a figure of speech for describing the sweeping away of evil. *Ruth 3:2; Isaiah 30:24; 41:16; Jeremiah 15:7; Matthew 25:24-26; Luke 3:17.*

WISE MEN

In ancient times magicians and interpreters of the stars. The courts of the ancient kings of Egypt and Babylonia kept wise men who were authorities on religion and predicted future events. The Hebrews were forbidden to deal in magic and divination. For them a wise man was one who had knowledge of right living. The book of Proverbs contains sayings of wise men and teachers of OT times. Some wise men sat at the gates of cities telling riddles and stories and settling disputes. In the Gospel of Matthew it is reported that wise men came from the East to worship the infant Jesus. These wise men had studied the stars to learn of the birth of Jesus and also how to find him. (See Magic, Magicians.) *Genesis 41:8; Exodus 7:11; Isaiah 19:12; Jeremiah 50:35; Daniel 2:12-14, 21, 24, 27; Matthew 2:1-12.*

WISE MEN

WITNESS

A person who has firsthand knowledge of a fact or an event. Biblical law required the testimony of two witnesses to establish guilt. If the person was condemned to death, the witnesses themselves threw the first stone. Bearing false witness was a serious crime. In the NT those who testified to the truth of God and those who testified to what they had seen or heard about Jesus were called witnesses. *Exodus 20:16; Deuteronomy 17:6; 19:15-18; Joshua 22:26-27; Judges 11:10; Ruth 4:9-11; Luke 24:48; John 3:11; Acts 1:8, 22; 7:58; 10:39-41; 1 Timothy 6:12.*

WOLF

A beast that preyed upon domestic animals, especially sheep. Because the wolf seemed greedy and cruel, the word is often used in the Bible to describe invading armies, unbelievers, wicked judges, and false prophets. *Isaiah 11:6; Jeremiah 5:6; Habakkuk 1:8; Zephaniah 3:3; Matthew 7:15; 10:16; John 10:12; Acts 20:29.*

WORD, THE

In the OT God's declaration of God's will and God's purpose. God's word and God's act were the same. For example, the heavens and the earth were created by God's word. Throughout the OT history of the Hebrews the word of the Lord was usually received through the prophets. In some places in the NT "the word" still has the OT meaning. In other places it becomes "the Word of Christ," the gospel which he first preached. In the Gospel of John and in Revelation "Word" or "Word of God" is used to mean Jesus Christ himself as God's clearest word to humankind. *Genesis 15:4; Deuteronomy 5:4-5; 1 Samuel 15:10; Psalm 33:4-6; Isaiah 1:10; Jeremiah 1:2; Ezekiel 1:3; Mark 2:2; 4:14-20, 33; 7:13; Luke 8:11-21; 11:28; John 1:1, 14; 2:22; Acts 4:31; 8:14; 13:7; 16:16; 19:20; 1 Corinthians 1:18; Colossians 3:16; 1 John 1:1; Revelation 19:13.*

WORLD, THE

To the ancient Hebrew of the OT, "world" was most often used to mean no more than the familiar lands around the Mediterranean Sea. By NT times the known world was as large as the Roman Empire. "World" was also used to mean not so much lands and nations as all the affairs and doings of humans. The word "world" in this sense distinguished the affairs and doings of humans from the kingdom of God. The word was sometimes used to refer to the whole created order. (See Earth.) *1 Samuel 2:8; Psalms 9:8; 24:1-2; 90:2; Isaiah 34:1; Jeremiah 25:26; Nahum 1:5; Matthew 13:22; Mark 14:9; 16:15; Luke 2:1; John 3:16-17; 9:32; 12:19; 14:17, 27; 15:19; Romans 1:8; James 1:27; 1 John 2:15-16.*

WORMWOOD

A variety of shrub with woolly, gray-green leaves. These leaves were used in making medicine and had a very bitter taste. Wormwood extract was poisonous if taken in large quantities. The prophets used it as a figure of speech to describe something that is hard or bitter to accept. "Wormwood" is used as a figure of speech to refer to the results of evil and to the judgment of God. *Jeremiah 9:15; 23:15; Lamentations 3:15, 19; Amos 5:7; 6:12; Revelation 8:10-11.*

alone. *Exodus 34:14; 1 Samuel 1:3; 15:30; 2 Samuel 12:20; 1 Chronicles 16:29; Psalms 22:27; 99:5; Isaiah 36:7; Matthew 4:10; 28:9, 17; Acts 13:2; 17:23; Romans 12:1; 1 Corinthians 14:25.*

WORSHIP

The English word, coming from an Anglo-Saxon word meaning "worth-ship," means an acknowledgment of worthiness, respect, reverence. In the Bible, worship is an act or attitude intended to recognize the worth of God, to honor God. In OT times worship was expressed with sacrifices and offerings. Psalms and musical instruments were used in the temple services. In later OT times the Jews gathered together in the synagogue for the reading of scripture, for instruction, and for prayers. In the NT, Christian worship centered in the Lord's Supper, in baptism, and in preaching. There was also singing of psalms, reading of scripture, instructions, and prayers. From the earliest times in the Christian church there has been both public or congregational worship and private worship in which an individual participates

ANCIENT WORLDVIEW

XYZ

XERXES

See *Ahasuerus*.

YAHWEH (YHWH)

(YAH-way)

An English-language version of the probable name by which the Hebrews thought of God. For the Hebrews the name of each person represented the person him or herself. Thus the name of the Holy God represented God's power and God's holiness (see *God, Names of.*) They regarded the name with utmost reverence. It is believed the name would have been pronounced, "Yahweh," but it was seldom spoken. In writing it only four letters, translated as YHWH and called the Tetragammaton, were used. Today in the English versions of the OT "Lord" is often used in places where the name of God is indicated. YHWH or Yahweh rarely appears except in footnotes.

YEAR

A division of time. The oldest calendar of the Israelites was borrowed from the Canaanites. It was an agricultural calendar. The day of cutting the first sheaf of grain was New Year's Day. The year was divided into seven periods of seven weeks plus one extra day in each period, a sacred day. Added to this were two seven-day periods in which were held the Feast of Booths and the Feast of Unleavened Bread. This way of defining time was used until the reign of Solomon. He borrowed the calendar of Tyre, based on the solar system with 365 days in a normal year. The year began with the autumn equinox—in late September. About 450 B.C. a lunar calendar was adopted which depended on the phases of the moon. In the fourth century B.C. the Jews began to reckon a day as being from sunrise to sunset. This lunar calendar developed into the calendar still used today for Jewish religious time-reckoning. *1 Kings 6:1; 2 Chronicles 9:24; 36:21; Psalm 90:9-10; Proverbs 4:10.*

YOKE

A wooden frame placed over the necks of two oxen to harness them together. To the middle of the yoke bar was connected a single shaft which pulled a plow, sled, or cart. Yokes were also put on prisoners of war and slaves. The word was used in the OT as a symbol of slavery. It was used by Paul in the NT to symbolize the bonds in which fellow Christians worked together as a team under Christ. *Numbers 19:2; 1 Kings 19:19, 21; 2 Chronicles 10:4; Job 1:3; Jeremiah 27:8; 28:11; Lamentations 1:14; Matthew 11:29; Galatians 5:1; 1 Timothy 6:1.*

YOUTH

According to the Bible, the time between a person's infancy and his or her years of greatest vigor and opportunity, but not years of greatest maturity and judgment. The early years of Israel were called the nation's youth by the prophets. *Job 33:25; Ecclesiastes 12:1; Jeremiah 1:6-8; 2:2; Ezekiel 23:19; Hosea 2:15; Acts 26:4; 1 Timothy 4:12; 2 Timothy 2:22-26.*

ZACCHAEUS

ZACCHAEUS

(zuh-KEE-uhss)

Chief tax collector of Jericho. The life of this man was changed when he met and talked with Jesus. *Luke 19:1-10.*

ZADOK

(ZAY-dok)

The priest of David in Gibeon and later in Jerusalem. After the death of David, Zadok backed Solomon in his struggle against his brother Adonijah for the throne. Until this time Abiathar had been equal in authority with Zadok. Solomon exiled Abiathar and gave Zadok complete charge of the temple. His family continued as the dominant priestly family. *2 Samuel 15:24-37; 1 Kings 1:22-39; 2:35; 1 Chronicles 16:37-41; Ezekiel 40:46; 43:19; 44:15; 48:11.*

ZEALOT

(ZEL-uht)

In NT times a member of a patriotic group of Jews who rebelled against all foreign rulers, especially the Romans. Simon the Zealot, before becoming a disciple of Jesus, had probably been a member of some group like this. *Luke 6:15; Acts 1:13.*

ZEBEDEE

(ZEB-uh-dee)

The father of the apostles James and John. He and his sons were in the fishing business with Simon and Andrew at Capernaum and seem to have been prosperous enough to have a fleet of boats and servants. *Matthew 4:21; Mark 1:16-20; Luke 5:10.*

ZEBULUN

(ZEB-yoo-luhn)

A son of Jacob and the ancestor of the Israelite tribe by that name whose territory was west of the Sea of Galilee. In the song of Deborah the tribe is mentioned for its bravery. *Genesis 30:20; Numbers 1:30-31; 2:7; 26:26; Judges 4:10; 5:14, 18; 12:11-12; 1 Chronicles 12:33, 40; Psalm 68:27; Matthew 4:13.*

ZECHARIAH

(zek-uh-RYE-uh)

1. A prophet about 520 B.C. after the return of some of the exiles to Jerusalem from Babylon. He was concerned with the rebuilding of the temple in Jerusalem. (See *Zechariah, Book of.*) *Ezra 5:1; 6:14; Zechariah 1:1, 7; 7:1, 8.*
2. The name of a king of Israel who ruled for six months in 753 and 752 B.C. and was murdered by Shallum. *2 Kings 14:29; 15:8, 11.*
3. The son of the priest Jehoiada. During the reign of Joash in the southern kingdom of Judah he preached against idol worship and announced the judgment of God. The people plotted against him, and Joash ordered him stoned in the temple. In Matthew this Zechariah is identified with the OT prophet, probably through a copyist's mistake. *2 Chronicles 24:20-25; Matthew 23:35; Luke 11:51.*
4. Father of John the Baptist. When he doubted the word of Gabriel, he lost the power to speak until after John was born. *Luke 1:5-25, 57-79; 3:2.*

ZECHARIAH WRITING

ZECHARIAH, BOOK OF

One of the twelve short books of prophecy in the OT. It consists of oracles and visions of the prophet Zechariah after some of the Jews had returned to Jerusalem from exile in Babylon. The last six chapters probably were written by later prophets and added to the collection. *See the book itself.*

ZEDEKIAH
(zed-uh-KYE-uh)

The last king of the southern kingdom of Judah, from about 597 to 586 B.C. He was placed on the throne by Nebuchadnezzar, king of Babylon, after King Jehoiachin had been sent into exile. Zedekiah rebelled against Nebuchadnezzar, and this led to the attack and destruction of Jerusalem. Zedekiah was taken prisoner. Nebuchadnezzar forced him to watch while his two sons were killed. Then the king's own eyes were put out, and he was led in chains to Babylon. The prophet Jeremiah was active during the reign of Zedekiah. *2 Kings 24:17–25:7; 2 Chronicles 18:10; 36:10-13; Jeremiah 1:3; 27:1-15; 37:1–39:7; 52:1-11.*

ZEPHANIAH
(zef-uh-NYE-uh)

A prophet in the southern kingdom of Judah from around 630 to 625 B.C. His work was done in the reign of King Josiah, who was a great religious leader and did much to encourage faith and worship among his people. (See *Zephaniah, Book of.*)

ZEPHANIAH, BOOK OF

Work of a Judean prophet of the seventh century whose great-great-grandfather was King Hezekiah. Zephaniah prophesied during the reign of King Josiah. In his oracles he denounced idolatry and warned that the day of the Lord would bring judgment on the Hebrews and on the surrounding nations. *See the book itself.*

ZERUBBABEL
(zuh-RUH-buh-buhl)

A Babylonian Jew who returned to Jerusalem after the Exile to become governor under the Persian king Darius I. He resumed the building of the temple about 520 B.C. although a start had been made by the first exiles who returned, around 538 B.C. However, more than twenty years had elapsed without the building's being finished. Zerubbabel was a grandson of Jehoiachin, the exiled king of Judah. *Ezra 3:2-13; 5:1-2; Nehemiah 7:7; 12:1, 47; Haggai 1:1-15.*

ZIKLAG
(ZIK-lag)

A town in Judah, north of Beersheba. David used it as a base for his raids against the Amalakites before he became king. *1 Samuel 27:6; 30:1, 14, 26; 2 Samuel 1:1; 4:10; 1 Chronicles 12:1-20; Nehemiah 11:28.*

ZIMRI

(ZIM-rye)

King of the northern kingdom of Israel for seven days in 885 B.C. He led a revolt against King Elah and murdered the drunken king, who had remained behind while his army was fighting the Philistines. When word of the king's death reached the army, the man acclaimed Omri, the commander-in-chief, as king. Zimri burned the palace and himself in it when he saw how things had turned against him. *1 Kings 16:18-20.*

ZIN, WILDERNESS OF

(zin)

In the OT a wilderness through which the Israelites passed on their way to Canaan. It was probably a part of the southeastern border of Judah toward the Dead Sea. *Numbers 13:21; 20:1; 27:14; 33:36; 34:3-4; Deuteronomy 32:51; Joshua 15:1, 3.*

ZION

(ZYE-uhn)

A fortified hill in Jerusalem under the Jebusites. "Zion" was often used as a name for the entire city. After the conquest of Jerusalem by David, Zion was renamed "city of David," and the ark of the covenant was brought there. When the ark was transferred to the temple, the name "city of Zion" was extended to include the temple area. "Daughter of Zion" is a poetic term for Jerusalem and its inhabitants. *2 Samuel 5:7; 1 Kings 8:1; 1 Chronicles 11:5; 2 Chronicles 5:2; Psalms 2:6; 69:35; 126:1; Song of Solomon 3:11; Isaiah 10:24; 16:1; 51:11, 16; 52:1, 8; 61:3;* *Micah 4:16-1; 51:11, 16; 52:1, 8; 61:3; Micah 4:2-8; Matthew 21:5; Romans 9:33; 11:26.*

ZIPPORAH

(ZIP-or-uh)

The first wife of Moses and daughter of Jethro. *Exodus 2:16, 21-22; 18:1-4.*

ZOAR

(ZOH-ar)

In the OT one of the "five cities of the valley" in the time of Abraham. It was probably located in the area now under water at the southern end of the Dead Sea. Lot, Abraham's nephew, escaped to Zoar when Sodom and Gomorrah were destroyed. Later he left out of fear. *Genesis 13:10; 14:2; 19:20-23, 30; Deuteronomy 34:3; Isaiah 15:5; Jeremiah 48:34.*

Art Credits

Page 12: Keith Neely; Page 13: Charles Jakubowski: Page 17: Keith Neely; Page 19: Cheryl Arnemann; Page 22: Keith Neely; Page 23: Randy Wollenman; Page 25: Charles Jakubowski; Page 27: Mike Muir ;Page 29: Patrick Soper; Page 31: Keith Neely; Page 35: Randy Wollenman; Page 37:Suzanne Snyder; Page 39: Dennis Hockerman; Page 41: Will Foster; Page 43: Keith Neely; Page 45: Randy Wollenmann; Page 47: Keith Neely; Page 49: Eddie Ross; Page 51: Keith Neely; Page 53: Keith Neely; Page 59: Lee Freppon; Page 61: Helen Kunze;Page 63: Keith Neely: Page 67: Keith Neely; Page 69: Randy Wollenmann; Page 71: David Gothard; Page 73: Keith Neely; Page 75: Keith Neely; Page 77: Yoshi Miyake; Page 79: Keith Neely; Page 81: Mike Muir; Page 83: John Ham; Page 85: Keith Neely; Page 87: Bob Pepper; Page 89: Randy Wollenmann; Page 91: Keith Neely; Page 93: Randy Wollenmann; Page 95: Marvin Jarboe; Page 97:Keith Neely; Page 99: Karen Pritchett; Page 101: Mike Muir; Page 103: Eddie Ross; Page 105: Eddie Ross; Page 109: Marvin Jaroe; Page 113: Carol Heyer; Page 115: Suzanne Snyder; Page 117: Eddie Ross; Page 119: Keith Neely; Page 121:Marvin Jarboe; Page 125: Jeff Preston; Page 127: Suzanne Snyer; Page 129: Keith Neely; Page 130: Bill Latta; Page 133: Cheryl Arnemann; Page 135: Lee Freppon; Page 137: Eddie Ross; Page 139: Bill Myers; Page 141: Suzanne Snyder; Page 143: Marvin Jarboe; Page 147: Cheryl Arnemann; Page 151: Keith Neely; Page 153: Keith Neely; Page 155: Charles Jakubowski; Page 157: Randy Wollenmann: Page 158: Keith Neely; Page 159: Bill Anderson; Page 163: Francis Phillipps; Page 165: Suzanne Snyder; Page 167: Keith Neely; Page 169: Keith Neely; Page 171: Eddie Ross; Page 173: Helen Kunze; Page 175: Suzanne Snyder; Page 177: Suzanne Snyder; Page 179: Robert Sauber; Page 179: Eddie Ross; Page 181: Lyn Martin; Page 185: Keith Neely; Page 187: Keith Neely; Page 189: Charles Jakubowski; Page 191: Keith Neely; Page 193: Suzanne Snyder; Page 195: Randy Wollenmann; Page 197: Karen Prichett; Page 199Mike Muir; Page 201: Suzanne Snyder; Page 203: Suzanne Snyder; Page 205: Francis Phillipps; Page 207: Suzanne Snyder; Page 209: Suzanne Snyder; Page 211: Suzanne Snyder; Page 215: Jeff Preston; Page 217: Lee Freppon; Page 219: Suzanne Snyder; Page 221: Suzanne Snyder; 223: Suzanne Snyder; Page 225: Suzanne Snyder; Page 227: Eddie Ross; Page 233: George Malick; Page 235: Dick Wahl 237: Suzanne Snyder; Page 239: Suzanne Snyder; Page 241: Eddie Ross; Page 243: Diana Magnuson; Page 245: Suzanne Snyder; Page 249: Suzanne Snyder; Page 251: Eddie Ross; Page 255: Mike Muir; Page 257: Suzanne Snyder; Page 259: Diana Magnuson; Page 261: Suzanne Snyder; Page 263: Suzanne Snyder; Page 267: Keith Neely; Page 269: Suzanne Snyder; Page 277: Keith Neely; Page 281: Suzanne Snyder; Page 283: Charles Jakubowski